D1648832

SUPPLY CHAIN
REVOLUTION

ALSO BY DON TAPSCOTT

The Blockchain Revolution: How the Technology Behind Bitcoin Is Changing Money, Business, and the World, Penguin Portfolio, 2018
Co-author, Alex Tapscott

Blockchain Revolution for the Enterprise Specialization
INSEAD and Coursera, 2019
Co-instructor, Alex Tapscott

The Digital Economy: Rethinking Promise and Peril in the Age of Networked Intelligence, McGraw-Hill, Anniversary Edition, 2014

Macrowikinomics: Rebooting Business and the World, Penguin Portfolio, 2010
Co-author, Anthony D. Williams

Grown Up Digital: How the Net Generation Is Changing Your World, McGraw-Hill, 2008

Wikinomics: How Mass Collaboration Changes Everything, Penguin Portfolio, 2006
Co-author, Anthony D. Williams

The Naked Corporation: How the Age of Transparency Will Revolutionize Business, Free Press, 2003
Co-author, David Ticoll

Digital Capital: Harnessing the Power of Business Webs, Harvard Business Press, 2000
Co-authors, David Ticoll and Alex Lowy

Blueprint to the Digital Economy: Creating Wealth in the Era of E-Business, McGraw-Hill, 1999
Co-authors, David Ticoll and Alex Lowy

Growing Up Digital: The Rise of the Net Generation, McGraw-Hill, 1999

The Digital Economy: Promise and Peril in the Age of Networked Intelligence, McGraw-Hill, 1997

Who Knows: Safeguarding Your Privacy in a Networked World, McGraw-Hill, 1997
Co-author, Ann Cavoukian

Paradigm Shift: The New Promise of Information Technology, McGraw-Hill Companies, 1992
Co-author, Art Caston

Office Automation: A User-Driven Method, Springer, 1985

Planning for Integrated Office Systems: A Strategic Approach, Carswell Legal, 1984
Co-authors, Del Henderson and Morley Greenberg

SUPPLY CHAIN REVOLUTION

How **BLOCKCHAIN TECHNOLOGY** Is Transforming the **GLOBAL FLOW** of Assets

Edited with a foreword by
DON TAPSCOTT
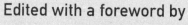
Co-Founder and Executive Chairman, Blockchain Research Institute

BARLOW BOOKS
fine books for enterprising authors

111 Peter Street, Suite 503, Toronto, ON M5V 2H1 Canada

Copyright © 2020 Blockchain Research Institute

The editor of this volume and its individual contributors have made every effort to provide information that was accurate and up to date at the time of writing. Neither the editor nor the contributors assume any responsibility for changes in data, names, titles, status, Internet addresses, or other details that occurred after manuscript completion.

This material is for educational purposes only; it is neither investment advice nor managerial consulting. Use of this material does not create or constitute any kind of business relationship with the Blockchain Research Institute or the Tapscott Group, and neither the Blockchain Research Institute nor the Tapscott Group is liable for the actions of persons or organizations relying on this material.

To refer to this material, we suggest the following citation:

> *Supply Chain Revolution: How Blockchain Technology Is Transforming the Global Flow of Assets*, edited with a foreword by Don Tapscott (Toronto: Barlow Books, 2020).

To request permission for copying, distributing, remixing, transforming, building upon this material, or creating and distributing any derivative of it in print or other form for any purpose, please contact the Blockchain Research Institute, www.blockchainresearchinstitute.org/contact-us, and put "Permission request" in the subject line. Thank you for your interest.

ISBN: 978-1-988025-53-7

Printed in Canada

1 3 5 7 9 10 8 6 4 2

Publisher: Sarah Scott/Barlow Books
Book producer: Tracy Bordian/At Large Editorial Services
Book design (cover and interior): Ruth Dwight
Layout: Rob Scanlan/First Image
For more information, visit **www.barlowbooks.com**

Barlow Book Publishing Inc.
96 Elm Avenue, Toronto, ON
Canada M4W 1P2

CONTENTS

LIST OF CONTRIBUTORS

LOUISA BAI (Chapter 1) is a senior manager in Deloitte's Technology Consulting practice and leads the firm's market development and partnerships in the blockchain ecosystem.

KSHITISH BALHOTRA (Chapter 1) is a manager in the Canadian consulting practice at Deloitte. He leads the Program Delivery for Blockchain for Deloitte Canada.

NOLAN BAUERLE (Chapter 2) is the director of research at Manhattan-based *CoinDesk*. His work with blockchain technology began in 2013 with a long-term study of cryptocurrencies for the Canadian Senate Banking Committee.

SOUMAK CHATTERJEE (Chapter 1) is a partner in Deloitte's Technology Consulting practice. He leads Deloitte's payments and blockchain team in Canada.

ALAN D. COHN (Chapter 6) is an attorney and consultant in Washington, DC. He is co-chair of the Blockchain and Digital Currency practice at Steptoe & Johnson LLP, and a principal of ADC/Strategy.Works LLC.

CARA ENGELBRECHT (Chapter 1) is an analyst in Deloitte's Technology Consulting practice. She assists clients with large-scale delivery and program management in financial services.

DR. STEFAN HOPF (Chapter 7) works in strategy and corporate development, electronics, and automated driving at the BMW Group.

RESHMA KAMATH (Chapter 5) is a law graduate of Northwestern University Pritzker School of Law, Class of 2017, and the inaugural NextGen fellow at the American Bar Association.

DR. HENRY KIM (Chapter 4) is associate professor at the Schulich School of Business at York University, co-director of Blockchain Lab, and one of the leading blockchain scholars in Canada.

DR. MAREK LASKOWSKI (Chapter 4) teaches data science at the graduate level at the Schulich School of Business at York University where he co-founded the Blockchain Lab.

VINEET NARULA (Chapters 8 and 9) is a customer success leader responsible for helping to build expert (supply) platform to support Intuit's global ecosystem.

PREMA SHRIKRISHNA (Chapters 8 and 9) works at the World Bank Group's technology innovation lab, where she evaluates the feasibility of emerging technologies such as blockchain for solving real-world problems.

VIKAS SINGLA (Chapter 1) is a senior manager in the Canadian consulting practice at Deloitte and leads the Canadian Blockchain team. He has led multiple blockchain-based experimentation projects.

DON TAPSCOTT (Foreword) is CEO of the Tapscott Group and co-founder and executive chairman of the Blockchain Research Institute. He is one of the world's leading authorities on the impact of technology on business and society.

ANTHONY D. WILLIAMS (Chapter 3) is co-founder and president of the DEEP Centre and an internationally recognized authority on the digital revolution, innovation, and creativity in business and society.

FOREWORD

Don Tapscott

When we first started working on this book, the corona virus (COVID-19) hadn't yet made headlines. In only a few months, COVID-19 has taken precious lives, devastated the global economy, and exposed serious shortcomings in our social contract, particularly regarding public health and household income.[1] The pandemic has also revealed chinks in our supply chains. Not only did manufacturers find themselves scrambling unsuccessfully to find new suppliers when their Asian sources shut down, but the Western world experienced across-the-board shortages of essential consumer packaged goods for the first time in decades.

Yes, the virus inspired admirable behavior, as many of us socially distanced ourselves, pitched in to help those in need, and self-quarantined with an abundance of caution. But it also fomented a fear that manifested in some antisocial behavior such as hoarding. Throughout the West, people jammed stores to clear shelves of everything from hand sanitizer to toilet paper. Worse, unscrupulous entrepreneurs attempted to resell these goods at exorbitant prices online. Lacking transparency into the supply chain, terrified consumers became their victims.

The global supply chain is a $50 trillion industry.[2] It's the foundation of commerce and our global economy. As I've become fond of saying, "If you've got it, a supply chain brought it to you." I suppose that, during these times, I could add, "If you can't get it, a supply chain let you down."

Information technology has certainly improved the flow of goods globally over the last decades. Enterprise resource planning systems, electronic data interchange, and standards like ISO 9001 and ISO 1401 have helped make the global supply of goods more efficient. But, as the COVID-19 crisis revealed, there is still critical work to do.

Today's supply chains are complex, with various manufacturers creating components of goods that move through trucks, planes, boats, and trains. Too many parties are still coordinating and conducting their transactions through a Byzantine network of computer systems with disparate applications like e-mail, phone, and fax. It is still slow, expensive, and very serial in nature. There are invoices, letters of credit, bank guarantees, bills of lading, tax forms, receipts, and numerous other documents navigating the labyrinth. Some parties make payments through a hodgepodge of intermediaries—banks, custodians, agents, lawyers, tax authorities, book keepers, and the like—and through batch-like processes. Consumers and supply-chain players alike struggle to get accurate information.

That's why, in a pandemic, an uninformed consumer might reasonably believe that toilet paper won't be available for many months. Hence, the hoarding.

Enter blockchain—the Internet of Value. For the first time in human history, individuals and organizations can manage and trade their assets digitally peer to peer. These assets can be digital like money, identity, and private information; or they can be physical assets represented by digital tokens. Parties to a transaction achieve trust not necessarily through an intermediary but through cryptography and clever code.

I can imagine a supply chain that is a high-metabolic shared network, with a real-time, single version of the truth about the location, quantity, and custody of goods. We could use smart contracts to make smart payments in the network, thereby reducing conflict, human intervention, and legal fees. We could redirect vital medical supplies to hospitals hardest hit. Things themselves could make real-time micropayments as they moved across the network. Costs would be lower. And consumers could see the flow of hand sanitizer throughout the economy, place orders for reasonable quantities, and be confident of the prices and delivery dates. Likewise, producers could track demand and adjust production in real time.

Bettina Warburg and Tom Serres, co-founders of Animal Ventures, got me thinking about the unprecedented volume of data that blockchains would be throwing off like this, enabling us to study large-scale supply chains as never before.[3] One of our conversations revved up my formulation engine and out popped the phrase, *asset chains*, in response to their description of the blockchains that would support the autonomous and distributed management of supply chains.

To understand the impact of blockchain on business and society more deeply, Alex Tapscott and I co-founded the Blockchain Research Institute (BRI), a global think tank on distributed ledger technology. Along with our editor-in-chief Kirsten Sandberg and our managing director Hilary Carter, we assembled some of the best minds in the space—Bettina and Tom among them—to investigate blockchain use cases and implementation challenges. Our multimillion-dollar program includes more than one hundred projects across ten industry verticals and nine C-suite roles in both public and private sectors. Our membership consists of large corporations, governments, nonprofits, and entrepreneurs from the start-up community.

After three BRI member summits and now with this pandemic, I'm more convinced than ever that

- Blockchain technology would transform the global flow of assets of all kinds, tangible and intangible.

- Any enterprise that was moving assets through global supply chains could join in reinventing global commerce as we know it.

So immense and immediate is the supply chain opportunity that we have assembled our research to date on the topic in this single volume. It is even more relevant in light of this global crisis, which is already having dire health and economic consequences.

We have placed Deloitte's foundational work on global trade up front. This first chapter explores how blockchain can improve global operations. For banks and financiers, blockchain technology streamlines processes, reduces costs and fraud, and fuels product innovation. Corporations benefit from greater access to capital, greater supply-chain visibility, and improved product quality and provenance of goods. Logistics companies such as freight forwarders benefit from greater visibility into the movement of goods along the supply chain, improved authentication of freight collectors, and real-time capacity monitoring.

Chapter 1 also explains the benefits of blockchain technology for regulatory bodies, insurance providers, and customs authorities. Led by Soumak Chatterjee, Deloitte's Canadian leader for payments and blockchain, the research team outlines the future of global trade, once blockchain technology is embraced and leveraged. The chapter provides practical analysis of the blockchain opportunities for enterprise leaders.

Chapter 2 features the Foxconn Technology Group, which operates one of the world's largest and most complicated supply chains from its headquarters in Taiwan. This chapter describes Foxconn's experiment with blockchain to transform its global operation. Nolan Bauerle of *CoinDesk* is the first to tell the story in depth. A well-known and highly regarded blockchain authority, he has beautifully articulated Foxconn's suite of digital relationships and its application of blockchain technology.

Nolan looks at Foxconn's application of advanced cryptographic techniques and decentralized networks to build trustable digital relationships among its many partners, suppliers, products, factories, tools, and customers. He also explores Chained Finance, the payments and supply-chain management tool launched by the finance arm of Foxconn to solve several integration problems. It should help readers to rethink how they currently grease the wheels of global trade.

Chapter 3 delves into trust and verification, two of the most important benefits of blockchain technology. The vast dollar amount of the diamond industry indicates how valuable a blockchain-based solution can be in reducing fraud and securing property rights. People will be confident that the stones they purchased are legitimate and stolen property can easily be returned to the rightful owner.

This chapter investigates how Everledger tackles these supply-chain problems in the diamond industry. Its author, Anthony Williams of DEEP Centre, explains how diamond trade's opacity has worsened human suffering and stripped developing companies of valuable resources without proper compensation. He focuses on Everledger's use of blockchain technology for the common good of all stakeholders. It should prompt readers to reexamine how they establish trust and accountability in the provenance of assets.

Chapter 4 covers various technologies, especially blockchain, that have real promise to transform agriculture in such areas as food safety, fraud reduction, and market access for small farmers. The first area is perhaps the most important, since foodborne infectious diseases can have disastrous effects on public health and local economies if unchecked in cross-border trade. This chapter shows how blockchain can track fresh produce and meat from farm to fork.

In addition to reducing hazards and screening out bad actors, blockchain and the Internet of Things can dramatically improve agriculture. The authors of Chapter 4, Henry Kim and Marek Laskowski of York University, show how blockchain, soil sensors, satellite monitoring, and drones can increase crop yields, improve quality of crops and soil, and reduce waste throughout the food supply chain—plugging small, independent farmers into the global supply chain, increasing local yields and capabilities, and moving excess supply to where people and animals are starving.

When the largest company in the United States deploys blockchain, we should all take note. Chapter 5 explains how Walmart implemented a blockchain solution to food provenance in two pilot projects—pork in China and mangoes in the Americas. Its author, Reshma Kamath, does a remarkable job detailing how these two foodstuffs get from farm to fork and how the blockchain captures and shares data along the way.

In combination with sensors and the global positioning system, blockchain helps increase food safety by optimizing supply routes for efficiency, minimizing impact on cargo, and monitoring health and treatment of livestock and the conditions of transport and storage of foodstuffs. Since bruised or damaged produce quickly loses value, this increased supply-chain visibility improves profitability. Walmart's experience in collaboration with IBM shows how blockchain technology can increase the accuracy, utility, and timeliness of data across a supply chain. In the event of a health issue, up-to-date and complete information helps to isolate and identify the problem and prevent it from becoming a public health crisis.

Chapter 6 details border control, a very important area of study. Not only does cross-border trade fuel the global economy, with customs a source of revenue for governments, but the volume of transported goods creates great costs and potentially lengthy delays in global supply chains. In addition, funds, products, and people crossing borders generate security and safety concerns and have legal and fee-generation implications. While we have made some technological improvements in this arena, blockchain has the potential to revolutionize how customs agencies operate.

Blockchain technology can increase safety and security by more accurately identifying the source and identity of money, goods, and people, while reducing costs and increasing processing speed. In this chapter, Alan Cohn of Steptoe & Johnson explores how best to achieve these goals, what the US Customs and Border Protection has learned thus far, and what readers should understand about blockchain at the borders in their supply chain.

Chapter 7 connects multiple supply-chain innovations: advanced robotics, additive manufacturing (3D printing), augmented reality, artificial intelligence, and big data analytics. Distributed ledgers can serve as the open platform to bind these technological advances together and achieve end-to-end digital integration across the supply chain, from sourcing to delivery.

This chapter also illustrates the concepts of smart products, smart factories, and mass customization through use cases. Its author, Stefan Hopf, understands both the scope and the magnitude of transformation underway in manufacturing as both a researcher and a practitioner in the space. Stefan provides thoughtful analysis and a clear assessment framework for readers to determine which blockchain applications would be most useful to explore for their supply chains.

Chapter 8 walks us through the complicated supply chain of an enormously complicated product, the airplane. It incorporates hundreds of parts from multiple manufacturers, and its owners expect to use it constantly for thirty years. Failure risk is catastrophic: precision, security, and quality are paramount. This chapter elaborates upon the efforts of Moog, a global designer, manufacturer, and integrator of precision motion control products and systems focused on the aerospace industry with its razor-thin margins.

The chapter's authors, Vineet Narula and Prema Shrikrishna, have done an extraordinary job of detailing how the combination of blockchain and additive manufacturing increases precision and reduces the costs of maintenance, inventory, and shipping, since custom parts can be printed on site and on demand. Vineet and Prema also illustrate how blockchain technology helps to ensure security, encourage innovation, preserve intellectual property rights, and enhance supply-chain visibility within a high-stakes/low-margin industry. Any company with valuable patents and designs will learn how to license it securely and to automate licensing within a supply chain—it is fascinating work!

Chapter 9 is a capstone chapter. It pulls ideas from the previous chapters into a foundational study of China's impressive "One Belt One Road" initiative. Inspired by the Silk Road, which originally referred to the Han Dynasty trade route connecting the Far East with the Mediterranean region, this twenty-first century version is connecting over 150 countries across Asia, Africa, Europe, and the

Americas by land and sea.[4] It is a massive multistakeholder project designed to implement China's economic development strategy.

In this chapter, Prema and Vineet describe the Belt and Road Blockchain Consortium organized to support governance of One Belt One Road. Chinese leaders believe in blockchain—and they are eager to use it to reduce business friction while improving transparency and trust. It is a bold vision of what is possible when diverse stakeholders come together with open minds, identify their common interests, acknowledge each other's concerns, and collaborate in governance networks to transform global supply chains.

A key theme of the book is *governance.* By governance, we mean *stewardship,* which involves collaborating, identifying common interests, and creating incentives to act on them. We do not mean *government,* regulation, or top-down or centralized control. Throughout, contributors explore governance needs at three levels:

- Protocol/platform (e.g., scalability, consensus mechanism)
- Application (e.g., oversight, skilled talent, user-friendly interfaces)
- Ecosystem/industry (proper legal structure, regulatory restraint, scientific research)

Given the COVID-19 crisis, we hope you find this book a helpful and hopeful glimpse into the fast approaching future of global supply chains, an ecosystem ripe for disruption at every level and in every role. Distributed ledgers—combined with the Internet of Things, artificial intelligence, machine learning, robotics, sensors, and the global positioning system—will transform the practices of operations, logistics, procurement and purchasing, transportation, customs and border control, trade finance and insurance, manufacturing, and inventory management, making the whole network more adaptable and responsive to demand and crisis. There are ideas and opportunities here for everyone to discuss with their collaborators, customers, and suppliers. Now is the time to participate in the blockchain revolution.

CHAPTER 1

BLOCKCHAIN IN GLOBAL TRADE

Revitalizing International Commerce in the Digital Era

Soumak Chatterjee, Louisa Bai, Vikas Singla,
Kshitish Balhotra, Neha Bhasin, and Cara Engelbrecht

 ## GLOBAL TRADE IN BRIEF

- Global trade has grown in complexity and magnitude over millennia, but its processes remain relatively unchanged. Blockchain technologies could help to modernize the industry and link together other capabilities for the twenty-first century.

- Each participant in the network of global trade stands to derive unique value from blockchain; however, the most successful implementation and commercialization of platforms will be contingent upon collaboration rather than competition.

- Activity in the global trade market confirms the interest of participants in pursuing blockchain endeavors and the notion that blockchain is disruptive. However, they have questions about the paths beyond prototyping and the value of paths unexplored.

- As blockchain matures, and prototypes in global trade applications prove successful, organizations will need to create a road map for their journey to implementation, a map requiring deliberation on business and technical fronts.

- These deliberations include such unresolved issues as blockchain ecosystem, governance, standards, regulation, and law; as well as issues of platform performance, scalability, interoperability, and integration.

GLOBAL TRADE: TIMELESS CONCEPT, TIRED PROCESSES

THE LANDSCAPE OF GLOBAL TRADE

International trading between countries and across continents has existed since ancient times. In its early days, cross-border trade occurred primarily for goods such as textiles, spices, precious metals and stones, and art. Through the Silk Road, the Spice Route, and myriad other trade networks, civilizations have cultivated trade patterns that have blossomed with industrialization and globalization.[1] For example, according to the World Trade Organization (WTO), world exports of manufactured goods increased from $8 trillion to $11 trillion between 2006 and 2016 alone.[2] The WTO also reported that, in the same decade, world exports of commercial services increased by $1.9 trillion, to a total of $4.8 trillion.[3]

While the general precept of global trade is simple and unchanged—to move goods and money from point A in one country to point B in another country—its reality is more complex. Its activities include financing trade, tracking and tracing goods within supply chains, and verifying the quality of those goods through provenance and product pedigree.

As global trade has grown in scale, its processes have become more numerous and intricate, yet they strain to accommodate the demands of increased trade volume among more participants—financiers, corporations as importers and exporters servicing various markets, freight forwarders, customs and port authorities, regulatory bodies, and insurance providers.

THE CHALLENGING STATE OF TRADE

On the operations side, global trade still relies heavily on costly, opaque, and time-consuming processes. Documentation is largely paper-based and handled manually; the astounding volume of documents is labor intensive. Approvals requiring sign-off from multiple parties often cause delay. There is little traceability of supply-chain hiccups: pinpointing breakdowns in quality control and compliance is difficult. Approvals at checkpoints on cross-border orders are susceptible to fraud. Such manual processing often proves costly for importers and exporters.

On the finance side, banks hesitate to provide deep-tier financing—that is, financing for companies further down a supply chain from the corporations with the strongest brand power—which reduces the ability of importers and exporters to obtain pre- and post-shipment funding. It also reduces the ability to perform invoice factoring effectively, which often enables companies to continue operating without tying up their cash in transactions. The frustrations of manual processes and the hesitations to extend financial services to smaller players contribute to an environment of distrust.

Parties throughout the supply chain—banks, freight forwarders, importers, exporters, customs and port authorities, and regulators—lean on preexisting relationships to avoid such complications. This environment of distrust, however, is what makes global trade suitable for blockchain use cases.

BLOCKCHAIN'S ROLE IN BREAKING DOWN BARRIERS

Discord and disruption are familiar to companies leading technological innovation. Recently, companies have addressed their many opportunities to innovate by launching transformation initiatives within organizational silos. But projects in different domains have sometimes, despite their boldness, failed to thrive on their own.[4]

For example, projects rooted in domain-specific cloud and analytics led companies to realize that complex predictive analytic capabilities deliver little value without big data—and vice versa.

Companies need to consider digital tools and technologies as part of a broader suite. To drive maximum value, disruptive technologies need to complement each other, like instruments in a symphony. Thus, a *symphonic enterprise,* such as Sysco or Vodafone, orchestrates several innovations, such that enterprise strategy, technology, and operations harmonize across all domains and boundaries.[5] Blockchain will be an important innovation for realizing new efficiencies in global trade.

Blockchain has potential for deep foundational re-architecture, meaning that global trade participants could use it to redesign processes and transform outdated business models. They could lean not on paper, but on cryptographically secure digital records and codified business rules. They could use smart contracts—distributed software applications that mimic the terms of agreements, run across multiple computers, and execute by consensus—to enforce business rules and deal terms automatically, even among untrusting parties.[6]

Blockchain also has the potential to secure global trade through the implementation of public key infrastructure, a means of authenticating participants and permissioning access. It could reduce the number of gatekeepers required to verify transactions along trade routes. It could also increase the immutability and traceability of data, assets, and documents. To realize such benefits, numerous efforts are underway to develop blockchain use cases for global trade.

In an ideal future, blockchain would help to optimize the entire ecosystem. That would require participants to re-evaluate the orthodoxies that underpin their systems. Then everyone in the ecosystem would need to collaborate end to end, across industries and geographies. Blockchain's key theme for global trade in the twenty-first century is collaboration. In the next era of the digital economy, where the symphonic enterprise thrives, the shift from competition toward cooperation is inevitable.

THE BLOCKCHAIN DIFFERENCE FOR THE GLOBAL TRADE NETWORK

To reimagine global trade fully, we need to understand the roles of the primary participants, their challenges as well as their constraints for blockchain adoption. A blockchain-enabled solution that works for all of them will take time to develop. Therefore, we see value in multiple approaches to addressing the diversity of needs. As the technology matures, the key will be interoperability among the successful initiatives.

BANKS AND FINANCIERS

Banks and financiers are the conduits of trade finance. By providing factoring and forfaiting services as well as products—such as letters of credit, promissory notes, bills of exchange, bank guarantees, and bank payment obligations—that protect exporters from nonpayment risk, banks and financiers help corporations to participate in international trade.

But manual processes expose these financial firms to the risk of fraud. Consider these examples. In 2018, India's Punjab National Bank disclosed a $1.8 billion fraud, where a deputy branch manager sent fake letters of guarantee to bank branches outside India, so that they would loan money to a group of jewelry companies.[7] In 2014, Standard Chartered Bank lost nearly $200 million at China's Qingdao Port when a Singaporean businessperson's companies used invoices several times for the same metals stockpiles, dipping into banks' finances repeatedly, for what should have been a single transaction.[8] In 2008, a transatlantic conspiracy defrauded banks like JPMorgan Chase & Co. for close to $700 million in loans on what turned out to be fictitious purchase orders and invoices for metal shipments.[9]

Banks also lack tools for tracking the movement and condition of goods between checkpoints, they cannot triage issues as they arise or before they are beyond rectifying, and so they bear the risks associated with delayed, damaged, or even undelivered goods.

The opacity of asset movement further prevents banks from offering innovative trade finance products that could cater to under-served market participants—like deep-tier financing to *small and medium-sized enterprises* (SMEs)—as banks already undertake significant risk with large clients who have proven track records. The risks associated with trade financing, particularly those that increase the already high cost of capital, increase the pressure on banks to reduce trade finance liabilities associated with Basel III regulation.[10]

Blockchain will enable banks to reduce paperwork and manual processing as well as transaction reconciliation. The digitization of trade finance processes could reduce operational and compliance costs by a potential 10 to 15 percent.[11] Blockchain infrastructure shared among participants could automate purchase order and invoice reconciliation.

TABLE 1-1

BANKS AND FINANCIERS

Challenges with current processes	• Manual processes, paper documents • High probability of fraud • Difficulty in asset tracking • Lack of innovative trade finance offerings • High pressure to shed trade finance liabilities from Basel III regulation
Needs align with these value characteristics	• Digital processes and documentation • Streamlined processes and reduced costs • Storage and sharing on an immutable ledger • Near real-time forensics analysis • Innovative products targeting underserved segments
Considerations for blockchain adoption	• Navigation of multiple jurisdictions • Data segregation and privacy of proprietary data • Integration with legacy information technologies • Implementation of KYC/AML-compliant digital identity network

Blockchain could also enable banks to serve underserved markets such as SMEs with limited financial histories. According to International Chamber of Commerce in its 2016 "Global Survey on Trade Finance," 58 percent of rejected trade finance proposals were SME applications, even though the SME sector submitted only 44 percent of all trade finance proposals.[12] With greater transparency in asset tracking, blockchain will enable banks to evaluate risk better, take on new customer segments like SMEs, and increase their credit offerings through more innovative trade finance programs.

While blockchain will disrupt the status quo of trade finance, it will add value only when the core elements of the business are ready to receive it. For example, blockchain could extend, enhance, and complement—but not entirely replace—a bank's existing technologies.

CORPORATIONS

As importers and exporters, corporations fuel what we know as global trade in supplying and demanding the goods that change hands. From trade finance to supply-chain track and trace, through to provenance and product pedigree, corporations play a vital role along each pillar of global trade activities.

Nowadays, corporations rely on highly latent, manual, paper-based processes for global trade. They often have limited visibility into goods movement. They also have limited ability to track assets or discover and address issues of product quality, logistics, or transportation as they arise. Because of poor visibility of parts availability in outsourced contractors, Boeing delayed the production of its 787 Dreamliner aircraft by six months, which lengthened to a revised timeline amounting to years.[13] After the announcement of the initial delay, Boeing's shares fell 2.7 percent.

According to the WTO, access to trade finance is increasingly competitive, as regulation pressures financiers to minimize margins and take on fewer trade finance liabilities.[14] It's so competitive that small and medium-sized exporters end up with inadequate access to trade finance. With limited visibility into goods movement, importers end up with high insurance premiums to offset financiers' perceived risk of fraud or nonfulfillment of goods.

Blockchain supports transparency across transactions. For global trade use cases, that attribute imparts visibility into the supply chain. With such visibility, banks and financiers will be better able to calculate the risk associated with extending financing to smaller companies, and those companies will be better positioned to access trade finance products. US start-up Wave has proven that the use of *distributed ledger technology* (DLT) can reduce trade transaction time from 20 days to a few hours.[15] This streamlined process will make for same-day payments, benefiting not only the exporters but also the importers and banks. Implementing blockchain in the network will unlock a wider marketplace for trade finance products. With more banks and financiers willing and able to diversify their products aimed at corporations, corporations could consider competitive offers.

Corporations can also leverage *Internet of Things* (IoT) technologies to collect data on their products during transportation and store the information on the blockchain. From sensor-collected data, corporations could draw insights that could help to improve product quality, improved provenance of product, certified product pedigree, optimization of transportation attributes, and other operational efficiencies. In the last quarter of 2015, Chipotle's profits were down 44 percent over the previous year because of the presence of E. coli in ingredients. Through improved supply-chain traceability and the use of IoT sensors, restaurants could avoid the impact of food contamination.[16]

Corporations will have to be mindful about how they share their data, especially proprietary information, over the blockchain. They will need to identify which trade partners should have access to which pieces of information. For example, if a corporation exports perishable goods and uses sensors to track their quality, then it could give certain trade partners permission to view the sensor data.

Corporations will also need to consider integrating their existing information technology (IT) infrastructure with the blockchain solutions they are looking to implement. If the new technology sits in a silo separate from that of *enterprise resource planning* (ERP) software, a company will not realize some of the operational efficiencies of blockchain in global trade. If the ERP software cannot access documents stored on blockchain, the user will have to double-down on document entry anyway.

TABLE 1-2
CORPORATIONS

Challenges with current processes	• Reliance on paper-based processes that are manual, slow, and costly • Difficulty in asset tracking because of opacity in supply-chain processes and movement of goods • Transactional complications like payment delay or nonpayment to exporters and delivery delay or failure to supply to importers • Barriers to accessing trade financing on two fronts: for SMEs looking to export and for importers seeking innovative products
Needs align with these value characteristics	• Improved access to capital via pre- or post-shipment financing, invoice factoring, and other trade finance products • Supply-chain traceability and trade financing enabled for deep-tier transactions • Streamlined processes and reduced costs with document digitization, storage and sharing on an immutable ledger • Improved product quality and provenance of goods from insights built on sensor-drawn data shared via blockchain
Considerations for blockchain adoption	• Data segregation and privacy of proprietary data defined to inform what can or cannot be shared via blockchain • Legacy information technologies that are fundamental to business operations working in step with new blockchains • Closer collaboration enabled with port and customs authorities to leverage blockchain to garner reliable estimates on processing time • Ease of use across key facets such as cost and specific business value as an importer or exporter

FREIGHT FORWARDERS AND CARRIERS

Freight forwarders and carriers provide a vital link in global trade by managing logistics of moving cargo in supply chains. Forwarders orchestrate the journey of goods between their origin and destination, while carriers execute the journey.

Freight forwarders and carriers rely on paper-based processes, much like other trade participants, and on manual (rather than automated) interaction with a majority of their partners. In a study of freight transport and logistics, the European Parliament found that, because of the lack of digital technology, freight forwarders incur nonessential costs such as premium freight.[17] Maritime transport invoicing and payment processing cost the industry an estimated $34.4 billion annually.[18]

Freight forwarders have limited visibility into transferring assets; this lack of visibility results in low margins and high insurance premiums. Such difficulties in asset tracking pose a high risk to the pharmaceutical industry: INTERPOL found that approximately one million people die each year from counterfeit drugs in the system.[19] Freight carriers want to prevent theft of cargo. The current system relies on manual verification, and so unauthorized individuals could slip through and collect cargo. In 2017, cargo theft in Canada amounted to $35.6 million, a nine percent increase from the previous year.[20]

Blockchain can enable the digital handling of trade documents, such as purchase orders and bills of lading. Near real-time sharing and verification of trade documents on the blockchain will also help streamline the process of asset tracking and offer freight forwarders visibility into the supply they do not have. DHL and Accenture are developing a blockchain-based serialization project to combat counterfeiting of drugs and false medication.[21] The solution will provide a sophisticated track-and-trace capability to show that pharmaceutical products have come from legitimate manufacturers and were handled properly from source to consumer. Digital handling of trade documents will help reduce processing time, expediting payments and communications between trade participants. We could pair document digitization with digital identities to reduce the risk of freight theft. Leveraging digital identities to authenticate claimant freight collectors will augment the level of security of existing verification processes.

Freight forwarders and carriers can also leverage IoT technologies and use blockchain to manage sensor-collected data. For example, capacity monitoring via IoT sensors in trucks and other cargo vessels can help determine volume-based cost of shipping freight rapidly and accurately. IoT sensors can also track quality of goods against product attributes and parameters, and such data can be stored on blockchain and communicated to parties interested in performing quality assurance.

TABLE 1-3
FREIGHT FORWARDERS AND CARRIERS

Challenges with current processes	• Reliance on paper-based processes and manual interaction with partners throughout the supply chain • Lack of technology resulting in the incurrence of nonessential costs, like premium freight • Difficulty in asset tracking because of opacity in supply-chain processes and movement of goods • Potential theft of freight because of reliance on manual processes for verification and authentication of cargo collectors
Needs align with these value characteristics	• Visibility into the movement of goods along the supply chain that will enable more informed decision-making • Reduced processing time through document digitization and faster receipt of payment • Improved authentication of freight collectors via verification of digital identities, and reduced risk of cargo theft • Real-time capacity monitoring based on sensor-collected data relayed to the blockchain
Considerations for blockchain adoption	• Navigation of multiple jurisdictions' recognition of smart-contract legitimacy when processing digitalized documentation • Data privacy and permissions, especially as data on customers' product attributes are tracked in real time using sensors • Ease of use across key facets, such as cost and specific business value

Before adopting blockchain, freight forwarders and carriers will need to identify standards for the documents they seek to digitalize. They must be able to attest to the legitimacy of documentation they present when crossing borders or delivering cargo in multiple jurisdictions. Standards-setting often involves extensive deliberation and discussion with the various stakeholders in global trade so that all will honor the digitalized documents upon presentation. An IBM-led trade finance project secured support from the government department, Dubai Customs, as well as the integrated electronic services provider, Dubai Trade. With Dubai's support, IBM was able to recruit different parties—Emirates NBD Bank, Banco Santander, freight company Aramex, the UAE-based telecommunications service Du, and an airline—to participate in the project and demonstrate the use of DLT and smart contracts in trade finance.[22]

Freight carriers will also need to consider how they wish to share data and with whom, and what sort of permissions they need to pair with their blockchain solutions, to maintain data integrity. With the proliferation of IoT sensors collecting proprietary data on goods in transport, permissioning will be especially vital, since freight forwarders and carriers bear responsibility for these data.

CUSTOMS AND PORT AUTHORITIES

Customs and port authorities approve and handle the transfer of goods at intersections of transport routes. With this transfer comes the need to sort through layers of logistical and regulatory data on the cargo's origin, destination, and the pathways between.

Within the freight supply chain, there are many stakeholders—each with its own set of platforms and methods. Multiple versions of the same document can inundate end users, especially if they need to input one set of data in multiple places. Such circumstances open gaps for fraudulent or malicious activity in the supply chain. How are authorities to give their stamp of approval on the entry of goods, based on inadequately processed documents?

In 2017, a European Anti-Fraud Office investigation revealed that UK Customs lost approximately €1.9 billion because of the under-valuation of textiles and footwear.[23] Saudi Arabia's customs also lost almost $30 million in revenue because of customs duty evasion.[24] Many processes, like customs-clearing, still rely on manual completion and paper documentation. Intermediaries can spend hours just monitoring the documents required to settle contracts. These processes are inherently vulnerable to human error.

By digitizing trade documents and storing them on a distributed ledger, port and customs authorities would have real-time access and insight into tariff codes, classification data, origin information, import and export certificates, customs values, and clearance status. Digitized trade documents on the blockchain would reduce the operational costs and volume of manual paperwork that currently support trade facilitation and customs enforcement.

TABLE 1-4

CUSTOMS AND PORT AUTHORITIES

Challenges with current processes	• Replication of document entry across multiple platforms and consequent variance between different versions of the same data • Inefficient container examination processes that rely heavily on paperwork and iterative coordination with the terminal • Counterfeit goods that slip through the gaps opened up by reliance on highly manual processes • Vulnerability to human error and slow processing speed that needs to be more predictable and cost-efficient
Needs align with these value characteristics	• Real-time and transparent access to accurate data, per establishment of a single source of truth • Improved data quality regarding corporations and freight carriers to enable reliable analytics and new insights • Streamlined processing that is faster, affordable, and digitized
Considerations for blockchain adoption	• Integration with port community systems to prevent process duplication between existing methods and blockchain • Navigation of multiple jurisdictions' recognition of smart-contract legitimacy when processing digitalized documentation

Asset tracking capabilities on blockchain would also provide customs and port authorities greater visibility and insight into the actual and anticipated flow of goods, so that they could plan better for demand and realize more operational efficiencies.

Currently, most port authorities connect primarily to their supply-chain partners, such as government bodies and businesses, via electronic platforms known as *port community systems* (PCS).[25] PCS offers transport infrastructure management. In the most technologically advanced trade communities, PCS interfaces with *maritime single window* systems and *trade single window* systems for transport and trade regulations, respectively.[26] To maximize blockchain's value for ports and customs authorities, any blockchain-based platform must be able to communicate with these systems.

REGULATORY BODIES

Regulators ensure sound trade finance practices and verify authenticity of exported or imported goods. Regulatory bodies operate at various tiers. At the international level, the WTO administers world trade agreements and negotiations and monitors national trade policies. Concurrently, nations have their own federal departments and even regional bodies overseeing trade-related activities. They work with banks and financiers to execute *anti–money laundering* and *know-your-customer* (AML/KYC) requirements and other industry anti-terrorism measures, and with customs authorities to confirm the legitimacy of traded materials.

But oversight is challenging because of the paper-based nature of transactions. Between January 2004 and May 2009, trade-based money laundering totaled more than $276 billion.[27] Global Financial Integrity estimated that 14 to 24 percent of the total trade for developing and emerging economies between 2005 and 2014 came from illicit inflows and outflows involving such schemes as misrepresentation of price, quantity, or quality of goods.[28]

To scrutinize transaction documentation, banks employ extensive teams of document checkers who highlight discrepancies between line entries or missing fields as well as contraventions of internal banking policies and state and port-specific sanctions. These teams also check for compliance with international trading standards and embargoes, per Uniform Customs and Practice for Documentary Credits (UCP) and the International Chamber of Commerce's International Standard Banking Practice. The intensive, heavily manual process of document scrutiny, however, leaves gaps for illegal activity.

Perhaps the most significant value regulatory bodies can derive from blockchain is direct oversight of global trade processes. The transparency of blockchain would enable regulators to have direct, instant, and full visibility into transactions related to asset transfers in near real time. Regulators could better analyze systemic risk and improve credit rating information.

RegChain, a proof of concept (POC) developed by the Bank of Ireland in collaboration with Deloitte Ireland, demonstrated a relevant use case in global asset servicing and fund management. Its goal was to create a regulatory reporting platform accessible to both the reporting entity and the regulator. Findings from the POC attested to blockchain's value in managing regulatory change requests and facilitating additional or new reporting requirements.[29] Within the blockchain, regulators can change code once on the platform and then push it across the network to all participants, in contrast with the legacy model, wherein each institution would manage a change request in its own operations.

KYC utilities, with improved KYC data storage security via blockchain implementation, can reduce the time that correspondent banks spend on repetitive due diligence processes. To satisfy KYC regulations, digital identities on blockchain would be a more efficient method of identifying clients and legal persons. Blockchain can also help regulators improve AML compliance. For example, smart contracts can hard-code rules that trigger an alert of a sanctions risk on the counterparty during a trade transaction.

To manage the unlocking of hard-coding in response to regulatory changes within a blockchain-based solution, regulators need to play an active role in blockchain endeavors involving multiple participants. That means collaborating with other stakeholders in global trade, particularly banks and financiers, to develop solutions that give regulators direct oversight over transactional data.

TABLE 1-5

REGULATORY BODIES

Challenges with current processes	• Manual examination and verification of paper-based documentation that is costly in terms of both time and resources • Slow propagation and adoption of changing regulations because of the paper-based nature of most global trade processes • Delayed access to data that is necessary for enforcing regulatory compliance
Needs align with these value characteristics	• Easier codification of rules via smart contracts, reducing dependency on independent change protocols, and streamlining adoption • Faster identification of clients and legal persons to satisfy KYC regulations via digital identities and KYC utilities • Improved AML compliance through automatic triggers and alerts for transactions where sanctions risks exist
Considerations for blockchain adoption	• Strategically partnering with other participants in the global trade network to create transformative blockchain solutions

INSURANCE PROVIDERS

Insurers are omnipresent in global trade. Across all activities, exporters and importers have reasons to seek insurance. First, they may want to insure against damage of goods in transit or storage. Exporters may have qualms about risk of nonpayment, credit worthiness of new customers, and costs associated with the return of goods deemed unacceptable or with related litigation. Conversely, importers may have qualms about exporters' failure to supply, delays in transport such as stalls at ports or customs, payment of duties on imported goods, storage of goods in bonded warehouses, and poor product performance or quality. Exporters and importers also need to protect themselves against currency fluctuations, in consideration of the full cycle of cross-border trade end to end.

Even with robust rationales for insurance, exporters and importers throughout the supply chain do not secure insurance directly. They liaise with specialist brokers to insure their products, but most insurance in global trade transpires between insurers and banks (for trade financing applications) or between insurers and freight carriers (for track-and-trace applications) and propagates through the supply chain accordingly.

Before insurers can issue a claims payment, they must navigate a lengthy claims management process through which they reconcile multiple versions of the same information, recorded in documents prepared separately by clients, brokers, retro- and reinsurers, underwriters, and claims managers. The document matching process is very time-consuming and costly. Such lack of certainty often muddles dispute resolution between insurers and claimants. Issuing a payment on a claim can sometimes take years.

In some applications where different supply-chain participants are clients of different insurers, assessing which insurer carries the risk is difficult, when goods are damaged or destroyed somewhere in the chain of custody. Insurers also generally absorb extra costs by insuring more often for maximum risk, rather than actual risk, based on the information available to them.

Compared to paper-based processes, blockchain-based processes are more tamper-proof. With blockchain, multiple untrusting parties can share information and documentation effectively under the tenet of immutability. All parties are privy to a single source of truth. Blockchain strips away the lengthy document reconciliation process that slows claims management today. Blockchain also offers more effective dispute resolution among insurers: greater visibility into the supply chain via asset tracking helps to pinpoint which insurer carries risk and when. Insurers will be able to track their exposure to and liability for risk in near real time.

Insurers can also look at applications at the intersection of IoT and blockchain. By using sensors to collect real-time data on goods or cargo—data on their location, the temperature of their container, and other attributes—insurers will be in a better position to offer innovative products tailored to their customers. They can share these data via blockchain and leverage it to offer niche products on demand. Similarly, pairing IoT sensor technology and blockchain can enable insurers to insure based on actual volumes of goods, instead of the maximum capacity of freight containers or warehouses containing goods.

TABLE 1-6

INSURANCE PROVIDERS

Challenges with current processes	• Lengthy claims management processes requiring reconciliation of ancillary contract documentation sourced from many parties • Lack of certainty adding levels of complexity and significant delay to dispute resolution on claims • Insuring for maximum risk instead of actual risk based on availability of data that is broad and not necessarily client-specific
Needs align with these value characteristics	• Single source of truth per tamper-proof and time-stamped nature of blockchain and document digitization • Visibility into the supply chain and corresponding chain of custody, which offers legal certainty to resolve disputes • Ability to offer precise and targeted products in near real time by making use of rich, sensor-collected data and sharing it via blockchain
Considerations for blockchain adoption	• Navigation of multiple jurisdictions' recognition of smart-contract legitimacy when processing digitalized documentation • Data segregation and privacy of proprietary data need to be defined to inform what can or cannot be shared via blockchain • Legacy information technologies fundamental to business operations will need to work in step with new blockchains • Implementation of a robust digital identity network to enable market-wide transactions in line with AML/KYC regulations

The constraints that insurers need to consider mirror those of banks and financiers. Smart-contract legitimacy will be particularly important to insurers, especially in the claims management process, which requires multiparty alignment on ancillary contract documentation.

CURRENT INITIATIVES AND PURSUITS

Participants in the global trade network realize the power of blockchain, and some have started acting on and executing their blockchain visions. Their actions align with three pillars of activity: trade finance, supply-chain track and trace, and product pedigree and provenance. To project where blockchain will take global trade, let's look at current shifts in the landscape and map out the path forward.

BLOCKCHAIN ACTIVITY IN TRADE, TO DATE

Case study 1: HKMA trade finance

"Nearly half of the trade transactions in Hong Kong fail to obtain financing because of the lack of trust and potential fraudulent loss," said Dr. Paul Sin, a partner and leader with Deloitte China's fintech practice.[30] In 2017, Hong Kong's total merchandise trade was just over $1 trillion. Hong Kong also manages a significant portion of the Chinese mainland's external trade. So the underserved trade transaction market there is quite sizable.[31] Enter the Hong Kong Monetary Authority (HKMA), with a mandate to uphold Hong Kong's status as an international financial center. HKMA recognized the opportunity to innovate in trade finance.[32]

In 2017, Deloitte China worked with HKMA and five leading banks in Hong Kong to identify, illustrate, and implement blockchain solutions in trade finance. The POC carved out for them a distinct market advantage rooted in operational efficiency, to overcome such challenges as the lack of trust between parties, unreliable provenance of goods, and nonstandardized, labor-intensive paper workflows.[33] Leveraging blockchain for data distribution, the POC's primary objectives were to:

- Prove the authenticity of all trade documentation—such as purchase orders, bills of lading, and invoices—by sharing the status of each transaction to all trade participants.
- Reduce fraud loss by creating alerts on duplicated financing.
- Minimize human effort in invoice reconciliations by using smart contracts to automate select processes.
- Protect customer privacy and proprietary business information from other participants in the network by allowing only authorized access to privileged data.[34]

The success of the POC has led HKMA to partner with the Monetary Authority of Singapore and the Financial Services Regulatory Authority of Abu Dhabi in using blockchain for trade finance on a cross-jurisdiction scale.[35]

Case study 2: we.trade trading platform

we.trade is an SME-to-SME international trading platform. Formerly known as Digital Trade Chain, we.trade launched as a joint venture among nine European banks—HSBC, Natixis, Nordea, Rabobank, Deutsche Bank, KBC, Santander, Société Générale, and UniCredit—with IBM providing technical support.[36]

SMEs connect with each other over the platform to order goods, and their respective banks provide financing. Freight carriers and forwarders, regulators, insurers, and other third parties connect through open *application programming interfaces* (APIs).[37] All parties can view transactional activity via Web and mobile applications. we.trade aims to be user-friendly and available 24 hours a day, seven days a week.

The joint venture delivered quickly on its platform, and it credits its fast pace to its narrow scope: by electing to focus on SMEs and their preexisting banking partners, we.trade was able to create a solution fit for purpose without a disorienting level of complexity.[38] This approach allowed it to prototype rapidly, conduct transactions early in the summer of 2018, and scale up as it entertained additional use cases. Since its launch, CaixaBank, Eurobank, Erste Group Bank, and UBS have joined as banking partners.[39] It now offers track-and-trace capabilities for 426 couriers.[40]

Roberto Mancone, global head of disruptive technologies and solutions at Deutsche Bank, said, "Later on, clients may start to rate each other, based on reliability, timely delivery and timely payment."[41] Similarly, Anne Gorge, global head of product management and trade services at Société Générale, hinted at we.trade's exploring pre-shipment finance in an application that would integrate the physical supply chain into the platform.[42] For now, we.trade plans to expand its platform's network beyond Europe and possibly to conduct intercontinental trade in 2019.[43]

Case study 3: Maersk-IBM streamlined shipping

In July 2017, shipping juggernaut Maersk recovered from the notorious NotPetya ransomware incident by reinstalling over 4,000 servers, 45,000 personal computers, and 2,500 applications over the course of 10 days.[44] In effect, Maersk IT staff was tasked with the equivalent of installing a new infrastructure from square one. For those 10 days, Maersk had to operate without any IT. Somehow, it managed to deliver on 80 percent of all its shipping volume under these conditions, at a pace in which a ship with 20,000 containers entered a port every 15 minutes.[45] Maersk's ability to navigate such stormy waters is a testament to its resilience. It was quick to investigate technology that could secure its transactions.

Fast forward six months from the ransomware attack to Maersk and IBM's announcement of their intent to establish a joint venture.[46] The two companies, which started collaborating in 2016, have launched a blockchain platform, piloted on an international scale by companies like Dow Chemical, DuPont, Tetra Pak, Port Houston, the Rotterdam Port Community System, the Customs Administration of the Netherlands, and the US Customs and Border Protection.[47] The platform itself is built on Hyperledger Fabric 1.0 and IBM Blockchain technology, delivered through the IBM Cloud.[48]

Citing the World Economic Forum, Maersk and IBM assert a potential increase in global trade of 15 percent through the reduction of barriers within supply chains alone.[49] The companies have selected two core capabilities in which they aim to streamline activities in freight forwarding:

- Shipping information pipeline that will provide end-to-end visibility in the supply chain and allow participants to exchange information related to shipment events in near real time.

- Paperless trade that will automate manual paperwork activities and reduce the time and cost involved associated with clearance and cargo movement.[50]

More global corporations are signing on to the Maersk-IBM platform.[51] General Motors and Procter & Gamble are looking to leverage it in streamlining their complex supply chains, and Agility Logistics is seeking to provide customs clearance brokerage, among other improved customer services, on the platform. Customs and government authorities such as Peruvian Customs and Singapore Customs, as well as global terminal operators such as APM Terminals and PSA International, will be collaborating with the platform to facilitate trade flows.

THE UNEXPLORED POTENTIAL OF BLOCKCHAIN IN GLOBAL TRADE

As blockchain applications come to life for global trade, leaders in global trade must be aware of how the digital enhancements reflect on value generation. Leading-edge firms are piloting blockchain projects in silos, along key verticals. Table 1-7 maps out the value chain to illustrate the pace of blockchain innovation in global trade and the focus on certain capabilities (e.g., document digitization, product tracking) over others (e.g., digital identities for AML/KYC). The industry still has a lot of ground to cover.

TABLE 1-7

LEVEL OF BLOCKCHAIN ACTIVITY IN THE VALUE CHAIN

PARTNER ONBOARDING	Know your customer requirements	Anti-money laundering requirements	Customer registration	Customs verification	Freight forwarding documentation	Product quality authentication
TRANSACTION MANAGEMENT	Payment tracking	Invoice management	Purchase order management	Post-shipment	Letters of credit, bills of exchange	
TRADE FINANCING	Factoring and forfaiting	Deep-tier financing (2nd and 3rd levels)	Pre-shipment			
OPERATIONS	Back office operations	Network interoperability	Payments			
SUPPORT SERVICES	Customs brokerages	Insurance				

Emergent	Active	Prolific

The rationale for pursuing certain use cases over others is sound. Paper processes are prevalent throughout global trade and notably sluggish, draining time and money. Paper trails—in their truest form—can be difficult to trace. Document digitization makes sense as an initial endeavor, because it does not "reinvent the wheel" but makes it a more efficient and secure method of capturing and distributing the same information. As platforms mature, however, the industry can leverage blockchain's capabilities elsewhere in the value chain.

For example, once competencies in digitizing such documents as letters of credit have been sufficiently proven, a next-use case worth exploring could be pre- or post-shipment financing, sometimes considered too risky for banks and financiers to participate in. Blockchain mitigates part of this risk by giving banks and financiers visibility into deep tiers of the supply chain. While pre- or post-shipment financing use cases may disrupt the status quo, banks and financiers will grow more comfortable with the technology as they adopt blockchain platforms for digitalizing documents. Then, adapting to a new norm for conducting pre- or post-shipment financing will be less disruptive. This approach to prioritizing use cases is akin to peeling back the layers of an onion: we start with the outside layer, the easiest to access, and work our way in.

JOURNEY TO A FUTURE STATE

In an ideal future, blockchain will be integral to the enterprise digital tool kit. Linking together organizations, industries, and technologies, and fostering an approach to collaboration that will drive new efficiencies, blockchain cultivates a kind of economy in which the symphonic enterprise is the norm. The journey to this future state has already started; the key now is to navigate the path ahead.

As participants in the global trade chain continue to embrace blockchain technology and ready themselves for the new paradigm of enterprise digital fluency, leaders need to create and put into use a road map for reaching their blockchain goals:

1. Think "we" instead of "I" and focus on shared problems among members of the trade network.

2. Evangelize the potential of new perspectives and new products; break out of current orthodoxies.

3. Identify *minimum viable ecosystem* (MVE) in the market, including legal and regulatory bodies.

   i. Define governance structure and the operating models that will guide the endeavor.

   ii. Define technology committee to support selection of platform, systems, utility, tools, etc.

   iii. Define voting structure for the executive committee, e.g., one vote per member.

4. Define executive committee to identify and mobilize use cases.

5. Mobilize the use case for blockchain development and implementation.

6. Engage subject matter experts and advisors who will help inform the build.

7. Build and integrate the solution with existing enterprise technology frameworks.

8. Deploy the solution and think agile: discover, design, build, and release.

9. Measure against business value framework to verify the solution's effectiveness.

10. Gather feedback and develop road map to scale; assess, reflect upon, and expand the MVE accordingly.

11. Identify complementary use cases and build on the solution foundation.

Following such a road map, decision-makers will be in a better position to unlock new benefits beyond operational and cost efficiencies. They will move beyond the linear transition of existing processes onto the blockchain. Setting out to implement blockchain frees business leaders to think differently and innovatively, explore beyond traditional markets, and grow top-line revenue by addressing unserved markets (e.g., deep-tier financing and financing for SMEs) via blockchain. Once assessed thoroughly, leaders can identify and make a business case for these opportunities.

The business case is just the beginning. From there, leaders will need to ensure that their blockchain is not only valuable but also fundamentally viable. If the business case is the "what" and the "why," and now is the "when," then the next fundamental questions are "who?" "where?" and—most important—"how?" How will the ecosystem develop the initial case? Which technology architecture will support the blockchain solution? Which standards and legal or regulatory constraints will guide the journey? How will partners make these decisions together? Answering all these questions is critical to implementation.

ENABLING CONSIDERATIONS

As leaders initiate their blockchain journeys for global trade use cases, they will have business and technology considerations.

BUSINESS CONSIDERATIONS

From a business standpoint, leaders need to consider how different industry participants might come together in shaping the future. What is the minimum viable ecosystem for development? Which governance structures and operating models might we use? How might we develop or influence the development of standards, regulation, and law?

Minimum viable ecosystem

Deloitte Insights' "Tech Trends 2018" report described the concept of a minimum viable ecosystem, a network of market players and business partners that an enterprise or consortium needs to assemble, to bring its commercialization strategy to life.[52] For the development and adoption of commercial-scale blockchain solutions, leaders need to consider their minimum viable ecosystem. At its core, blockchain encourages collaboration over competition, but different partners in an ecosystem still play different roles; and so a commercially viable blockchain solution needs to make sense for all players along a value chain.

For global trade use cases, the minimum viable ecosystem may include financiers alongside freight forwarders and corporations, with involvement from regulators and assorted authorities. Once the enterprise or consortium defines and organizes its minimum viable ecosystem, project leaders can shift toward solution scalability and consider the type of governance crucial to growth.

The key strategy for managing the ecosystem of a blockchain endeavor is to start small and branch out gradually. Since no single blockchain solution will likely rule all of global trade, and reaching critical mass within the industry will center on the interoperability of multiple chains, the most pragmatic adoption approach is to involve only those necessary to demonstrating and mobilizing the solution. With each iteration of proof, growing the minimum viable ecosystem will be easier and less risk-laden.

Governance

As blockchain endeavors evolve from exploratory to commercially viable, an enterprise or consortium will want to identify the parameters of governance. With the uptick of blockchain adoption at the enterprise level, and the plethora of successful prototypes to show for it, consortia en route to commercialization must be ready to tackle standardization issues head on. A clear mechanism for facilitating consensus will prove essential, since developing standards will involve political navigation, especially with cross-border trade.

To ensure accuracy and trustworthiness among participants, consortia should firmly establish a governance model, of which there are three primary sorts: the working group, the joint venture, or the statutory organization.[53]

A working group, though not a legal entity, enables members to decide by consensus as an organization. This model has been popular among consortia for developing initial POCs and prototypes. In the working group model, all members have an equal say, and there is no central party to manage the onboarding of new parties onto the network. Within a working group, participating members contribute resources to drive progress toward a common objective. Each member has a voice at the table for negotiating and decision-making.

Working groups come with certain benefits, because members are empowered to scale together rapidly because of pooled funding and distributed liability of risks. The working group model has two potential drawbacks: decreased speed to consensus on decisions among members and misaligned incentives among members that hold up development. For these reasons, a working group can prove effective initially but is not well suited for blockchain endeavors moving toward commercialization.

A joint venture is an autonomous legal entity that develops and wholly owns the blockchain platform and any other associated intellectual property. Funded equally by founding members, a joint venture has a mandate to offer the developed platform as a utility for participants running their own nodes. While founding members hold status as core stakeholders in this model, the joint venture has an independent management team and technology architecture team. Since the venture is funded equally by founding members, the financial, technological, and regulatory costs, as well as any risks or revenue, are also shared equally.

Potential risk is somewhat offset, since the joint venture stands up with a high level of independence. There is a reduced risk of project failure, since founding members have mutually agreed to use the platform before it is built (i.e., the platform won't be built in isolation). There is also an inherent transparency and accountability of costs incurred by the venture. The joint venture model enables rapid decision-making, since it is a separate legal entity and can quickly reach consensus on critical decisions and prevent bias toward any founding member. As the joint venture has full autonomy, its management team can drive single, unified processes and rally consensus among core stakeholders or founding members. The drawback of this model is the barrier to entry for smaller players who may not be able to provide equal funding or bear equal risk.

The third model, a statutory organization, is a body whose operations and funding are primarily directed by a regulatory body. It operates as a separate legal entity that provides and manages the common platform. But a regulatory authority—like a government agency or a shared infrastructure operator—acts as key facilitator and owns the nodes. In a statutory organization, participating members follow the overarching directives and contribute toward a common objective. The organization bears any associated risks associated with the blockchain platform and owns any intellectual property, which it licenses to participants in the network at a fee designed to sustain operational costs.

This model is particularly useful for ensuring compliance with regulation. The model is also associated with a high level of governance of transparency and strong data governance, minimizing the risk of participants. The statutory organization also facilitates a level of cross-border cooperation in its active role as regulator and its inherent dedication to standardization.

For commercializing blockchain platforms after successfully demonstrating prototypes, companies may find that the joint venture or statutory organization models offer them the most formalized and low-risk mechanisms for governance. These models, in contrast with the working group, encourage taking action rather than ruminating endlessly, and they help distribute the risk of adopting new technology.

Standards, regulation, and law

Standards speed up widespread adoption of new technology. For example, ISO 20022 and the 1987 UN/EDIFACT standards helped spread adoption of financial messaging based on extensible market language, used by organizations like Visa, the Society for Worldwide Interbank Financial Telecommunication (SWIFT), and the International Swaps and Derivatives Association.[54] Unfortunately, the development of technology and the development of the standards that guide its use are not always in sync, as has been the case for blockchain. In a positive move, the National Standards Authority of Australia proposed to standardize blockchain and distributed ledger technologies for interoperability and data interchange among users, applications, and systems.[55] Its proposal, presently dubbed ISO/TC 307, is before the International Organizations of Standards for consideration.

As more proposals for blockchain standards come forth, trade participants should look to build relationships with standard-setting bodies, especially at a global scale. For early adopters of blockchain, the opportunity to collaborate with these bodies is also an opportunity to lead in the space, especially in an industry vertical. For example, nonprofit bodies—such as Blockchain in Transport Alliance in the global trade space and the Sovrin Foundation for digital identity standards in the public sector—have formed to establish blockchain standards that address industry-specific requirements.[56] Members of these bodies have voices in the standards discussions.

The development of appropriate technical standards is also critical to blockchain's success in global trade. Existing standards—such as UCP 600 for letters of credit and SWIFT's MT 798 for the import, export, and guarantee of letters of credit—act as codes of practice for financiers and other participants in trade finance.[57] A blockchain-enabled digital refresh will allow businesses to access documentation, like letters of credit, at a faster pace and with more visibility than before.

Rigorous review of new or revised electronic data standards is imperative. For example, standards like ISO/IEC 27001 for information security management will still apply to blockchain solutions but may need revision or bolstering by additional standards for information security.[58] Furthermore, any new standards should not only bring old processes into the future but also provide for smart-contract management, new security, and new interface protocols.

The smart contract, a key facet of blockchain technology, has potential to bring about swift enforcement of agreements and accelerate the pace of global trade transactions. Whether governments will recognize smart contracts as legal documents is unclear, and that lack of clarity could be a roadblock. Remember, a smart contract is a type of distributed application written in a programming language such as Solidity. For smart contracts to have the same legal status as normal contracts, state-level legislatures must enact laws to identify them as legal agreements on a par with paper-based contracts, and multiple jurisdictions must simultaneously formalize and agree upon a single, enforceable definition of a smart contract.

Another unique quality of the blockchain is the user's ability to share select data with select participants: users could give regulators near real-time access to data. With this transparency, regulators have an opportunity to rethink how they regulate participants. Before commercializing a blockchain solution, trade participants will want to discuss data protection and intellectual property rights with legal and regulatory bodies and agree on protocols and guidelines. Looping in regulators for unsegmented, undisturbed oversight reiterates the need for participants to foster the right relationships with regulatory bodies. Those who adopt the right solutions first will reap the rewards first. For streamlining regulatory processes, both regulators and trade participants stand to collect.

TECHNOLOGY CONSIDERATIONS

Blockchain technologies, though growing and improving rapidly, are still nascent. Blockchain is not necessarily made for the "plug-and-play" installation approach sometimes taken with more established enterprise technologies. From a technological standpoint, there are three key considerations: performance and scalability, interoperability among multiple blockchains, and integration with existing enterprise technologies.

Performance and scalability

Performance and scalability are two irrevocably important determinants in maximizing the value derived from a blockchain solution, but they pose a conundrum for solution developers. Frequently, characteristics associated with performance and scalability will fend off one another, leading to a set of trade-offs that innovators must consider when designing a blockchain solution. Vitalik Buterin, co-founder of Ethereum, uses the term, *trilemma*, to describe how a blockchain can have, at most, any two out of the three properties of decentralization, scalability, or security.[59]

As developers create different blockchains to address different challenges, they will apply different performance criteria such as latency, throughput, or resiliency. Also, new fixes for scalability are on the rise. Developers can investigate approaches like sharding, datalink layers to off-chain state channels, increases to block size, different consensus mechanisms, or side chains to speed up transaction times.[60]

Blockchain platforms are continuing to mature, and researchers and developers will likely discover new ways to improve performance and scalability with time. Meanwhile, developers should design the desired solution with performance and scalability constraints in mind. Awareness of the limitations of various platforms will help to inform the acceptability of trade-offs, at least while blockchain technology is in its infancy. Such awareness will also help to ensure that the developed solution reflects the qualities of paramount importance.

Interoperability

As we have highlighted, companies and consortia are developing specific blockchain use cases in global trade. Their progress is phenomenal, and the eventual need for interoperability among these solutions should not discourage them. Blockchain platforms, as the technology matures, will solve for interoperability. The connecters will come forward. Worrying about different chains interacting is premature. Right now, global trade participants should focus on improving performance and making sure that the blockchain solution integrates with other enterprise technologies.

If this laissez-faire approach does not soothe initially, then consider putting interoperability concerns on the back burner, something evocative of the early days of developing the Internet. The US Defense Advanced Research Projects Agency (DARPA) Internet protocol—also considered *the* Internet protocol—had a top-level goal to "*inter*connect *net*works."[61] It had seven secondary goals, of which the first three were:

1. Internet communication must continue despite loss of networks or gateways.

2. The Internet must support multiple types of communications service.

3. The Internet architecture must accommodate a variety of networks.[62]

The 2018 paper, "Towards a Design Philosophy for Interoperable Blockchain Systems," by authors from the Massachusetts Institute of Technology draws parallels between these objectives of the DARPA Internet protocol and the characteristics of an interoperable blockchain structure.[63] It reminds us that the Internet and its many applications were not developed overnight.

The Internet, as we know it, is inherently interoperable; but its predecessors were not. Neither were its early applications. The inspiration for the World Wide Web and the semantic web came from a CERN-led project called ENQUIRE, which satisfied requirements for compatibility but not interoperability.[64] The takeaway is straightforward: the advent of any technology requires some prioritization of technical development. For blockchain, that does not mean that interoperability is not important; rather, it is not important *yet*.

Integration

While interoperability is a technical concern for the future, integration considerations are more pressing. Blockchain will require integration with other key components of an enterprise's information and communication technology, including:

1. Middleware such as Web services like representational state transfer or service-oriented architectures, and asynchronous messaging protocols like message queuing telemetry transport, extensible messaging and presence protocol, or Java messaging service

2. Web-based, on-demand, or hosted software—also known as software-as-a-service products—including Salesforce, Adobe Creative Cloud, Amazon Web Services, Box, Marketo, and others

3. Legacy systems such as ERP software—like SAP or Oracle products—and mainframe technologies

Successful integration will require the validity of data—via the application of existing business rules to raw data as it is entered into or pulled from the system—while maintaining an interface to the data. In this regard, an issue unique to blockchain implementation is the segregation of data that is stored on the blockchain (on-chain) from that stored off-chain.[65]

On-chain data are public data obtained by looking at the blockchain itself. Off-chain data are typically derived from remote servers, client devices, or decentralized storage systems like InterPlanetary File System.[66] Off-chain data are those that enterprises will want to protect, as the data may be sensitive and not explicitly part of transactional information that must be stored on-chain, or information that is subject to change daily.

Distinguishing between data stored on-chain versus off-chain is essential, but the divide must be navigable so that smart contracts may be enacted. Smart contracts are triggered upon fulfilling specific, predefined conditions; the data used to verify whether the conditions are met is usually found off-chain. An oracle is a trusted off-chain data source to which smart contracts can refer, to execute an action or transaction on the blockchain.[67]

The creation of oracles that can automatically trigger smart contracts is not trivial, though. Because off-chain data are stored off the blockchain, they are less tamper-proof and therefore less trusted by other parties. A key challenge will be determining how to imbue off-chain data with the same level of reliability that on-chain data inherently have.

Regarding a simpler facet of data integration, APIs can interact with message queuing systems or service bus applications to provide interoperability. Blockchain APIs are typically written in common language (e.g., JavaScript, .NET, or Python), and their primary purpose is to read and write data. They can be worked into higher-level programming layers that can integrate with an *enterprise service bus* (ESB), a middleware component that facilitates interaction with legacy systems such as ERP products or mainframes.

The mechanism of API and ESB interfacing is less complex than other aspects of blockchain integration. The most crucial consideration informing its successful implementation is the quality of the general data architecture. While data will be stored either on- or off-chain based on its attributes, legacy data will need to be analyzed and possibly transformed before loading into the blockchain interfaces, through a standard extract-transform-load process with appropriate controls for data quality, where the technological limitations of other platforms require it.[68]

Blockchain cannot operate in isolation if global trade participants want to unlock its maximum potential. Enterprise leaders must consider integration, from both data and technology perspectives, if they want to maximize the benefits of new technology while minimizing shock to the system.

FINAL THOUGHTS ON GLOBAL TRADE

Brian Behlendorf, Hyperledger's executive director, said it best in an article published in January 2018: "I can't say you will be out of business in two years if you are not using it, but there will be some sectors that have meaningful use soon."[69] As we've seen with HKMA, we.trade, and Maersk, the world of global trade is one of the first sectors seeing meaningful use. How do incumbents remain competitive in the fast-paced world of blockchain? It starts with mentality and exploration.

- **Embrace nontraditional opportunities,** especially where they arise organically. The evolution of blockchain endeavors from exploratory to production-ready shows that the market is prepared to go beyond modernizing traditions to creating new ones. Start with the problem and then think of technology enablement. Ultimately, the genuine convergence of business and technology frames of thought will yield the most success. Through alignment, organizations can better channel their energies into pursuing one common goal and cultivating a solution that overcomes current orthodoxies.

- **Ideate, investigate, evaluate, and reiterate.** Take a page out of we.trade's playbook and scale up incrementally. To date, many big players have moved in early, and moved in big, on blockchain—but they have not necessarily seen the results they were hoping for. Acting quickly on the wrong use cases can be demoralizing and can slow down momentum in the long run. Evaluating the return on investment and thoroughly assessing where blockchain will have the most impact are essential to developing the solution that will really make a difference. We have discussed the idea of starting with the minimum viable ecosystem and growing as you go, following the road map when embarking on your blockchain journey, and letting it lead you to blockchain solutions that thrive commercially.

- **Collaboration trumps competition,** when it comes to blockchain initiatives. Once you've identified a problem, leverage ecosystem partners to develop a blockchain solution. Others in your ecosystem may already be working on a solution and formed a consortium you can join. If a relevant consortium does not exist yet, you have an opportunity to lead efforts in your sector and mobilize a consortium. Focus on value in terms of the entire trade network, not just the individual enterprise. Blockchain's unique selling point is its ability to connect parties; the best solutions will be those that speak to multiple stakeholders' needs.

Overall, blockchain technology has proven to be an enabling technology in many use cases. The successful case studies of HKMA, we.trade, and Maersk have one thing in common: their leadership didn't think in terms of how their organizations work today, but how they will work and give value in the future.

CHAPTER 2

FOXCONN 4.0

How Blockchains Can Handle the World's
Most Complicated Supply Chain

Nolan Bauerle

 ## FOXCONN IN BRIEF

- Computer companies rarely make computers any more. The big technology brands outsource their manufacturing and often their design to the electronics manufacturing industry. The industry is dominated by one player: Foxconn Technology Group.

- Foxconn is the second-largest private sector employer in the world with over a million employees who coordinate the roll out of its enormous product line, which accounts for over 40 percent of consumer electronics sold in a year.

- While Foxconn has made history as the most important contract manufacturer of its time, its value chain has grown into a complex web of relationships and responsibilities. To continue making history, its leadership must effectively manage this complexity.

- The company's operational strategy has blockchain technology at its core. Foxconn is building out a digital backbone, which will deploy blockchain to

  - Secure supply-chain management
  - Safeguard its own Internet of Things
  - Transform its network into a commodities marketplace

- Offer new types of commercial relationships that benefit its customers.

- Integral to these capabilities is a set of blockchain-based trade finance tools that will create deep-tier finance opportunities for its suppliers.

- Foxconn's blockchain strategy aims to position it as a leader of the fourth industrial revolution and among the most important manufacturers in the second era of the Internet.

INTRODUCTION TO FOXCONN

The Asian Miracle—the financial success of the four original Asian Tigers of South Korea, Taiwan, Hong Kong, and Singapore—grew from the contract manufacturing business model. This model spurred the miracle because it was good for the attraction of foreign buyers whose capital fueled growth.

Named Hon Hai Precision Industry when the Taiwanese company started operations in 1974, Foxconn rose to become the largest contract manufacturer in the world. Along with its partner Apple, Foxconn made history with important products and industrial processes. While Apple's product innovation is prolific, it is also regarded as an important innovator for supply-chain management and procurement. Steve Jobs himself performed this role until he recruited future CEO Tim Cook to relieve him of those duties.[70]

Apple chose only partners that shared a goal to make history. No partner met this criterion more than Foxconn. In the process, Foxconn grew to be the world's second-largest private employer after Walmart, and the largest employer in China. An estimated 40 percent of all consumer electronics sold worldwide in a year come from Foxconn's factories.[71] Now Foxconn is looking to be a leader in the fourth industrial revolution, including the Internet of Things—hence, Foxconn 4.0.[72]

FOXCONN TECHNOLOGY GROUP AT A GLANCE

Actual name: Hon Hai Precision Industry Co., Ltd.[73]

Headquarters: Tucheng, New Taipei, Taiwan

Opened: 1974

Employees: 1.3 million

Company type: Contract manufacturer

Impact: Manufactures 40% of worldwide consumer electronics sold annually

Total assets: $80 billion

Total revenues: $134 billion

MANAGING SUPPLY-CHAIN COMPLEXITY

Foxconn's goal with blockchain technology is no less than to continue making history as the most important manufacturer of its time. This vision centers on the management of the complexity of the entire company. Jack Lee, CEO of FnConn, the finance arm of Foxconn, leads these creative efforts:

> We see it at the heart of everything we do. With our entire network, we can arrange how we finance agreements with partners and suppliers, how we manage procurement and logistics, what we produce and sell, and how we engage with our customers. All of our departments, everything we do across our operation. It is seen as a core technology.[74]

This study spotlights Foxconn's efforts to bring blockchain technology into the core of its complex business activities and to help manage the complexity. In short, it takes a close look at the application of advanced cryptographic techniques and decentralized networks to build trustable digital relationships among Foxconn's partners, suppliers, products, factories, tools, and customers.

TOTAL SUPPLY-CHAIN UPGRADE

The first spike for FnConn's work is Chained Finance. Launched this past year, it's a payments and supply-chain management tool. At its most general level, it's designed to solve a number of integration problems. Jack Lee described the logic behind the design decision this way:

> I see it in three parts. There's the information flow—purchase orders and procurement. There's the logistics flow—the flow of the actual goods. And there's the payment flow—the money movements. These three systems cannot talk to each other. They are not integrated. We see this as a gigantic opportunity. Information, goods, and money all integrated for the whole system.[75]

The integration needed to solve these problems prompted FnConn to enter into a partnership with Dianrong, nicknamed the Lending Club of China because its founder and CEO, Soul Htite, co-founded the peer-to-peer Lending Club headquartered in San Francisco. Together, FnConn and Dianrong launched Chained Finance—a finance platform which, as Lee pointed out, aims to integrate the flow of information and agreements, the flow of goods, and the flow of money all into the same place.

FnConn recently tested the platform and successfully moved $6.5 million in loans among a number of partners.[76] In the process, records of transactions about agreements, the flow of goods, and the flow of payments moved between multiple parties, were collected in one place and in the correct order. Through this platform, the entire story of each trade became easy to track. The simple application of this integration is a vast improvement on current practices. For the last two hundred years, the flow of money alone has been difficult to follow. The flow of money over this period was processed through a network of correspondent banks.

The correspondent banking system is a network of banks in different countries that hold accounts with each other. Because two particular banks in two different countries might not hold accounts with each other, the sending banks push transactions into a network of banks that do have relationships. The money then charts a wandering path through a string of correspondent banks until it hits on the final destination bank.

Money transferred this way flows through its own information communication network, SWIFT. Created in 1973, SWIFT standardizes messages and thus expedites the information flow among correspondent banks. While this network moves money, it does not account for the movement of goods. Industry practice puts goods in motion before money moves, thus creating a delay between two tiers/links in a supply chain. The more tiers/links in the chain, the longer the delay, as each tier/link waits for its financing to come through.

DEEP-TIER FINANCE

Because of these delays, banks' financing terms for suppliers farther down the chain are less favorable. Banks give great financing terms to direct suppliers of companies like Apple. They do not for suppliers caught up in the delays inherent in the higher tiers of a supply chain. Consequently, the latter group of suppliers either sells deeply discounted invoices or holds unpaid invoices for months at a loss because of currency changes or loan interest. Lee pointed out that,

> Over the years, Foxconn has dealt with the biggest banks in the world. For Foxconn, finance is easy. We're a direct supplier, financing can happen. When we talk with those banks about financing our suppliers, tier-two suppliers, the answer from the

banks is no. Only a large multinational bank like Citi will budge, and its answer is basically the following: "We can partially finance, but with the guarantee of 30 percent." That's 30 percent cash. When we ask about a third-tier supplier, it answers, "Impossible." Eighty-five percent of SMEs in China are unable to get financed. They have to go to shadow bankers. It's inefficient and costly, especially for the upper-tier SMEs. We realized this problem a year ago, and that's why we decided to launch Chained Finance.[77]

Foxconn's complex supply chains can stretch as deep as eight or nine tiers. The stretch of Foxconn's network gives Chained Finance the chance to extend invoice financing and credit straight through all the tiers in Foxconn's supply chain. As Lee put it,

We can leverage Foxconn's supply chain and do deep-tier finance for our partners. We can hook in the payment data with procurement data, and supplier data. Also, we can have the direct supplier invite the tier-two supplier and tier-three supplier and so on. This payment data will be within the accounts payable for Foxconn. If suppliers need working capital, they can get it from Chained Finance on the platform.[78]

DIGITAL MARKET MAKERS

As a contract manufacturer, Foxconn has grown into one of the largest companies in the world, with $136 billion in revenues and a network of thousands of suppliers, partners, and customers.[79] Foxconn's visibility and coordination of trade relationships through Chained Finance hints at an even greater power around market formation.

For its own production processes, Foxconn gets wholesale prices on such materials as atomized aluminum used in the body casing of tablet and phone devices. Through Chained Finance, Foxconn plans to offer the wholesale price on aluminum it receives to any member of its vast network. Lee said, "We can use the integrated tool to build a powerful marketplace. We can grow the value and efficiency of our network. We can help our suppliers this way."[80]

The idea is to form transaction parameters for network members to find trade partners and secure deals for certain products. This collaboration builds on Foxconn's deep-tier finance work and allows its network to be used by all members of the network in an efficient and useful marketplace structure built from price discovery.

CHAIN OF CUSTODY AND PROVENANCE

The flow of money and agreements plus the creation of markets is not the only core complexity problem Lee believes can be managed. As mentioned, for trade, only after the money flows can the goods flow. The flow of the goods themselves is important and is another vital quality that can be strengthened through blockchain technology. Lee said,

> Yes, Chained Finance is aimed at the painful problems SMEs have for finance. However, we think the most important aspect of this for us will be tracking and provenance. Tracking the flow of goods, information, and procurement. So, we pay high attention to how to track goods. We want to integrate supply chains and procurement and the money flow all on the blockchain. That's why we are a founding member of the Trusted IoT Alliance along with Cisco and Bosch and a handful of blockchain start-ups.[81]

The Internet of Things, a relatively new and powerful technology, allows manufacturers to use data produced by physical assets. McKinsey Global Institute predicts the value of the Internet of Things to surpass $11 trillion by 2025.[82] The $30 Raspberry Pi demonstrates how inexpensive and ubiquitous strong computing power is and will continue to be.[83] The effective use of data is central for industries as they enter a new era.

DIGITAL AUTHENTICATION

The Trusted IoT Alliance—launched in January 2017 with blockchain start-ups BitSE, Chronicled, ConsenSys, Filament, Skuchain, and Slock.it—partnered with corporate giants BNY Mellon, Bosch, Cisco, and Foxconn to work on standardization of machine interactions.

The Trusted IoT Alliance has started its work with tests on authentication schemes: how to secure the schemes individually and within the network, and how to process the data from all these devices in a useful way. The first protocols they've established are for multiple weaker identities, including serial numbers, QR codes, RFID tags and *universal product codes* (UPCs). The protocol links these to stronger cryptographic identities that use private keys to sign transactions. The goal is to strengthen the bond between the physical object and the digital world to provide registration that commercial legacy systems can deploy immediately.

These digital identifiers are an important feature for manufacturers going forward as they can be leveraged for improved supply-chain management. An alliance partner of Foxconn, Chronicled, is a San Francisco-based start-up with this idea as its business plan. In partnership with Brooklyn-based GREATS, a shoe company partly owned by NFL running back Marshawn Lynch, Chronicled embedded RFID tags into pairs of Lynch's signature shoe, the Beastmode Royale Chukka, and hashed each individual shoe's identity into the Ethereum blockchain.[84]

This has powerful implications to fight counterfeiting and to supply the assurances many brand names require to satisfy their customers. Foxconn has long fought against counterfeit products and has a bird's-eye view for what the marketplace needs. Its current work with the alliance is about the creation of a cryptographically provable anti-counterfeiting technology, not just to expedite investigations and lawsuits but also to deter counterfeiters and minimize the need for legal action in the first place.

NEW ECONOMIC RELATIONSHIPS AMONG PEOPLE AND THINGS

But authentication for products is only one small step in the integration of machines into our contractual relationships. Foxconn's physical assets add to the complexity of the massive company. Buildings, machines, tools, and inventories drive the production process. The effective use of data derived from these physical assets is central for industries as they enter a new era.

A contract is a sort of meeting of the minds. What happens when one mind is not a mind at all, but a microprocessor, cryptographic keys, and a programmed set of instructions? How do they have the legal capacity to contract?

Take this scenario: a car whose manufacturer installed sensors to augment the driver's capabilities, and yet the driver is in an accident. An insurance company performs a forensic assessment of responsibility. With a connected car, who's at fault? The driver? The software maker? The hardware sensor maker or actuator? The auto company that bundled them? The owner of the vehicle? A hacker?

This was once a relatively simple question for investigators. With the questions mentioned above, answers are now confusing and difficult to ascertain with certainty. But answers must once again be straightforward so that we can properly integrate the IoT into industry and allow it to assume the legal responsibility that machines will require in a world of hundreds of millions of connected devices.

Through key possession and signed transactions arranged and time-stamped in a distributed database, it is possible to establish a system that would help in any forensic audit of responsibility. For example, a proximity sensor failed to alert a driver and a collision ensued—the sensor's failure could easily be identified in the travel log of all digital interactions for every component in the vehicle if these technologies were orchestrated on a blockchain.

For Foxconn, the goal is to integrate the physical assets within its vast and complex factories. This work gives Foxconn insight into what is needed in the market for products that can safely harness the IoT. That means more sensors and actuators along with their attendant keying material. Another unit of Foxconn, Engineering Services, works as a consultancy and tech provider to grow the institutional capacity needed to produce safe IoT devices for the market.

NEW CONSUMERS AND RELATIONSHIPS

When Foxconn opened its doors, it entered into a niche inside manufacturing. It was not consumer facing—it was a contract manufacturer that few had ever heard of. But in an era where the relationships among manufacturer, product, and consumer are in flux—where digital ties that bind have established new relationship capacities throughout the value chain—Foxconn has pivoted to a consumer facing brand.

In 2016, it acquired Sharp, a Japanese electronics company, for $3.8 billion.[85] It focused Sharp's growth strategy on connected cars and smart homes, now the anchor products in Foxconn's new consumer IoT. Through this IoT focus, Foxconn plans to create new sales mechanisms and ownership models for its customers. This is another example of the product as a crucial information carrier. Complex products, like jet engines for example, have long been sold with sophisticated ownership models that reflect the data produced by the product.

In the early days of private jets in the 1960s, Bristol Siddeley built jet engines and offered a revolutionary ownership and servicing contract that hints at the future of the combination of data, product, and ownership. Bristol Siddeley introduced the "power by the hour" system. It offered a better way to forecast costs of jet engine ownership by offering a fixed-sum per flying hour that included all-engine servicing. The manufacturer's relationship with the new owners was for the lifetime of the product. While the power-by-the-hour name is trademarked by Rolls-Royce, which acquired the engine maker, it is now a generic term to refer to other jet engines sold and managed this way by GE, Pratt & Whitney, and Bombardier.

Between shoes and jet engines, virtually all products can now carry information that will affect ownership and sales models. Products that carry information can solidify relationships between manufacturer and consumer, ensuring they last much longer—perpetual even—down the value chain. This idea involves an extension of blockchain technology straight through to a perpetual relationship with consumers. We may describe blockchain technology as a "database innovation," but this tells only part of the story. Blockchain technology represents an innovation to *systems of record*. A system of record is more than a database or snapshot in time. It is data in its context, data with a history of itself. It takes note of all transactions, amendments, drafts, or anything else related to the story of the data.

While some analysts have scoffed at the idea that a contract manufacturer can enter consumer electronics sales and predict the kinds of growth that have come out of corporate projections, Foxconn is confident. As Lee explained, "Through Sharp, we are going to pioneer ownership models that will allow us to better serve our customers, save them money, and earn more revenue for ourselves. It's about the most efficient and helpful relationship we can have with customers."[86]

CYBERSECURITY

It is unsurprising that authentication is at the top of the Trusted IoT Alliance's list as well as a focus for Foxconn. Authentication is an important weakness in our current cybersecurity arrangement. The list of companies involved in important hacks and cybersecurity breaches keeps growing –Sony, JPMorgan Chase, Home Depot,

Anthem Healthcare, and now Equifax. Reputational damage from these attacks is difficult to mitigate.

The weakness in our systems is rooted in centralized authorities created to organize authentication schemes. It is the act of centralization itself that has characterized "trusted third parties as security holes."[87]

In a centralized authentication scheme, people share their mother's maiden name or their dog's name with an authentication authority whose centralization endangers the whole system. Bitcoin offers an example of decentralized authentication performed through the simple deployment of public key cryptography. Possession of a private key equals ownership in the case of bitcoin, or authentication in the case of blockchain technology, deployment in supply-chain management, or customer relationships.

If we use cryptocurrency, where the possession of the key means ownership of some finite data, we can authenticate machines as owners of assets or parties with responsibilities or obligations. The demands of bitcoin wallets have catalyzed the use and development of new microchips that have trusted encryption enclaves that allow for keys to reside on a device without exposing themselves to the Internet. Keying materials (wallets or other devices that store, generate, or use keys to sign transactions cryptographically) have begun to leverage this technology and several bitcoin wallet providers have branched into the IoT sector. So, IoT devices will likely come with software and hardware that functions and looks like a bitcoin wallet.

REGULATORY COMPLIANCE AND PRIVACY BY DESIGN

One of the great advantages to such a system for digital authentication is that it makes it easier to adhere to many of the privacy laws about to come into force in Europe. The concept, called *privacy by design*, was first coined by a study by the privacy commissioner in the province of Ontario in the 1990s.[88] The idea has grown to be an important feature of privacy law and is the basis for a major exclusion from the EU's *general data privacy regulation* (GDPR).[89] These new regulations, to come into force in 2018, bring sweeping penalties and wide applicability to anyone gathering data on consumers who live in the EU member countries.

Lots of speculation and concerns have been raised on how onerous the rule change will be. This is partly because the law places responsibility on companies when dealing with any kind of authentication information. The exclusion, privacy by design, works as follows:[90]

> Encryption and decryption operations must be carried out locally, not by remote service, because both keys and data must remain in the power of the data owner if any privacy is to be achieved.

Furthermore, in the instructions:

> If the personal data is pseudonymized with adequate internal policies and measures by the data controller, then it is considered to be effectively anonymized, and not subject to controls and penalties of the GDPR.

Much of blockchain technology is actually based on the exception in this rule. Many blockchain projects have as a business model the personal guard and control of cryptographic keys. The security by design exclusion helps pave the way for the technology to proliferate, especially for machine-to-machine, machine-to-person, and machine-to-corporation dialogue and contracting.

Cybersecurity and customer privacy strategies are integral for companies as they seek to meet the forces of the digital revolution. Foxconn's work with its finance platform, Chained Finance, as well as through its IoT Alliance is part of the company's strategy to protect its operations, secure its relationships, and protect its customers.

KEY TAKEAWAYS ON FOXCONN'S BLOCKCHAIN BACKBONE

- Foxconn has grown into such a complex company that we could more accurately describe it as a planned society. Like any society, leadership has difficulty coordinating the many relationships, responsibilities, and obligations that the company has undertaken.

- Blockchain technology offers a tool for managing this complexity. Foxconn's goal is to create a backbone upon which the company can arrange and organize its operations as it continues to lead as the most important manufacturer of its era.

- Foxconn has leveraged blockchain technology to create a tool for the movement of money, goods, and agreements to be orchestrated in one place. This tool leverages Foxconn's network and turns it into a useful market for its partners.

- Digital authentication schemes are a focus for the company, both for the goods produced and for the data they transmit. These new authentication schemes are useful for the integration of machines into Foxconn's contractual obligations and responsibilities.

- Through work on advanced cryptographic techniques for authentication, Foxconn has put cybersecurity at the forefront of its plans.

CHAPTER 3

DIAMONDS ON THE BLOCKCHAIN
Building a Global Digital Ledger for Valuable Assets
Anthony D. Williams

 ## DIAMOND PROVENANCE IN BRIEF

- Having thrived for decades on the integral role of diamonds in romantic relationships, the $80 billion-dollar diamond industry confronted a grave threat to its brand in the early 2000s by embracing a multistakeholder effort to eradicate conflict diamonds.

- The so-called Kimberley Process brought significant progress by requiring diamond-producing countries to certify that exports of rough diamonds are conflict free. However, the largely paper-based diamond certification process has been plagued by corruption, forgeries, and inefficiencies, resulting in many conflict diamonds entering the supply chain illegitimately.

- Efforts to ameliorate the often-harsh realities of the global diamond trade have also fallen short in the eyes of the industry watchdogs, which point to ongoing violence and human rights violations in diamond-producing countries such as Angola, Zimbabwe, and the Central African Republic as further evidence of the Kimberley Process' failure.

- A London-based company, Everledger, is using emerging technologies including blockchain to create a global digital ledger for diamonds that enables producers, consumers, insurers, and regulators to track the flow of individual diamonds through the supply chain, from the mines where they are unearthed right through to jewelers' display cases.

- Incorporating blockchain into the diamond supply chain has several other benefits, such as eliminating insurance fraud and reducing the potential for corruption, money laundering, and other problems associated with the diamond trade.

- The case sheds light on the potential for blockchain to verify the authenticity, provenance, and custody not only of diamonds but also of a wide range of high-value items, from luxury automobiles to rare wines and priceless works of art.

THE DIAMOND SUPPLY CHAIN AND THE PROBLEM OF CONFLICT STONES

For decades, the diamond industry has deliberately and carefully crafted a brand for diamonds as objects of love. Highly successful marketing campaigns targeting old and young couples alike have ensured that diamonds are an essential and ongoing part of romantic relationships. Meanwhile, diamond suppliers like De Beers operate quietly in the background, attracting little public attention. Yet, the image portrayed by De Beers and other diamond suppliers stands in stark contrast to the frequently harsh realities of the diamond supply chain.

In countries such as Angola, Zimbabwe, and the Central African Republic, where oversight is scant and crime and corruption are rampant, diamonds continue to provide hard currency for rebel groups and terrorists to purchase weapons and wage war on elected or internationally recognized governments.[91] According to the United Nations, *conflict diamonds* are "rough diamonds used by rebels to finance armed conflict aimed at overthrowing legitimate governments."[92] The result, according to investigative journalists and human rights observers, is prolonged conflicts and terrible human rights violations.[93] Violence, mutilation, and even kidnapping (as a means of military recruitment) have destroyed the social and economic foundation in many countries where diamonds are mined. Ironically, a precious natural resource that has enriched diamond producers has also produced some of the harshest living conditions in the world.[94]

Like other valuable natural resources, a well-managed diamond trade is a potentially lucrative driver of economic development, providing the funds required to improve living conditions, create jobs, and build social infrastructure. However, the brutal civil wars and human rights violations that diamonds fund in some producing regions are completely at odds with the purity of the images sold to consumers.

AN OPAQUE SUPPLY CHAIN COMES UNDER SCRUTINY

In the past, the diamond brand was protected by the extreme opacity of the diamond supply chain. Diamonds moved easily from one country to another, making it difficult to pinpoint their true origin.[95] The aggregation, sorting, and reselling of diamonds in markets such as Antwerp only compounded these difficulties. The rough diamonds that flow through the De Beers supply chain, for example, eventually land in London where they are aggregated and sorted at De Beers' charterhouse street facility, which at any given time may hold up to $1 billion worth of rough diamonds.[96] These diamonds are then divided and sold in multimillion-dollar lots to special customers that De Beers calls sightholders. Ironically, these sightholders do not actually see these diamonds beforehand. De Beers determines which diamonds go into which lots, and even sets the prices. Customers are buying "sight unseen" at fixed prices, a process De Beers executives termed "feeding the ducks."[97] This opacity not only made it difficult to track the true source of rough diamonds but also obscured public visibility into corruption and violence that the trade in diamonds fuels.

Public awareness of the problems created by the diamond trade began to increase when well-organized advocacy networks emerged to call attention to what became known as "conflict diamonds." These organizations included NGOs such as Partnership Africa Canada, Global Witness, Amnesty International, and Human Rights Watch, along with prominent international organizations such as the United Nations and the World Bank. A report published in early 2000 by Partnership Africa Canada was particularly damaging.[98] Robert Kaplan, director of Rex Diamond Mining Corporation, said the company "lost market value of $600 million in the three days following the *Globe and Mail* article about the report." "Perhaps more important for the long term," said Kaplan, "is that no public company, including us, will be likely to invest in the diamond industry in Sierra Leone into the indefinite future."[99]

THE KIMBERLEY PROCESS AND ITS DISCONTENTS

Growing public exposure made it essential for the diamond industry to deal with the conflict diamonds issue before further damage could be done. Two years of lengthy discussions between the diamond industry, 50 countries, and several NGOs produced the *Kimberley Process* (KP): a voluntary agreement that established a certification and tracking mechanism for diamonds that can ensure their origins are known.[100] The system, which went into effect in 2003, includes a "chain of warranties" that creates an audit trail for any given diamond that stretches from the mine where it is unearthed to the jeweler's shop where it is cut and polished. The transparency of the certification process, and a commitment to independent monitoring, was intended to establish trust that meaningful action is being taken to reduce the flow of conflict diamonds into the supply chain.

Today, KP has 55 participants representing 82 countries, which account for 99.8 percent of the global extraction, trade, and manufacturing of diamonds.[101] Despite its widespread adoption, views differ on how effective the Kimberley certification process has been in eliminating the problem. The diamond industry estimates that conflict diamonds account for as much as 3.7 percent of the world's multibillion-dollar rough diamond trade. KP claims its certification process has succeeded in eliminating nearly all these conflict stones from the legitimate diamond trade.[102]

NGOs such as Global Witness and the Diamond Development Initiative, on the other hand, claim the share of conflict diamonds is closer to 20 percent and have documented a long list of apparent instances of noncompliance, smuggling, money laundering, and human rights abuses occurring in countries that claim to comply with the KP's voluntary requirements.[103] In fact, Global Witness pulled out of the Kimberley Process in December 2011, arguing that "the industry's 'system of warranties' lacks independent verification" and that the KP had failed to address breaches of its rules, instances of corruption, and state-sponsored violence in diamond-producing regions.[104] Andrey Polyakov, president of the World Diamond Council, countered that "well-timed and concerted industry actions have alerted authorities to counterfeit products, stopped the export of conflict diamonds and encouraged responsible operating practices."[105]

What all participants seem to agree on, including the KP itself, is that this well-intentioned certification scheme suffers from flaws that are undermining its efficacy and credibility. These flaws, in turn, have leaders in industry, government, and civil society turning to blockchain as a source of solutions. Fortunately, a new company harnessing blockchain is building a global digital ledger for diamonds that will help address the problem of conflict diamonds and a variety of other problems plaguing the industry.

EVERLEDGER AND THE GLOBAL DIGITAL LEDGER FOR DIAMONDS

Founded in 2015, Everledger is the first company to build a global, digital ledger that tracks and protects valuable assets throughout their lifetime journey. Everledger starts by collecting an asset's defining characteristics, history, and ownership to create a permanent record on the blockchain. This digital incarnation, or thumbprint, is used by various stakeholders in a supply chain to form provenance and verify authenticity. The challenges in the diamond industry, including those associated with conflict diamonds, made the global diamond supply chain the perfect test case for Everledger's digital ledger.

ESTABLISHING PROVENANCE AND FIXING A BROKEN CERTIFICATION PROCESS

Provenance is the life story of an item and in the world of luxury goods like diamonds, provenance matters, because we cannot separate the value of an item from its origin and its history. The problem, according to Everledger's founder and CEO, Leanne Kemp, is that the world's provenance is locked in paper, with the diamond certification process a perfect example.

After mining and cutting, diamonds are sent for certification. Certificate houses inspect the diamonds, while laboratories grade them using the 4Cs: cut, carat, clarity, and color. Certification houses then typically serialize the stones and issue physical certificates with all the attributes of the diamond, including the girdle dimensions and hand-drawn line pictures. These certificates follow the diamonds into retail chains and increase the price of the stones considerably.

A major problem with the antiquated process is that there is no central database for information. Diamond traders depend on certificates of authenticity and origin that are still largely paper-based. The paper-based system is not simply inefficient; the physical records themselves are vulnerable to tampering and outright forgeries. "Not only are the certifications not readily available to the public, you have to trust the certificate houses, which are not necessarily immune to corruption," said Kemp.[106]

In fact, forged documents accompanying rough diamonds have always been the Achilles' heel of the Kimberley Process, making it possible for diamonds borne out of some of the worst human suffering to be sold at legitimate outlets worldwide. The KP has worked for over a decade to fight this problem, but has not yet prevailed. Even today, it acknowledges that traders have been presented with fake documents purporting to be Kimberley Process certificates in the Democratic Republic of Congo, Angola, Malaysia, and Ghana.[107]

PUTTING THE DIAMOND SUPPLY CHAIN ON A SINGLE DIGITAL NETWORK

Everledger's core value proposition is putting the entire diamond supply chain onto the same digital network, creating a single version of the truth for all parties involved in the diamond trade. Using the Hyperledger-based IBM Blockchain on LinuxOne, Everledger's platform meets the diamond industry's requirements with a hybrid technical model that combines the high security of the public blockchain with permissioned controls in private blockchains.

The process of adding certified diamonds to the digital ledger starts at the diamond sorting offices in places like India, Israel, and Belgium where Everledger creates what Kemp called a forensic view of each individual diamond. Using machine vision, Everledger records 40 metadata points to create a unique thumbprint of each stone. The diamond's unique physical properties, along with key details such as its place of origin and chain of custody, are then added to the blockchain, creating an audit trail to make each stone completely traceable.

If Everledger fulfills its ambition, every diamond that makes its way to legitimate international markets will have a secure digital record on the blockchain. To date, over 1.8 million diamonds have been encrypted onto Everledger's digital ledger. Master certificates of the Kimberley Process certified rough diamonds are also digitally stored on the blockchain.

Adding digital records and certificates to a digital ledger is just the first step. A partnership with IBM is extending the capabilities of Everledger's digital ledger even further by using cognitive analytics to spot automatically instances of noncompliance with the Kimberley

Process and other international protocols. "With Everledger, we set out to strengthen the integrity of this process by leveraging IBM Watson to incorporate artificial intelligence into the blockchain," explained Arvind Krishna, senior vice president at IBM Research.[108] According to Krishna, IBM Research created a new AI-enabled approach to help ensure that all of the diamonds linked in Everledger's digital ledger are authentic and compliant with thousands of regulations, including those imposed by the United Nations to prevent the sale of conflict diamonds.

In what IBM claims is an industry first, cognitive analytics are performed directly within the blockchain where the data reside, eliminating the need for data to be extracted for analysis, which makes it susceptible to fraud.[109] Krishna explained that Watson cross-references each diamond certificate on the blockchain with myriad regulations and records as well as supply chain and Internet of Things data, including time and date stamps and geospatial information.

Going a step further, the system can then start to analyze the shared characteristics of noncompliant certificates such as their value, the signatures on their documents, and the countries in which they originated. "No longer will humans have to spend countless hours checking reams of paper regulations and certificates to ensure a diamond's authenticity, compliance, and worth," said Krishna.[110] The efficiencies gained from ensuring regulatory compliance using cognitive analytics extend well beyond diamonds to countless other domains of international trade.

A SINGLE DIGITAL LEDGER TACKLES FRAUD

While the issues concerning conflict diamonds, black markets, and ethical trade capture the headlines, Everledger's bread and butter is tackling the problem of insurance fraud. The insurance sector considers fraudulent claims for lost or stolen jewelry a major problem resulting in billions of dollars in annual losses. Conventional industry wisdom has held that about 10 percent of the property/casualty insurance claims are fraudulent.[111] Based on this estimate, property insurance fraud in the United States alone amounts to approximately $33 billion in losses a year, with jewelry-related fraud constituting about $2 billion of that total.[112] A 2013 survey of 143 US insurers suggested the losses could be even higher, with 31 percent of insurers estimating that up to 20 percent of claims are the direct result of fraud.[113] Meanwhile, 57 percent of the insurers surveyed said they anticipate a rise in losses due to fraud on personal insurance lines.[114]

With respect to diamond jewelry fraud, there are many possible scenarios, such as using fake receipts or fake certification and appraisal records to make a false claim against jewelry that never existed, or staging a robbery when valuable jewelry is falsely alleged to have been stolen. Another type of fraud occurs where one stone is claimed across similar timelines with multiple insurers. Much of this fraud is only possible because the value of jewelry relies on paper-based records that can be forged or tampered with.

Participants operating closer to the consumer end of the supply chain—including merchants, banks, insurers, and consumers themselves—are intrigued by blockchain because it provides a permanent, secure, and immutable ledger that records assets, participants, and transactions. This means an insurer, for example, can verify that an asset (a diamond in this case) is legitimate, and that makes Everledger's solution a compelling proposition. Kemp explained that at the same time that a policyholder insures the diamond, Everledger is providing verification that *that* diamond is real. "Using our platforms, insurers can trust that policyholders are not trying to insure a $40,000 stone when in reality it is a fake diamond. We can also verify that claims against the policy are legitimized and that the diamond hasn't been used in previous multiple claims."[115]

A DIGITAL VAULT FOR ART, WINE, AUTOMOBILES, AND OTHER VALUABLE ITEMS

Tackling conflict diamonds, as well as mitigating risk and fraud, provided proof that blockchain is integral to enabling supply-chain transparency. Everledger's ultimate ambition, however, is to become the digital vault for a wide range of tradable commodities and high-value assets. The company is gradually expanding its reach and has partnered with other organizations—Britannia Mining for commodities trading, Chai Consulting for wine, Vastari for art, and SAP Ariba to help track the identity and movement of a variety of other risky goods in their procurement platform across global supply chains.

The fine wine industry, for example, is another where problems with document tampering and fraudulent activity continue to affect the supply chain, with an estimated 20 percent of international sales involving counterfeit wines.[116] As with diamonds, the provenance and authenticity of fine wines is fundamental to establishing value.

The Chai Wine Vault, a joint venture of Everledger and fine wine expert Maureen Downey, addresses by issuing a digital certification to bottles authenticated through Maureen Downey's Chai Method.[117] The certification captures 90-plus data points about the bottle, in addition to high-resolution photography and records of a bottle's ownership and storage, and creates a permanent, digital incarnation of the bottle that is written permanently into the blockchain.

This digital proof travels with the bottle as it moves between different supply-chain participants, with ownership and storage records updated as the wine changes hands. Licensed retailers, warehouses, auction houses, and other sale platforms can ping the Chai Wine Vault to verify the bottle's identity at any point, thus preserving the bottle's value over its lifetime.[118]

Like fine wine, fine art dealers, buyers, and exhibitors face similar concerns about the authenticity and provenance of precious works of art. In this case, Everledger partner Vastari maintains a fine art and exhibition database and acts as a middleman between art museums that are looking for new pieces and private art collectors who want to increase the value of their art by getting it exhibited in public. Together, they are building a global digital ledger of fine art, in which data about the art are written into the public blockchain, as well as Everledger's own permissioned ledger.[119] The data consist of four key elements: the provenance, including its history of ownership; the exhibition history; the literary works in which the artwork has been referenced; and the physical characteristics of the work of art such as its size, appearance, and the medium.

Kemp explained that rights to modify or even read data on the permissioned blockchain state are restricted to trusted users. "One might imagine a consortium of 15 art institutions, each of which operates a node and of which 10 must sign every block in order for the block to be valid," said Kemp.[120]

As for what's next, Kemp believes there are a wide range of valuable assets for which an indelible digital incarnation can establish provenance, increase trust, and lower transaction costs in trading relationships. "Our goal is to expand into more markets where provenance matters and continue our sustained efforts in enabling radical transparency along the supply chains," said Kemp.[121] The key is knowing when and where provenance and transparency matter. From there, Everledger can build a business model around each of the use cases and sector solutions it develops with industry partners. The company expects to generate revenue by selling the data it collects about valuable assets, charging for search and recovery of data, and potentially licensing its platform to third-party developers.

KEY TAKEAWAYS OF DIAMOND PROVENANCE

- **It takes education and compelling solutions to unlock opportunities for blockchain-enabled innovation.** Traditional industries like diamond mining and manufacturing tend to associate blockchain with cryptocurrencies. According to Kemp, a first step in fostering the adoption of new solutions is to ensure decision-makers appreciate the broader applications of blockchain. "When we started out with Everledger in 2015, awareness of blockchain was still growing and mostly in relevance to Bitcoin," said Kemp. "We had to educate traditional industries on what we were developing and work hard to understand the potential applications to the problems that needed solving in traditional industries."[122] Knowledge networks that bring industry, solution providers, and researchers together could play a valuable role in raising awareness of the broader applications of blockchain.

- **Blockchain's essential value proposition for global supply chains is the enablement of trust, transparency, and efficiencies.** Kemp explained that shifting the paper-based processes and documents into a digitized version on the blockchain creates better security and visibility for stakeholders and helps build trust along the supply chain.[123] Trust and transparency, in turn, help grease the wheel of global trade by mitigating risk and fraud in the markets, whether for diamonds, fine wine, precious works of art, or other valuable assets.

- **Blockchain and AI provide synergistic solutions for data-intensive supply chains.** The marketplace for blockchain solutions is increasingly competitive, so winning companies can't stand still. Kemp said Everledger is continuously investing in R&D to extend the capability and effectiveness of its products and the technologies that underpin them, including artificial intelligence and cognitive analytics through partnerships with leading companies such as IBM. "Ultimately blockchain and AI can work together in synergy for data scalability and querying purposes," Kemp explained. "With any supply-chain-intensive business, including the diamond industry, there are huge data sets being created. By modeling those data sets, we can channel the information to help customers understand exactly the information they need from the supply chain; what, why, where, when, and how, which is the provenance of the item."[124]

- **Successful blockchain solutions need a business case that sells itself.** Traditional industries like diamond mining and distribution are not normally synonymous with risk-taking and innovation. Indeed, a general culture of conservatism when it comes to investments in technology puts a premium on the business case that solution providers such as Everledger can bring to decision-makers in these industries. In building a global digital ledger for valuable assets, Everledger's business model rests on providing a zero sum game for the industries it serves. "The costs to our clients of our technology are more than offset with benefits and savings associated with the reduction of risk and fraud and reduction in friction across the supply chain," said Kemp.[125]

- **Commercializing blockchain solutions is a marathon, not a sprint.** "There is a lot of pressure being a start-up, in particular focusing on blockchain," said Kemp. "We started with lofty ambitions: solving global problems like blood diamonds with a novel technology that most people thought is interchangeable with cryptocurrencies. It was never going to be easy." Kemp pointed out that, while awareness of blockchain has increased exponentially in the past couple of years, it is still considered a nascent technology for many industries. "One of the key challenges is to find a way to cut through the hype and arrive at a solution that adds value to clients. This is a marathon, and finding the right people who have the same purpose, passion, and goal to join you is essential."[126]

CHAPTER 4

AGRICULTURE ON THE BLOCKCHAIN

Sustainable Solutions for Food, Farmers, and Financing

Henry Kim and Marek Laskowski

 ## AGRICULTURAL SUSTAINABILITY IN BRIEF

- This research explores applications of blockchain across the agricultural sector, beyond the typical finance use cases. In considering agriculture itself as a chain, a network that reaches from farm to fork, we analyze blockchain efforts to improve safety, efficiency, and accountability at every stage of the process.

- Provenance tracking or traceability across the various stages of the global food supply chain ensures food safety both for direct consumers as well as for a global community vulnerable to a food-born pandemic.

- Smart contracts and chain-of-custody records can mitigate instances of food fraud and identify untrustworthy middlemen and business practices that exploit both independent farmers and cooperatives.

- Sustainable agriculture and "local economy" cooperatives—such as AgriLedger with pilot programs in Kenya, Myanmar, and Papua New Guinea—can generate economic activity and retain more value locally, even to the extent that the community operates within its own economy complete with distinct cryptocurrency and tracked exchanges.

- Instantaneous transactions, accountable origin, and route tracking of goods such as Provenance's blockchain for the Grass Roots Farmers' Cooperative in Arkansas can transform a sprawling, complicated, and decentralized food market into a local one with high trust and quality.

- Agriculture finance innovations, especially for developing world farmers, include transparent and efficient futures contract payment platforms, smart-contract insurance against crop catastrophes, and microfinancing opportunities for underserved communities that can grow from subsistence-level loans into investments in new businesses.

THE CHALLENGES OF AGRICULTURE WORLDWIDE

According to the UN Food and Agriculture Organization, 2.5 billion people in developing economics derived their livelihood from agriculture in 2011; that was over a third of the world's population.[127] Yet, without farming sophistication, business knowledge, financial resources, and leverage against much larger buyers—not to mention corrupt intermediaries and government officials—developing world farmers receive only a tiny share of the ultimate value of their crops. For instance, Kenyan farmers reported receiving only 30 cents per kilogram for their coffee, which retailed for more than 100 times that price.[128]

Blockchain is a revolutionary technology that implements a shared ledger or database to deliver an immutable, single version of the truth among numerous, sometimes adversarial, stakeholders. Blockchain provides transparency to inefficient and corrupt business practices by enabling equitable participation for farmers and other stakeholders on the global food value chain, leading to greater prosperity for developing world agricultural workers.

Where in agriculture can we best fulfill this promise? First, it is in *provenance and traceability* for food safety. Every year, one in ten people fall ill—and 400,000 die—because of contaminated food.[129] Food safety failures are magnified, last longer, and cost more because of lack of access to information and traceability. In the summer of 2017, the US Food and Drug Administration took two months to trace salmonella-tainted papayas consumed in the States back to a Mexican farm where the contamination originated.

Using blockchain, global supply-chain participants can gain permissioned access to trusted information regarding food provenance. They could then access data on the blockchain network to trace contaminated products expeditiously, stemming public health outbreaks, and potentially saving lives.[130]

A second class of blockchain applications is the support of *farmer cooperatives* at the local level, especially in developing worlds. Cooperatives pool individual farmers' resources, giving the collective more leverage over large buyers and inefficient or corrupt middlemen. As legal stakeholders, co-op members are inherently interested in sustainable agriculture practices that "minimize tilling and water use, encourage healthy soil by planting fields with different crops year after year and integrating croplands with livestock grazing, and avoid pesticide use by nurturing the presence of organisms that control crop-destroying pests."[131]

Blockchain can help co-op farmers retain more of their profits, ensuring that they will not have to forsake long-term sustainability practices in exchange for the short-term need to turn a profit. Sustainable agriculture is complementary to local, community-based economics, wherein the goal is to have producers and buyers transact locally and, therefore, retain economic value in the community.

A third class is *agriculture finance*, which comprises financial services for agricultural enterprises. Many applications leverage transparency and smart-contract automation features of blockchain to make financing and insuring farmers—especially those in the developing world—more viable.

Finally, a fourth class is *precision agriculture*, which describes very precise and granular data-driven decision-making facilitated by advancements in data collection and analytics technologies. Using blockchain, data from sources like soil sensors, weather satellites, drones, and farm equipment improve decision-making and automation both at the individual farm level and the community level via pooling and analysis of those data.

THREE CLASSES OF AGRICULTURAL USE CASES

FOOD SAFETY

The application of blockchain for provenance tracking is central to the most developed and highly publicized blockchain case studies in agriculture. The Walmart-IBM food ecosystem has received much coverage.[132]

Lesser known is the Chinese e-commerce giant Alibaba's partnership with food suppliers in Australia and New Zealand, as well as Australia Post and PricewaterhouseCoopers on another blockchain pilot for food traceability.[133] Nimble start-ups are also addressing food safety and traceability. For example, a key pilot by Provenance ensures blockchain use for near real-time monitoring and traceability in the seafood chain emanating from Indonesia. The network can detect and address wholesaler fraud within hours, once the offending wholesalers are uniquely identified and confronted, as opposed to days or weeks of investigation, during which the offender can disappear without consequence or hide behind another name and business ID.[134] Other endeavors have so far focused on specific items to trace: Bureau Veritas/Stratumn for tuna, Chai Wine Vault and Wine Blockchain EY for wine, and ZhongAn for poultry.[135] In many cases, the focus remains on the farm side of the equation, rather than on the entirety of the farm-to-fork chain.

Mitigating the risk of animal-borne disease is central to food safety. According to the World Health Organization, consuming or even having contact with infected poultry or livestock presents a vector for introducing zoonotic diseases such as avian influenza into human communities, potentially resulting in a global pandemic. The mobile app Intellichain employs distributed AI agent-based simulation and virtual reality visualization of blockchain data for monitoring and analyzing infectious disease spread. Public health officials could apply Intellichain to data from an agrifood blockchain to monitor spread within both animal and human populations, diagnose the jumps from animal to human populations, and highlight where along the agrifood chain this jump might have taken place—and how.[136]

The question for decision-makers in the food industry is not if, but how to incorporate blockchain into their food safety systems. There are several issues to consider. The first is that blockchain is not a panacea, though in concert with IoT, the traceability capability that it provides is revolutionary. According to Mitchell Weinberg, head of INSCATECH, whose agents identify counterfeit and mislabeled food,

> The problem is the data is only as reliable as the person providing the data. In most supply chains, there is one or more "unreliable" data provider. This means blockchain is likely useless for protecting against food fraud unless every piece of data is scrutinized to be accurate.[137]

Blockchain is far from useless, but its effectiveness is constrained by missing or unscrutinized data. To minimize this constraint, we ought not develop a system for IoT, blockchain, and smart contracts in isolation, but in a sociotechnical context—flagging locations, for example, where regulatory inspection of food is compromised by frequent local corruption.

Another issue is that industry players such as grocers and restaurants have notoriously slim profit margins, and investment in food traceability systems incurs costs without necessarily increasing revenues. As a result, the profit motive is often not compelling for investing in this type of innovation. Mammoth, powerful grocers like Walmart have the capital and incentive to comply with regulators and inspectors, but even then, such industry players are often motivated to develop systems designed to meet minimal compliance, and no more. The industry could end up with multiple blockchains for food traceability that are minimally useful and unable to communicate with each other. In the event of large-scale food contamination, the available systems might not be up to the task of rapidly identifying the source.

We spoke with Brian Sterling, former managing director of the Global Food Traceability Center in Washington, DC. According to Mr. Sterling, the key to addressing this issue is to think, "Traceability is free."[138] In Total Quality Management and Six Sigma improvement initiatives, "quality is free" expresses the notion that processes are managed so well in a world-class operational system that high quality is a free by-product of the system itself. In a similar vein, his perspective is that a world-class value chain would operate so well that traceability would be a capability inherent in the chain's systems rather than delivered via alternative systems. To date, the traceability blockchains of Walmart, Alibaba, and Provenance appear to be such alternatives to the systems of JDA Software, SAP, Oracle, or custom implementations. Extending Mr. Sterling's perspective, we believe that Walmart's blockchain for food traceability, for instance, will reach an important milestone when and if it is so integrated with the company's own excellent supply-chain management system. Then Walmart and its partners can declare, "Traceability is free."[139]

A third issue for food industry decision-makers, and certainly for blockchain providers like IBM, is that because food is truly ubiquitous—more than cars, smartphones, or shoes—the global food supply chains look much more like a complex, entangled hodgepodge than other industries' supply chains. For the vision of global blockchain-enabled food safety, the blockchains of Alibaba, Provenance, Walmart, and others ought to interoperate, or at least communicate, with each other. The Tapscotts have conceptualized a governing structure for chain interoperability.[140] Aion Network (formerly Nuco Inc.) is taking the first steps toward the Tapscott vision by building an infrastructure network to bridge different blockchains.[141] It's focusing on lower, protocol, or hardware level interoperability.

However, more work is needed. Additional initiatives—such as the use of ontologies for blockchain interoperability from York University Blockchain Lab—will be required for different food blockchains to communicate among themselves.[142] To achieve chain interoperability, we must enable them to communicate at a higher, more semantic level through shared vocabulary and industry terms among different chains. Somehow, global supply-chain standards like GS1 or data reference models like United Nations Centre for Trade Facilitation and Electronic Business (UN/CEFACT) International Supply Chain Reference Model (ISCRM) must be implemented in the blockchains so that different food chains can "talk to each other."

SUSTAINABLE AGRICULTURE AND THE LOCAL ECONOMY

Agricultural entities range in scope from global consortia to local farming communities. Historically, cooperatives have been key pillars in many farming economies. There are some blockchain initiatives harnessing this ethos, specifically for sustainable agriculture to leave a smaller, community-based carbon footprint and to contribute to the local food economy.

Especially in developing worlds, cooperatives of small farmers have emerged to negotiate collectively with notoriously exploitative intermediaries. However, even with cooperatives, there are losses due to inefficient and fraudulent paper handling and the use of informal and verbal agreements. AgriLedger is a philanthropic initiative vying to move farming co-op data and transactions onto the blockchain to mitigate these losses. Participating farmers would access the blockchain using mobile phones, which are pervasive even in developing communities. AgriLedger has developed pilot programs in Kenya, Myanmar, and Papua New Guinea.[143]

Provenance is developing a blockchain for meat-product monitoring for the Grass Roots Farmers' Cooperative in Arkansas. This co-op was launched and funded by Heifer International, a nonprofit that establishes sustainable agriculture and commerce in impoverished international and US communities. It employs sustainable practices like micro broods and herds, hormone-free grass feed, use of local suppliers and services, and local delivery to homes and restaurants. This last point is important because it means reliable traceability: "farm to fork" is simple and hence comprehensive data collection, scrutiny, and tracking are possible. Information about meat products will be registered on the blockchain and labeled on the packaging as QR codes. Customers can scan QR codes to learn not only about meat quality, but also how the animal was raised and who was involved in production.[144]

Blockchain holds promise to store much more intensive data about meat, even down to the DNA level. We spoke with Dr. Ellen Goddard, professor of agricultural marketing and business at the University of Alberta, Canada. She participates in the Canadian Cattle Genome Project, a multimillion-dollar initiative between scientists and the cattle industry to sequence the genome of Canadian cattle breeds and create a reference library for future breeding decisions.[145] She sees the blockchain as an opportunity to leverage genomics. In her view, food safety is an obvious area of leverage. Consider arc-net, a blockchain start-up for traceability that aims to provide a unique ID for food items where the ID is comprised in part by the item's DNA code.

Dr. Goddard also sees how genomics and blockchain can contribute to sustainable agriculture practices. The tendency to breed dairy cows for optimal milk production has led to a loss of genetic diversity. There are concerted efforts to counter this trend. Moreover, blockchain can contribute by enabling transparent and tamper-proof recording of genetic markers of a cow's biodiversity—that is, the extent to which the cow's lineage is diverse. By accessing this information on the blockchain along with production traits that mark a cow's milk production capabilities and functional traits like fertility, health, and calving ease, dairy farmers can make more sustainable breeding decisions.[146]

We also spoke with Marieke de Ruyter de Wildt, founder of The Fork, an Amsterdam-based software company with a network of blockchain and food supply-chain experts. One of its engagements, for instance, is a proof of concept for managing certificate information of South African grapes to farmers, auditors, standard-setting organizations, and retailers in Europe. She believes that one of the subtle but potentially powerful uses of blockchain is fostering greater customer intimacy between the consumer and the grower—say, between a Dutch consumer and a South African orchardist. De Ruyter de Wildt believes that blockchain can help the consumer know more about, for example, South African grapes, the orchards of origin, and the transit conditions for the grapes.[147] This transparency leads to a greater connection to the food, as if it were sourced locally. That is, blockchain might help consumers experience global food with local proximity.

Blockchain can store information beyond what is required strictly for traceability for food safety. For instance, Grass Roots co-op made animal welfare and production personnel data available to its customers via the blockchain because that additional transparency enables the co-op's health-conscious and sustainability-minded customers to recognize more value in their food. Whether it's Grass Roots co-op or The Fork, blockchain enables something interesting: blockchains for food safety are being co-opted to demonstrate sustainability and "local economy" benefit.

Another effort that does exactly this is an early stage initiative called FarmShare, which is billed as a decentralized blockchain-based platform for local economy/community-based economics.[148] Through the FarmShare platform, a local community would be able to set up and operate a virtual farmers' market. It would allow other local economy exchanges to be linked, so that its users could trade, for instance, apples for solar energy with another user on a community microgrid. FarmShare plans to enable this trade by issuing and using its own native currency, called the farmshare token. As FarmShare is developing on the Ethereum blockchain network, customers and farmers would need first to possess Ethereum cryptocurrency, ether, which they would exchange for farmshare tokens. Customers would pay tokens to farmers and schedule weekly deliveries as well as pay in real time if they bought in a face-to-face transaction at a physical farmers' market. The tokens would also represent shares in FarmShare, such that if activity and economic value increased in many farmers' markets operated by FarmShare, the tokens would appreciate relative to ether.

The major issue for this application is quite simply who will pay to build these blockchains. Local-economy participants usually lack deep pockets and technical and business sophistication to seek out, develop, and fully realize the business value of a blockchain-based solution, even when *return on investment* (ROI) is demonstrable. In the AgriLedger and Grass Roots co-op examples, charities stepped in and funded the blockchains. FarmShare was conceived as a for-profit venture. It would not necessarily charge transaction or maintenance fees but would receive ether in exchange for its tokens. The market for ether (around $21 billion as of Oct. 2018) is so liquid that it is easily converted to cash.[149] In addition, by decree, FarmShare would create and hold large amounts of tokens that would appreciate—just as stock shares appreciate as buyers bid up the shares in a stock exchange—as economic activity in the various markets it operated within increased. As a very early stage start-up, FarmShare faces many challenges and is currently on hold, but there might be merit in its business model.[150]

In sum, local-economy participants might be unwilling or unable to fund blockchain solutions. However, others might be willing to invest on their behalf because the economic activity spurred by the blockchain might be of value to charities or governments that do not necessarily have a profit motive. Alternatively, the blockchain provider might be incentivized to invest because they can directly convert an increase in activity as a realizable increase in monetary value.

AGRICULTURE FINANCE

There are also novel blockchain applications on the farmer transaction and payment side. In December 2016, 23 metric tons of wheat were delivered within Australia, and that transaction was recorded on the blockchain:

> The deal was "auto-executed" by a smart contract run by commodity management platform AgriDigital. This smart contract performed a series of tasks, including valuing the delivery, verifying that the buyer had sufficient funds, and securing the funds in the grower's name pending delivery. Once the grower made the physical delivery, the title for the grain was transferred to the buyer as the grower's payment was simultaneously created from the reserved funds.[151]

Blockchain can be used by governments and NGOs to level the playing field for developing world farmers in the global futures market. Buyers purchase price contracts for West African cocoa or Indian sugar cane before the season. However, if the futures prices of those commodities make those contracts unprofitable, the buyers will sometimes renege on those contracts. Because these farmers are very under-resourced, the buyers renege knowing that there is not much recourse for the farmers. Even if the farmers can scramble and find another buyer, they will have to sell at a reduced price, and if there is a time lag in the scramble, significant spoilage in their crops might have occurred reducing the amount that can be sold, leading to further losses.

AgriDigital is also tackling this problem "by enabling real-time transactions for farmers through 'smart contracts' that run on blockchain. Because pre-approved logic can be built into a blockchain—as long as all parties have opted in—payments can be made immediately following the transfer of asset ownership."[152] This discourages reneging as payment is automatically scheduled and if the buyer actively stops payment, there is a well-documented evidence trail that can be used against them in litigation.

Etherisc, a start-up using blockchain to provide decentralized insurance, has conceptualized how they can help the plight of farmers in the developing world. Crop insurance is underutilized in these countries even though the need is great: these farmers typically lack substantial financial reserves and would greatly benefit from insurance against natural events that are catastrophic for their crops. However, there are instances where farmers have been unable to collect against crop insurance they held because they could not navigate the complex, sometimes corrupt claims process, or didn't fully understand terms of their insurance. Often, farmers simply can't afford the premiums. Etherisc uses *parametric insurance*, wherein processing would be done by smart contracts that are triggered when certain events occur (modeled as certain parameter threshold values being reached).

In one use case, a developing-world farmer would be insured for one or two dollars a month, a rate that a traditional insurance provider could not viably offer. Etherisc would execute a smart contract so that if the rainfall in the region of a farmer is below a threshold specified by insurance it would be paid out to them automatically. Rainfall information would be sourced from a trusted weather database. There would be little human intervention for claims processing, keeping costs low. More importantly, the farmer would receive timely payment, without having to deal with potentially corrupt bureaucrats. Etherisc is working to integrate insurance processing with M-Pesa, the cell phone-based payments infrastructure used in much of developing Africa.[153]

Another example is the start-up Everex's blockchain use to offer microfinancing to the developing world.[154] Inevitably, much of that money will be lent to farmers. Microfinancing is the notion of offering small, low-barrier loans to businesses or individuals who would be otherwise shut out by their region's traditional bank lending practices. The major problem of microfinancing is that loans often go for subsistence, not necessarily for growing, businesses. As a result, borrowers might be further burdened with loan repayments. Lenders often charge exorbitant rates (e.g., a large Mexican bank charged as much as 200% per annum), effectively transforming a well-intentioned program into a loan-sharking scheme. From the lender's perspective, given the borrowers' high-risk profiles and small loan sizes, as well as the possibility of corruption, administrative costs per dollar lent for providing these loans is relatively high. By offering transparency, automating processing using smart contracts, and speeding up money transfers, Everex can significantly lower costs for the lender, which could lead to better terms being offered to borrowers, who then can take on larger loans to drive business growth beyond subsistence.

We spoke with Anne Connelly, the founding team member of ixo Foundation, a nonprofit based in South Africa that is optimizing impact to achieve the UN Sustainable Development Goals.[155] ixo is building a protocol that enables sustainable development organizations to create an impact claim around the work they have achieved. Claims could include such impacts as improving farm production yields, delivering vaccines, or increasing access to education. The claim is then verified by an evaluator or an oracle, creating *proof of impact* through ixo's decentralized impact exchange. This proof enables organizations to access funding like social impact bonds and government subsidies, and funders can reduce the evaluation costs associated with their investments.

The data from the verified impact claims is stored in the Global Impact Ledger, an open data commons that funders, organizations, researchers, and governments can use to make more informed decisions about their work and optimize their impact. The ixo Foundation has partnered with UNICEF, with whom it has been running field trials of an application called Amply that tracks preschool attendance on the ixo protocol.[156] It is operating in over 72 schools across South Africa and has recorded 44,000 attendance records, improving access to government subsidies while creating valuable data about access to education.

The top two of the 17 UN sustainable development goals are "No Poverty" and "Zero Hunger," hence numerous UN projects focus on improving agriculture in the developing world. Connelly hopes that ixo can improve the effectiveness of such projects and become a shining example of how blockchain can positively affect developing-world farmers.

Finance was the first area to which blockchain was applied. Not surprisingly then, some of the examples presented here adapt blockchain designs born of finance to the agriculture space. In contrast, blockchain solutions in food safety, sustainable agriculture, and local economy are directly conceived to address issues in agriculture. There are fast-paced innovations in blockchain for finance, and so the issue for agriculture decision-makers is to determine whether and how applications in that space can translate into agriculture solutions.

 KEY TAKEAWAYS FOR AGRICULTURE

Traceability for food safety is thus far the most adopted application of blockchain for agriculture. As blockchain initiatives in food safety reach widespread acceptance, we make the following recommendations for decision-makers to stay ahead of the curve. The blockchain pioneers we interviewed contributed to these insights.

- **Experiment with, and add blockchain capability to, your organization's food safety programs.** Be sure to include a sociotechnical perspective to provide the right incentives and context to address the weakest link in traceability—false, incomplete, or missing data.

- **Plan to partner with champions and key personnel of your organization's value chain systems** (e.g., implementations from SAP or Oracle). Such partnerships lead to tight coupling between the blockchain and the value chain system and a world-class traceability capability that will be a by-product of your organization operating a world-class value chain.

- **Participate in global standards initiatives like GS1 and UN/CEFACT.** Your organization will need to ensure that your blockchain maps to these standards to bridge with other blockchains and enable global-scale food traceability.

- **Get personally and socially involved in learning about blockchain and agriculture.** According to de Ruyter de Wildt, The Fork's meetups are particularly informative because they not only are about blockchain but also are based on use cases. They gather diverse perspectives from software developers, agriculturalists, brand managers, and government officials. She told us that she has been able to enlist companies to invest time and money in The Fork's initiatives partly because of these meetups.

- **Invest in your own proof of concept.** Obviously, the most motivated companies should invest in their own proofs of concepts, such as The Fork's managing certificates for South African grapes, ixo's proof of impact exchange, Etherisc's crop insurance smart contracts, AgriLedger's co-op data collection, FarmShare's local economy exchanges, and Everex's microfinancing platform.

- **Contribute time and money to a third-party or consortium blockchain initiative.** De Ruyter de Wildt's corporate collaborators told her they wanted to dip their toes, view first-hand how The Fork consortium would work, and collaborate with partners in their ecosystems, all while mitigating the risk of going it alone.

- **Perform due diligence before contemplating participating in any ICO.** Connelly at ixo Foundation told us that UNICEF as a founding partner of ixo will be a "coin holder" if ixo does an ICO, another means of funding and investment with less regulatory oversight and fewer hurdles than initial public offerings. Not only would UNICEF be a key user of ixo's blockchain that measures the impact of development projects, it would also effectively be a key shareholder.

- **Consider buying coins or tokens of third-party partners who help build your blockchain.** Coin purchases in combination with direct payments can constitute total remuneration to such partners as ixo, FarmShare, AgriLedger, or Etherisc. Agricultural organizations can amplify their ROI, as they receive direct cost or profit benefit from their blockchains *and* as their coins appreciate.

Blockchain holds great promise to revolutionize agriculture. We hope that this research will help stakeholders in the global agriculture ecosystem get their journey started.

CHAPTER 5

FOOD TRACEABILITY ON BLOCKCHAIN

Walmart's Pork and Mango Pilots with IBM

Reshma Kamath

 ## FOOD TRACEABILITY IN BRIEF

- Walmart, a leader in global retail, is tackling food safety and delivery with blockchain technology in response to food contamination scandals worldwide. It is collaborating with the food system to have a complete and interconnected view of the supply chain.

- In 2016, it established the Beijing-based Walmart Food Safety Collaboration Center and announced its plans to invest $25 million over five years to support research projects, the results of which will enhance food safety.[157] Using IBM's blockchain solution based on Hyperledger Fabric, Walmart has successfully completed two blockchain pilots: pork in China and mangoes in the Americas.[158]

- With a farm-to-table approach, Walmart's blockchain solution reduced time for tracking mango origins from seven days to 2.2 seconds.[159] Frank Yiannas, Walmart's vice president of food safety, lauded blockchain's potential in promoting shared value and transparency across Walmart's food supply chain.[160] Brigid McDermott, IBM's vice president of blockchain business development, called it "complete end-to-end traceability."[161]

- This research examines why Walmart conducted food traceability pilot tests in blockchain, how it partnered with IBM to leverage blockchain in food safety, and what participants learned through the two pilot projects. The case highlights the overall challenges of implementing blockchain technology in the food supply chain and the opportunities for deploying blockchain solutions throughout the global food ecosystem to increase safety and reduce waste.

BROKEN FOOD CHAINS

A RISE IN FOOD CONTAMINATION SCANDALS

Health hazards from food mismanagement and contamination are well documented. The Centers for Disease Control and Prevention (CDC) estimates 48 million people in the United States contract foodborne illnesses every year.[162] Moreover, the World Health Organization estimates that one out of every ten people suffers from food poisoning worldwide, 420,000 of whom die each year.[163] This figure includes a staggering number of children and youth. The compromised integrity of food chains has caused food-related illnesses worldwide.

European Union: The horsemeat scandal

In 2013, bad actors in the EU supply chain replaced lamb and beef with horsemeat.[164] The illegal substitution affected more than 4.5 million processed products representing at least 1,000 tons of food.[165] This collective and deliberate fraud drastically affected the EU food and beverage industry, which took a massive hit in profits and corporate image.[166] According to a study by PwC and Safe and Secure Approaches in Field Environments, food fraud is estimated to cost the global industry $40 billion a year.[167]

China: Mislabeled pork and adulterated donkey meat

Economically motivated food adulteration, commonly referred to as *food fraud*, occurs worldwide. In 2011, China witnessed a massive pork mislabeling debacle, along with the donkey meat contamination hoax in which donkey meat products were later recalled because they were found to include fox meat.[168] Many Chinese believed that adulterated meat was seeping into China's retail markets. Additional contaminants such as melamine, Sudan red, clenbuterol, Sanlu toxic milk powder, and trench oil, all of which had breached the food supply chain, further eroded Chinese trust in food markets.[169] With arcane agricultural food logistics systems, China continued to face an agrifood loss ratio of 25 to 30 percent annually.[170] A report by the Office of Economic Cooperation and Development identified several challenges, among them deficient information at each stage of the food value chain, decentralized storage of food on farms rather than in commercial or government facilities, waste in the restaurant and catering sector, and a lack of coordination among relevant regulatory agencies and ministries.[171]

The Americas: From suspicious spinach to impure papayas

In North America, isolating bad actors in the spinach *E. coli* outbreak in 2006 wasted time, energy, and the resources of the entire ecosystem (wholesalers, retailers, farmers, and regulators), severely shattering public trust in the supply chain.[172] American consumers stopped eating spinach altogether, while restaurateurs and grocery stores pulled all spinach off their shelves and menus. Health officials took almost two weeks to identify the source of the contaminated spinach. At the end of the day, the contamination was linked to one supplier, one day's production, and one lot number. The inability to rapidly track and trace the source of the contaminated spinach resulted in significant economic harm to all spinach farmers and erosion in consumer trust of the commodity.[173]

In July 2017, papayas in the US market were linked to a multi-state outbreak of salmonella.[174] By mid-August 2017, the CDC reported 173 cases of salmonellosis, 58 hospitalizations, and one death across 21 states.[175] Initially, health officials advised all Americans to avoid eating papayas and retailers not to sell them. Even by replicating measures in the spinach outbreak, health officials took almost three weeks to trace the source of the contaminated papayas back to one farm in Mexico. Once again, papaya farmers from unaffected areas, such as other Central American countries and Hawaii, suffered economic loss because of inefficiencies in the ability to rapidly track and trace food products.[176]

"ONE UP, ONE DOWN" APPROACH IS INSUFFICIENT

In these cases, the challenge is usually the inability to trace records in the supply chain because participants use disparate record-keeping methods.[177] Moreover, the widely accepted industry approach of "one up, one down" (OUOD)—where food supply-chain participants need to identify only the immediate supplier (one link up the chain) and the immediate customer (one link down the chain) of a food stuff or ingredient—is simply insufficient.[178]

In suspected contamination outbreaks, investigators typically have to review paper documentation step by step. Erroneous or incomplete data can further delay their investigations.[179] With multi-ingredient foods including materials from a variety of food chains and countries, importers end up relying on the arcane traceability systems (if any) of other countries up to the point of import. Traceability gets even more complicated in mixtures and bulk containers.

As a precautionary step, entire shipments are thrown out under the current OUOD parameters. With blockchain technology, such food shipments "will be identified as being safe at a much earlier juncture," while saving millions in sales as well as valuable human lives.[180]

WALMART'S BLOCKCHAIN PILOT FOR FOOD PROVENANCE

To aid in strengthening trust in food supply chains, Walmart had to go beyond OUOD traceability.[181] With a history of collaborating, Walmart worked with IBM to develop and implement its food provenance pilots.[182] According to Brigid McDermott, "Blockchain solves business problems where trust is part of the solution—you can't do that with a database."[183]

She identified two key features of blockchain that differentiate it from standard databases and help to build trust: first, data immutability, and second, speed and security of dissemination leading to a single version of the truth. "When records are stored on a blockchain, everything ranging from dates and times to temperature controls (or whatever at each step and stage along a supply chain) becomes tamperproof," she said. "Secondly, technology enables information to be both disseminated rapidly and simultaneously protected. With combined speed and reliable, immutable data, the stage for trust is set."[184]

Leaders at IBM recognized that they could accelerate the adoption of blockchain and avoid a proliferation of internal systems and data formats by using existing open standards such as the Global Specifications 1 (GS1), specifically its Electronic Product Code Information Services (EPCIS) and Core Business Vocabulary (CBV).[185] In conjunction with these standards, blockchain enables Walmart to track and trace individual items in the supply chain.[186]

Interoperability among participants was crucial. "By removing barriers ... including those caused from disparate entry systems, [blockchain] solidifies that trust even further," McDermott said. "That's why we are working with our clients and collaborating with other industry leaders to implement GS1 open standards into the work that we do."[187]

IBM's blockchain is based on Hyperledger Fabric, which supports modular architecture and plug-and-play components as needed, such as consensus and membership services.[188] It allows both efficient data capture and data control.

Most importantly, users have a shared view of the truth at any time. "In food safety, you don't want anonymity. You want transparency of who has responsibility for the food at what given time."[189] Capturing value-added attributes to reflect transparency is an integral conversation in blockchain tracking. McDermott explained:

> People could do without blockchain what we are trying to do, which is provide information across the ecosystem. They choose not to because they worry they will lose control over information or they will be disadvantaged with others using information. ... Blockchain gives comfort that people have ownership and control over their information.[190]

For the food chain, it becomes a record keeper of step-by-step conduct (e.g., audits, treatments, identification numbers, manufacturers, available device updates, known security issues, granted permissions, and safety protocols). Such data are chronologically logged in real time and permanently stored as e-certificates.

This foundational trust has a flywheel effect. Said McDermott, "The trust it delivers enables more efficient and complete sharing of the critical data that drives enterprise transactions."[191] The next two sections look more closely at Walmart's pork pilot in China and its mango pilot in the Americas.

PORK CHAINS ACROSS CHINA

According to the Economic Research Service (ERS) of the US Department of Agriculture, China is a leading importer of pork, and it produces approximately half of the world's pork.[192] In its report, "China's Pork Imports Rise Along with Production Costs," the ERS noted that larger, industrialized pork production systems similar to those in the United States were quickly displacing small-scale "backyard" pork producers.[193] In line with this trend, government officials in China called for the country's pork industry to modernize its production system from farm to fork.

As customer focus in China has shifted to food safety and quality, trust has become a fundamental element in customer purchasing decisions. Therefore, the Chinese government is investing heavily in its food system by upping food inspection and safety methods, putting pressure on production systems, and partnering with corporate retail giants. The government's concern was an opportunity.

Given the country's sizable population and its immense appetite for pork as a source of animal protein (with an annual consumption of 12.7 million tons), Walmart had an incentive to explore new technologies for food provenance in China.[194]

COLLABORATION, COLLABORATION, COLLABORATION

In October 2016, Walmart launched the Food Safety Collaboration Center.[195] At the center's opening, Doug McMillon, president and CEO of Walmart Stores, said, "By bringing together the best food safety thinkers from across the food ecosystem, from farmers to suppliers, retailers to policy regulators, we'll accelerate food safety awareness and help make Chinese families safer and healthier."[196] The center's staff started researching foodborne contaminants and developing food safety risk assessment models globally that other corporations and organizations will be able to use.[197] Walmart also invested in food-related technologies to detect foodborne illness and harmful bacteria, and to monitor packaged food for unusual patterns of contamination in the supply chain.

Frank Yiannas, Walmart's vice president of food safety and a special adviser to the center, saw blockchain's potential to empower small and local businesses to retain control over their systems in the produce supply chains.[198] Walmart had a collaboration with IBM on food traceability. Its pilot project in China used blockchain technology to track and verify food provenance in a secure and transparent manner.

Cooperation with governmental entities was crucial to the success of Walmart's blockchain pilot. The good news was that regulators were enthusiastic about blockchain technology and its potential, as it aligned with their work.[199] Never had there been so much interest and excitement in regulatory bodies for a technology.[200] With collaborators in place and a green light from regulators, Walmart was ready to apply features of blockchain technology to pork safety and supply-chain management.

THE POTENTIAL OF BLOCKCHAIN IN SUPPLY-CHAIN GOVERNANCE

The permissioned nature of IBM's blockchain solution allows for a governance policy designed to meet the needs of all participants in a particular ecosystem. The solution is built on the IBM blockchain platform and can leverage the platform's voting process, which "collects signatures from members in order to govern the invitation of new members, the distribution of smart contracts, and creation of transactions channels."[201] The point is that blockchain is more than a technology solution; it is a means of instantiating business rules in an ecosystem—such as membership requirements and commitments, data permissions, data ownership, and decision rights—before any transaction occurs.

For pork, the process begins at pens—where every pig is smart-tagged with bar codes—and follows the product all the way to packaged pork. While using RFID (radio frequency identification) and cameras, participants record the pig's movement as well. Additional cameras installed in slaughterhouses capture the entire production process.

These efforts add to livestock optimization, protecting piglets from injury, providing individual care for the sow and piglets, and modulating temperature for piglets to stay warm while the sow stays cooler.[202]

In pork production, shipping trucks have deployed temperature and humidity sensors, along with global positioning (location) and geographic information systems, to ensure the meat arrives to retailers under safe conditions. Using these technologies, Walmart can trace whereabouts of trucks and monitor conditions in each refrigerated container. If conditions exceed established thresholds, the system will send alerts to prompt corrective action.[203]

WALMART DISTRIBUTION CENTER AND STORE TRACKING

With blockchain, procurement managers can remotely and seamlessly trace all information, from expiration dates to warehouse temperatures, in an immutable and tamper-proof ledger.[204] Blockchain network participants can leverage information about farm origination, batch numbers, processing data, soil quality and fertilizers, and even storage temperatures and shipping details. All this can be uploaded on an e-certificate and linked to the product package via a QR code.[205]

Walmart's blockchain pilot involved different systems of data capture and improved speed and accuracy in providing relevant information from the farm to the store.[206] Such systems typically include

Global Trade Identification Number (GTIN) with a handler's production lot or batch number, or less used possibilities include serialized GTINs (e.g., sGTIN) and Unique Identification Numbers (UID) as used by the United States Department of Defense or a Globally Unique Identification Number (GUID) as used by other manufactured product industries.[207]

The traceability system aims to improve food safety and public confidence in pork. The hope is that, should anyone become sick after consuming tainted food, the traceability system can better pinpoint which products should be removed, while keeping the safe products in stock.[208]

Throughout the product life cycle, supply-chain participants record, cross-check, and ensure a product's authenticity and trace its movement and quality.[209] With a holistic traceability model, this blockchain solution has the potential to cut costs of product recalls and reduce process inefficiencies, enabling retailers to track digitally individual pork products in seconds, not days.[210]

MANGO CHAINS IN THE AMERICAS

Walmart concurrently conducted a mango pilot in the Americas. The food ecosystem's inability to trace quickly the source of contaminated produce (such as spinach and papayas) was a key driver in this pilot project. According to IBM's McDermott, if ever there were a recall of spinach or similar produce again, blockchain traceability would enhance public trust in the information about the produce— which product was bad, which might be bad, and which was safe to consume.[211]

As mangoes are popular in several markets, mango origins and derivatives are shipped worldwide. Moreover, like other produce items, they are susceptible to listeria and salmonella contaminations.[212] Therefore, Walmart's mango blockchain pilot had to demonstrate transferability and accountability across borders.[213] The US blockchain pilot project was straightforward: Walmart used IBM's Hyperledger-based blockchain to trace sliced mangoes from South and Central America to North America.[214]

FOOD PRODUCTION (PRE-SEEDLING)

In mango production, mangoes can suffer from such fruit disorders as "fruit decay, surface defects, internal breakdown symptoms, chilling and heat injury, disorders during ripening and more."[215] They need great care from pre-seedling to post-harvest.

Because of the seasonal nature of agriculture, the production phase tends to require an all-hands-on-deck approach.[216] Producers may cut corners by using contaminated fertilizers, allowing children to work, paying poverty wages, or requiring laborers to work extremely long days. Workers may have no permanent contracts and no trade union to defend their interests.[217] To participate in a food supply chain that uses distributed ledger technology, suppliers may be required—or may require each other, depending on the ledger's governance policy—to record data that could raise red flags as to these practices.[218]

In addition, blockchain can include marginalized farmers who have limited information on market prices and production inputs, limited quality control, and nonexistent bargaining power with traders.[219] By bringing these farmers together and recording their transactions and agreements on its blockchain, blockchain-enabled supply chains can empower them to participate in the market. Any mistreatment from using small suppliers to "balance the books," when required, and giving them unauthorized price reductions, through stringent price reductions, can be decreased.[220]

Blockchain technology can also help to resolve problems arising from small-scale farmers who buy and arrange their own farm inputs such as fertilizers and pesticides. Blockchain can store any variation of these inputs from farmer to farmer, usually because of resource availability and accessibility.

FOOD PROCESSING (WAREHOUSE STORAGE STAGE)

Greater perishability of agrifoods mandates an exacting check of temperature and moisture in Walmart's logistics process.[221] For mangoes, Walmart analyzes fruit quality at all levels in the supply chain—on the tree, at harvest, at the packing shed, at wholesale markets, and at retail outlets—to determine the fruit quality at each stage, acceptable to the market. This analysis helps Walmart anticipate potential losses caused by sap burn, bruising, physical damage, diseases, and other disorders, including poor methods of harvesting and poor transportation from the packing shed to whole-sale markets.[222]

Blockchain can store data on impact of harvest maturity, method of harvesting, desapping, fruit packing, and mode of transportation. At all independent stages, participants can collect and store data to benchmark the industry performance beyond traditional industry practices.[223]

FOOD DISTRIBUTION AND AGGREGATION (SHED STAGE)

At mango importer facilities and retail distribution centers, food chain members inspect for quality, measure and record shipments, account mango shipper's responsibilities, document proper certificates, ascertain cargo and temperature excursions, fulfill temperature measurement and fruit sampling at arrival, and evaluate external and internal quality.[224] All of this information can be stored and traced on a blockchain.

Suppliers package the mangoes according to the end-customers' needs and expectations. For example, if mangoes are traveling to retailers and traders, then the mangoes are packed in boxes made of wooden strips that recipients can easily dismantle. Aligning with third-party transport operators that provide box-moving services, blockchain will help transporters' management policies and practices such as choice of vehicles.

Finally, in the distribution process, blockchain-connected devices such as cognitive IoT devices and smart sensors will eventually be able to sense and record any produce damage caused by excessive sunlight or any rotting of meat because of temperature and humidity.[225]

Walmart is engaged in dialogue with shipping and logistics providers. Such conversations can improve data capture of original electronic bills of lading (or warehouse warrants) and propel invoice consents, dispute resolution, and cargo provenance and tracking. For example, distributed ledger technology has the ability to record any updates to legal agreements and platforms, thereby ensuring both legal and security integrity.[226] In an article, "Walmart Explores Blockchain for Delivery Drones," *Fortune* reported on Walmart's patent application for a "delivery management system" involving distributed ledgers, robotics, and sensors.[227] IBM is also developing blockchain solutions for cross-border supply chains in collaboration with global transport and container logistics giant Maersk.[228]

MARKETING AND RETAILING (SUPERMARKETS STAGE)

Traceability is a major competitive advantage for supply-chain participants.[229] Supermarkets will be able to connect their enterprise resource planning and point-of-sale systems to the blockchain-enabled platform and trace every item sold. Yiannas told *Bloomberg Technology*, "With blockchain, you can do strategic removals, and let consumers and companies have confidence."[230] Every retailer should be able to generate rock-solid customer loyalty by showcasing the available-for-all records through blockchain technology during the shopping experience.[231] In turn, retailers could slash recall costs and create a huge uptake in profits, while improving their legal positions.

HOUSEHOLD AND FOOD PURCHASING (CONSUMER STAGE)

Walmart's blockchain pilot demonstrates retailers' concerted efforts to pull dangerous products off their shelves before anyone is hurt. Bloomberg reported that, should a consumer fall ill, "Walmart will be able to obtain crucial data from a single receipt, including supplies, detail on how and where food was grown and who inspected ... from the pallet to the individual package."[232]

While improving supply-chain visibility, customers can also provide retailers with specific feedback regarding quality that can be linked to growers and sources.[233] In addition, customers can get the added benefits of cost-cutting, getting fresher produce, and knowing ahead of time when groceries will arrive. Restaurant owners and managers of school and government cafeterias will also benefit. Recent findings by IBM Institute for Business Value on blockchain in the supply chain stated that, by "digitally tracking the provenance and movement of food throughout the entire supply chain, purveyors have instant quality assurance that the products they receive and serve customers are safe."[234] Food inspectors could include restaurant or cafeteria health and safety ratings on the blockchain as well.

POST-CUMULATIVE DATA CAPTURE (R&D STAGE AND POST-HARVESTING OR FINISH)

Whether pork or mangoes, Walmart's blockchain pilots have the capacity to document post-cumulative losses from potential supply-chain inefficiencies.[235] Such digital tracking helps enhance food safety mechanisms, provide quality assurances, smooth supply-chain disruptions from food wastage and spoilage, and factor into R&D. A proof of record will be evident in each transaction from the pre-seedling stage to the consumer's table at home, even noting any consumer health issues from food ingestion. Combined with data analytics and existing industry standards, the entire supply ecosystem will benefit from such a comprehensive data snapshot, thereby adding shared value.

Regarding the success of these pilots, Yiannas told *Fortune* magazine, "We were so encouraged that we really quickly started reaching out to other suppliers and retailers as well."[236] In August 2017, IBM announced a collaboration with Walmart and nine other food industry giants—Dole, Driscoll's, Golden State Foods, Kroger, McCormick & Company, McLane Company, Nestlé, Tyson Foods, and Unilever—to evolve Walmart and IBM's supply-chain solution and apply it to the global food system.[237]

KEY TAKEAWAYS ON FOOD TRACEABILITY

Walmart's successful blockchain pilots for food traceability document what we can do now with distributed ledger technology to improve food safety and efficiency. Throughout, we have explored blockchain's potential beyond these two pilot projects and looked at other types of information that a supply chain might record on a blockchain through various means of data capture. What is clear is that blockchain provides greater transparency, veracity, and trust in food information; and it is information that supply-chain members can act on, should problems arise. Following are key takeaways from Walmart's blockchain pilots that food industry participants can take to heart:

- **Identify the problem warranting a distributed ledger solution.** "Blockchain is not solving a technical problem, it is solving a social problem," said McDermott.[238] Walmart's need for traceability arose from its focus on food safety, so as to prevent or respond quickly to contamination, fruit and animal disease, harmful drug or pesticide residues, or attempted bioterrorism.[239] Thus, with prevention, preparedness, and proof, Walmart's blockchain pilots serve a larger purpose. It also has a positive effect on the Walmart brand.

- **Make the business case for a pilot.** Yiannas emphasized that Walmart's blockchain solution needed to be "business-driven and technology-enabled."[240] Walmart's blockchain solution has the capacity to solve myriad business problems in food supply chains such as time efficiencies, cost reduction, long-term good will, and revenue generation. Ensuring shared value for all participants in the ecosystem is critical to adoption; all participants need to have a strong value proposition to join. Walmart's pilot programs improved confidence in the supply chain—breeders/farms, processing plants, cold storage facilities, distribution centers, retail stores, and more. All can have access to and input into the same immutable record.

- **Engage and prepare members of the supply chain.** To maintain whole-chain traceability, this kind of initiative requires leadership to coordinate stakeholders and promote awareness of different technology solutions. "This is not about competition, this is about collaboration," said Yiannas. "[It's about] creating a solution that offers shared value for stakeholders."[241] Throughout the product life cycle, supply-chain participants were able to record, cross-check, and ensure a product's authenticity and trace its movement and quality.[242] This information gave all participants greater control over their brands and businesses and supported deeper learning capacities from enhanced gathering of data and analytics. Such a supply-chain network could eventually include research and development centers, primary production facilities, aggregation and mobilization providers, farm input supplies and materials such as soil types and food additives, trading and grading participants, wholesalers, retailers, and customers.[243]

- **Identify the relevant data to combine.**
Blockchain technology enables food traceability
to the item level, not just batch level, so that
participants can trace each item in the supply
chain.[244] Walmart's blockchain pilot identified which
data were relevant to capture from supply-chain
participants. Anyone contemplating a pilot should
compile a list of mandatory attributes for their
business problem (e.g., for food safety, attributes
could include lot number, pack date, quantity
shipped, unit of measure, purchase order number,
shipment identifiers) and a list of optional attributes
(e.g., carton serial numbers, pallet number, harvest
date, buyer identifier, vendor/supplier identifier).
Consistency is key. Pilot leaders should adopt data
structures (e.g., product lot numbers) that align
with standards (e.g., the GTIN) and develop
requirements for master data and guidelines for data
retention.[245] This supply-chain portrait accounts for
interoperability among ledger participants with an
in-depth grasp of data.

- **Leverage existing processes and information
systems.** According to McDermott, Walmart
chose IBM's blockchain solution because it was
"not recreating supply chain, but leveraging existing
technologies to enhance supply-chain traceability
using Hyperledger."[246] Like Walmart's blockchain
pilot, "traceability systems that are integrated with
existing company business practices are more likely
to be maintained and more likely to be accurate
than stand-alone traceability systems."[247] "Visibility,
optimization, and demand" are key challenges in
creating interoperable devices and platforms.[248]

- **Participate in governance networks.** Members of partnerships and collaborations need to have a voice in the development of industry standards and interoperability of any technology used.[249] For example, Walmart has taken a three-pronged approach to cultivating a knowledge network in food safety and delivery in China. First, Walmart is collaborating with China Children and Teenagers Fund, a nonprofit in China that provides food safety education developed for children. Second, it has brought together American and Chinese academics and Chinese poultry producers to study safety in poultry supply chains. Among the participants are University of Arkansas, South China Agricultural University, China Agriculture University, Zhejiang University, and Zhejiang Academy of Agricultural Sciences, Fujian Shengnong Food Co. Ltd., New Hope Liuhe Co. Ltd., and Guangzhou Jiangfeng Industry Co. Ltd. Third, it has pooled talent from top academic institutions—Massachusetts Institute of Technology, Zhejiang University, and Tsinghua University—to leverage supply-chain analytics and superior technology.[250] This approach will instantaneously predict and detect areas of greatest vulnerability and threats for food adulteration in China's food supply chains.

- **Invest to test and learn.** Walmart will continue to experiment, scale, and learn from its blockchain pilots as it builds coalitions within the supply-chain ecosystem where members are seeking to implement blockchain applications more broadly.[251] Walmart's investments and proactive stance will reap benefits, while uplifting food quality and safety worldwide.

Blockchain is bigger and broader than the pork and mango pilots. However, for Walmart, blockchain technology was deployed specifically to solve societal issues of broken food chains. Leveraging existing devices and sensors, Walmart's blockchain pilots identify systemic vulnerabilities in the food supply chain and go beyond technology and business to regain people's trust and confidence in food.

CHAPTER 6

BLOCKCHAIN AT OUR BORDERS

US Customs and Border Protection Explores
the Promise of Blockchain Technology

Alan Cohn

 ## CUSTOMS AND BORDER PROTECTION IN BRIEF

- As people, goods, and money flow across borders, national customs and border agencies must reduce processing and wait times and improve the user experience, while also seizing illicit and harmful goods that might hide within the vast volumes of lawful trade.

- Customs duties are among the largest sources of revenue for national governments, even in the developed world. This case analyzes how US Customs and Border Protection (CBP), the US national customs and border authority, looks to blockchain technology to aid its people and processes.

- CBP believes that blockchain's architectural advantages might make it well suited for the cargo and trade environment, with benefits for many participants in global supply chains.

- CBP's deep industry relationships, its international partnership, and its leading role in international organizations focused on customs practices all give CBP the opportunity to drive the global development of governance for how blockchain technology can be harnessed to enhance the safety and security of global trade.

CUSTOMS, BORDERS, AND BLOCKCHAIN

FOUL PLAY, FRICTION, AND FRAUD: THE PROBLEMS TO BE SOLVED

Over one million travelers—and $6 billion worth of imported goods—enter the United States every day. Of the people, 320,000 cross the border by airplane, while the remainder cross by car or on foot. In 2013, approximately 1.2 billion short tons of imports arrived in the United States by sea, truck, pipeline, rail, mail, and (the majority) by multiple modes. US government agents inspect 80,000 shipping containers every day.[252]

Overseeing both passenger entries and cargo imports into the United States, US Customs and Border Protection (CBP), part of the US Department of Homeland Security (DHS), is responsible for intercepting illicit and dangerous items, funds for crime or terrorism, and individuals wanted by law enforcement or attempting to enter the country without requisite travel or immigration status. Additionally, its approximately 23,000 officers and trade specialists are responsible for enforcing customs codes and collecting customs revenues, which total about $40 billion per year.[253] CBP's challenge is doing all of this in a way that is least disruptive to legitimate trade and travel and with limited personnel and other resources.

There is enormous potential for fraud concerning the flow of people and goods across any border. For instance, corruption and invoice fraud result in losses from false invoicing or double invoicing of goods. Disputes arise concerning who had physical and legal possession of goods at a particular time or geography. Payment of customs duties often leads to fraud and public corruption. In the United States, the government collected more than $50 million in customs fraud litigation in fiscal year 2016.[254] In the same year, CBP imposed over $30 million in penalties for attempted evasion of or negligence relating to antidumping and countervailing duties.[255] Despite these successes, these sums likely represent only a small fraction of the proceeds from overall customs fraud; in 2012, eight people and three corporations fraudulently imported more than $100 million of commercial merchandise *in a single case*, evading an estimated $10 million of duties and taxes before the scheme was uncovered.[256]

Attempts to cross borders without proper authorization are also widespread. A primary concern in many countries is that terrorists and criminals can exploit legal openness, geography, and interconnectivity (particularly global travel networks) to bypass border authorities and other law enforcement. Spurred by the events of 11 September 2001, many customs and border agencies began to look for technological tools.

CBP is one of the most innovative agencies in the US federal government, especially for an agency that traces its history back to an early act of the US Congress in 1789. It has been at the forefront of technology adoption for identity and traveler information and customs and import processes. CBP began automating cargo processes in the early 1960s, with the majority of trade transactions taking electronic form in the late 1980s. CBP, together with the US State Department and the Government Printing Office, were among the first government agencies in the world to begin development of biometric, machine-readable passports and scanning systems.[257] CBP launched a "mobile passport" facial recognition trial in 2015 and began rolling it out to the remainder of the United States a year later.[258] CBP has maintained an *advance passenger information/passenger name records* (API/PNR) system called the Advance Passenger Information System (APIS) since 2001.[259] This system is used to screen individuals on no-fly lists among other things.

Nevertheless, challenges remain. The key to efficient and effective customs and border processes is reliable advance information. With respect to people, advances such as the use of API/PNR data and biometric-enhanced and machine-readable passports help customs and border agencies standardize passenger screening for entry into global travel systems. However, with the wide variance in supply-chain and trade finance practices and the lack of digitization of these processes across many parts of the world, information is not always available; and when it is, it isn't always reliable. While the 9/11 attacks in the United States spurred efforts to safeguard the global travel system, these efforts are not foolproof. We have opportunities to apply cutting-edge technologies that can further support cargo, trader, and shipment identification, authentication, and risk assessment.

SOLUTIONS TRIED TO DATE: SORTING FLOWS AND PUSHING OUT BORDERS

After 9/11, US government agencies both increased the amount of information they collected and enhanced their linkages to other government data holdings in order to identify known or suspected illicit actors, goods, and money. The US government has used that knowledge to create watch lists, no-fly lists, and other tools for front-line officers in screening people, goods, and money, even in routine customs interactions. This capability divided the inflow into two categories: "known/suspected bad" and "unknown," lumping the vast majority into the latter and leaving analysts and officers to apply judgment and intuition. While officers conduct targeted searches of a small percentage of this "unknown" inflow, the process is often compared to finding the proverbial needle in the haystack.

To reduce this pool of unknowns, lessen the burden on the officer at the front line, and speed cross-border travel and trade while increasing security, CBP introduced "trusted traveler" and "trusted shipper" programs such as Global Entry, NEXUS, SENTRI, FAST, and the C-TPAT (see box).

US TRUSTED TRAVELER AND SHIPPER PROGRAMS

Customs-Trade Partnership Against Terrorism (C-TPAT): For large importers of commercial goods into the United States (companies must meet extensive security/eligibility requirements).

Free and Secure Trade (FAST) for Commercial Vehicles: Incoming commercial goods shipped via truck and truck drivers (citizens and residents of USA, Canada, and Mexico eligible).

Global Entry: All incoming international travel through airports (citizens of USA, India, Colombia, UK, Germany, Panama, Singapore, South Korea, Switzerland, and Mexico eligible).

NEXUS: Travel through all ports of entry in USA and Canada (citizens and residents of USA, Canada, and Mexico eligible).

Secure Electronic Network for Travelers Rapid Inspection (SENTRI): Incoming travel through southern land border by car (all citizens eligible).

The concept behind "trusted traveler" and "trusted shipper" programs is to introduce a third category of people, goods, and money transiting the border: "known/trusted." By conditioning acceptance into trusted traveler and trusted shipper programs on prior submission of information, collection of biometric information (for people), and conduct of site inspections or endorsement of third-party inspections (for goods), CBP can screen inflows before they reach the border. "Known/trusted" pools can then use "fast lanes" at the border itself, both speeding their transit and relieving frontline officers.

By creating three categories—"known/trusted," "known/bad," and "unknown"—national customs and border agencies have sped greater quantities of people, goods, and money through borders with a higher degree of assurance in the security of that traffic. These agencies can focus their limited frontline resources on finding and intercepting the "known/bad" pool, and more effectively sorting the "unknown" to focus interventions on those posing a higher risk.

For people, CBP has gone further, seeking to reduce wait times while increasing the screening of travelers prior to boarding aircraft by instituting "preclearance" operations at foreign last points of departure, in order to push as much of the screening and confirmation burden away from the physical border crossings as possible. In effect, CBP has reduced border bottlenecks and placed greater distance between threats and US borders by pushing the borders out. Operational in six Canadian airports, several Caribbean island nations, Shannon, Ireland, and Abu Dhabi, United Arab Emirates, the program is expanding to an additional slate of countries.

For cargo, the United States began screening at foreign last points of departure initially to detect nuclear and radiological materials. The first such effort was the Container Security Initiative, which began in 2002 and as of 2015, was operational in 50 ports globally.[260] The initiative now prescreens 80 percent of containerized inbound maritime cargo, and employs risk analysis algorithms and radiographic scanning (e.g., X-rays) to interdict cargo that may be a security risk.[261] In 2007, CBP expanded its efforts to prescreen nuclear and radiological materials with the Secure Freight Initiative, which deployed US government personnel and assets to foreign ports.[262] In 2008, CBP debuted the Importer Security Filing rule, more commonly known as "10+2," which requires shippers to transmit information about higher risk cargo 24 hours in advance of arrival at a US port.[263]

CBP and partner agencies throughout the US government have also modernized customs and import processes in other ways. Through the Automated Commercial Environment (ACE) and the implementation of the International Trade Data System Single Window ("single window"), the government has minimized paper filings to reduce the burden on US importers. The European Union and other countries such as Canada and Mexico have similar single-window projects aiming to automate and streamline customs and import processes.

All of these efforts are intended to increase the amount of data that governments can use to keep travelers and residents safe and to increase the trust that governments can place in said data. Seeing the benefit of digitization and integration, the World Customs Organization (WCO) declared that 2016 would be the "Year of Digital Customs." However, progress is uneven, despite the obvious benefits of automation and digitization.

CBP must continuously find ways to do more with less. In January 2017, the US Government Accountability Office (GAO) found that DHS's staffing level of CBP officers was about 10 percent (838 officers) below authorized strength, and that the agency's own models estimated that it would need to increase its staff by an additional 2,000 officers to meet service demands.[264] This staffing shortfall also affects trade inspection. CBP officers interviewed by the GAO reported being pulled from trade assignments to screen air passengers and to reduce secondary inspection lanes in order to provide the minimum acceptable number of primary inspection lanes.[265] This all underscores the need for CBP to continue to add to its analytics and inspection capacity in ways that do not rely on substantially higher levels of staffing.

ADDING BLOCKCHAIN TO CBP'S TOOLBOX

Blockchain technology encompasses three salient elements:

- A peer-to-peer network of "nodes" for conducting transactions without an intermediary

- A data store or append-only database for recording those transactions

- A consensus mechanism for validating the transactions and preventing fraudulent or false transactions

A *blockchain*—a chain of previously validated blocks of transactions—is a permanent, auditable record of successive, validated peer-to-peer transactions that is extremely difficult to falsify, disrupt, or alter. Blockchain technology also provides a platform for applying business logic in order to perform functions such as identity validation and automated smart-contract processes.

Don and Alex Tapscott, in their book *Blockchain Revolution*, characterize the blockchain simply as "the trust protocol." William Mougayar, in his book *The Business Blockchain*, summarizes blockchain's various promises: from a technical perspective, it is a back-end database, but one that "maintains a distributed ledger openly"; from a business perspective, it is a peer-to-peer exchange network for value; and from a legal perspective, it is "a transaction validation mechanism not requiring intermediary assistance."[266]

While traditional shared databases work well in a variety of circumstances, blockchains bring certain unique characteristics. Unlike a traditional shared database (and depending on the design of the blockchain), no single entity controls the ability to review or add to a blockchain ledger. Likewise, no single store of data exists to be hacked or corrupted. As a result, blockchains can form a neutral platform on which multiple parties in a supply chain, who may not otherwise trust one another, can interact. Because copies of the ledger exist across all "nodes" in a blockchain, the system is resistant to disruptions and data losses due to corruption, destructive attack, or disaster.[267]

Given blockchain's obvious applications to environments with multiple parties, potentially low trust, and the need for high-integrity data and transaction records, CBP is exploring its application. "We are initially focusing our efforts in three areas: flow of cargo, flow of passengers, and cybersecurity," said Kevin K. McAleenan, acting commissioner of CBP.[268] "These touch a wide range of systems within CBP."

Currently, CBP is examining the application of blockchain technology to challenges such as digital identity, passenger interactions, and cargo security and customs revenue collection, working together with DHS's Science and Technology Directorate (DHS S&T).

Anil John, DHS S&T's program manager for the Identity Management and Data Privacy Research, Development, and Transition Program, in the Cyber Security Division of DHS S&T's Homeland Security Advanced Research Projects Agency, explained:

> The four areas that have come up consistently across the broad Homeland Security Enterprise regarding blockchain technologies are:
>
> 1. Immutable logging of Internet of Things and sensor data
>
> 2. Facilitating, enhancing, and securing travel flows
>
> 3. Facilitating, enhancing, and securing trade documentation
>
> 4. Exploring alternatives to paper documents that are resistant to counterfeiting and fraud. Interestingly, CBP has touchpoints and need across all four areas.[269]

McAleenan explained further why CBP is investing in blockchain:

> The attractiveness of blockchain as a technical architecture is the immutability, the ability for non-trusted parties to reach consensus, and auditability. Given CBP's mission to facilitate the legitimate flow of trade and travel, we see several mission areas where these features could be transformative. For example, there are potential applications in the flow of cargo and passengers where blockchain could improve the quality of data we receive, and make that data easier to share with partner border enforcement agencies in other nations, which would enable better decision-making and ideally more rapid flow of goods.[270]

DHS S&T has already funded experiments on the border in another context: proving the integrity of the data flowing from the thousands of IoT devices deployed on the border such as security cameras. In two grants awarded to Factom, DHS has funded a proof of concept project to prevent spoofing IoT devices by maintaining a distributed record of their properties and past records.[271]

PILOT PROJECTS AT CBP/DHS

BlockCypher is developing a blockchain platform for interoperability among multiple blockchains.

Digital Bazaar is working on a verifiable claims project.

Evernym is developing online user-focused identity management technology.

Factom is developing a project to secure border technology and data, specifically a distributed record of IoT properties to prevent spoofing of IoT devices.

As McAleenan explained, these early efforts are helping to build confidence in blockchain technology:

In partnership with DHS S&T, we are currently actively engaged in a cybersecurity pilot with a start-up company, Factom, to see how its technology can help secure our border technology and data. We are looking to launch similar pilots in the cargo and passenger space over the next year. Thus far, our work with Factom has shown great promise in providing additional cybersecurity to support our border technology.[272]

The Factom pilot applied blockchain technology for immutable logging of IoT device and sensor platform data, to ensure its resiliency and integrity while allowing for its independent validation. To understand the implications of using blockchain technologies in this context, CBP and S&T worked with Factom on a proof of concept to provide immutable logging of imagery from border cameras.

The lessons learned from this experience informed DHS's understanding not only of blockchain but also how best to integrate blockchain technologies into its existing technology and processes. In particular, it shaped the choice of technical architecture and design, such that sensitive data remain within the DHS infrastructure while simultaneously allowing the ability to validate that sensitive data publicly, without actually storing it on the blockchain. As DHS S&T's John noted, "The Factom effort was significant in that it was about not just the viability of the technology but also how best to architect the system to ensure that it could be integrated with our existing technology and processes."[273]

DHS S&T has also backed general cybersecurity uses of blockchain. In May 2017, it announced small business grants totaling about $2.25 million to Evernym to develop online user-focused identity management technology, BlockCypher to develop a "blockchain platform for multiple blockchains," and Digital Bazaar for a "verifiable claims" project.[274] The issue for CBP is data that are *available* and *reliable*. As McAleenan explained:

In our mission, a key issue is having good data to make good decisions. For example, we want our trade partners to be correctly and thoroughly completing their documentation—such as the bill of lading—so that CBP can make an accurate risk assessment. If blockchain helps develop a universal ledger type of capability that allows for stakeholders to provide better data and make better decisions with that data, we can reduce "friction" in the supply chain and in turn create more value. If this ledger can be expanded to other partner customs agencies, then it would be even more powerful.[275]

HOW CUSTOMS AND BORDER AGENCIES CAN USE BLOCKCHAIN

Blockchain presents numerous advantages to customs and border authorities regarding the movement of people and goods across national borders. CBP is already working on proofs of concepts involving both.

BLOCKCHAIN, BORDERS, AND PEOPLE

The advantages of using blockchain to track the crossing of borders by individuals is similar in concept to using it to track the movement of any tangible good across any blockchain-enabled network. Specific characteristics of a traveler can be described in a blockchain hash, and changes in status or location are transmitted to all nodes that are part of the network, creating an immutable chain. This can be used, for instance, to give digital identities to those who have lost or do not have traditional government-issued identification such as migrant and trafficked workers. These identities can then be verified through employers and law-enforcement encounters.[276]

The advantages for customs and border officials are numerous. First, as noted above, digital identities can be provided to individuals for whom no traditional, government-issued identification can be issued. Second, border officials can examine individuals' movement across borders and changes in status more efficiently and with greater assurance than, for instance, a paper solution or one that relies on exchanges among international, official databases and other systems. Indeed, blockchain-based systems can help address the challenge of tracking entries and exits more confidently, since with multilateral agreements multiple countries could access these types of notations, and one country's entrance is inextricably linked to the last country's exit. Third, with traditional, more centralized data systems, there is greater risk of fraud or information loss as traveler records are built on individual exchanges between systems that can be altered or conducted unsuccessfully.[277] Blockchain as a distributed system reduces these risks.

BLOCKCHAIN, BORDERS, AND CARGO

There are two compelling use cases for customs and border officials concerning blockchain's application to trade: (1) enhancing duties and fees automation, and (2) ensuring the integrity of trusted flows, including greater fidelity on origin information.

The current process for paying duties and fees relies on a large amount of self-attestation. Shippers often declare and pay expected fees and duties before ships arrive in the country of destination; however, proof of receipt and payment are still done through an antiquated exchange of documents called *bills of lading*. While not working directly with CBP, a number of blockchain start-ups like Hijro and Skuchain are working on smart contracts to automate certain functions of the shipping process, among other things.

Smart contracts encode automated if-then statements with respect to certain functions. For example, if goods reach a certain geographic point and if physical custody is transferred, then a payment is made from one party to another. Smart contracts can also be encoded based on applicable legal or regulatory requirements. For example, if goods arrive at port for unloading, then the payment of required customs duties is made.

A digital mechanism for monitoring and measuring external events, referred to as an *oracle*, replaces self-reporting and provides an objective determinant of these conditions. For example, an oracle could be programmed to monitor a ship's *automatic information service* (AIS) transmitter and trigger payment of appropriate customs duties when the ship crosses a territorial boundary or enters port. Because these smart contracts would be encoded on the blockchain and would be triggered by objective events rather than by a single process owner or person, blockchain-based smart contracts can speed the collection of duties and reduce fraud while leaving an immutable, reviewable record of ownership, chain of custody, and duty payment.

Customs and border agencies can also use blockchain to help ensure the integrity of flows to cleave a larger part of the incoming flow of goods into a trusted channel that requires less inspection. The concept is similar to trusted-cargo processes in place, in which shippers or importers become trusted by shipping low-risk goods, and by giving additional information to customs authorities. There is more efficiency, greater visibility, and less risk by conducting the exchange of necessary information over blockchain.

For example, customs officials could designate certain types of bulk goods as low risk. Upon importation, customs officials could check a digital, blockchain-based manifest and shipping history to ensure that all is as expected. For certain types of higher-risk goods such as items of high value or electronic goods, CBP can verify the blockchain-based description of goods with scanning technologies like those mentioned in the first section.

With both smart contracts and trusted flows, there is a major adaptation advantage: blockchain technology has the potential to be the definitive platform for digitizing global trade documentation and transaction of assets. Banks, shipping companies, major retailers, and other participants in the global trade system, as well as many start-ups, have invested time and money in developing and piloting blockchain-based approaches to global trade.

For example, Bank of America is working with Microsoft to create a blockchain-based framework to make trade finance transactions quicker, safer, and more transparent.[278] The R3CEV consortium completed two prototypes demonstrating that smart contracts can be used to process accounts receivable purchase transactions and letter of credit transactions.[279] New pilots focusing on different aspects of global trade continue to emerge on a regular basis.[280]

Brenda B. Smith, CBP's executive assistant commissioner for the Office of International Trade, described some of blockchain's appeal: "CBP is interested in supply-chain transparency—who is participating in the process and when movements take place. In addition, we are interested in a 'track and trace' capability for sensitive products, ranging from food to intellectual property."

Why blockchain? Again, data availability and reliability. Smith explained, "We've learned that collecting information from the right party at the right time is critical to data integrity and low-cost data collection." According to Smith, "the greatest value would be gathering information that would help us make good risk-based decisions." Good risk-based decision-making would "improve trade facilitation" and "allow us to focus on effective trade enforcement." Within CBP, the focus is education. Smith said,

> We have primarily worked on educating ourselves about the technology itself and engaging with our private-sector and international partners to evaluate pilots already underway in the private-sector space. We are also working to define use cases where blockchain could be helpful, so that we can work with private-sector partners to support further testing.[281]

McAleenan echoed this sentiment:

> My goal is to ensure that CBP staff are educated and ready to adapt our business processes to technologies that are potentially "disruptive"—such as blockchain. We are achieving this by actively engaging with industry partners—such as Walmart and Maersk—to get educated on their pilots with blockchain, working with our colleagues at DHS S&T, and running our own pilots.

INTERNATIONAL STANDARDS AND BEST PRACTICES

Another dimension of this challenge for CBP is engagement with international partners. As Smith explained, "CBP can have a role in advancing blockchain or other new technologies in the international environment."[282] CBP has assumed a leadership role within the WCO in exploring the potential uses of blockchain for international travel and trade on a global scale.

International adoption of blockchain and distributed ledger technology, with its open architecture, decentralized and consensus-based approach to validating transactions, and immutable record of transactions, has the potential to solve this global problem. Blockchain could enable digitization in a manner that would increase transparency and enhance efficiency.

Digitization based on blockchain and distributed ledger technology could greatly benefit customs and border authorities, by automating processes for sharing information; determining provenance of goods; reducing fraud, inaccuracy, and error; verifying identity; and enabling the automated payment of customs duties. Each of these advances could improve efficiency and speed of processing and increase the accuracy and effectiveness of risk-based targeting. Customs and border agencies could audit supply chains in real time, trace the provenance of suspect goods, locate problematic goods in transit, and identify parties all along a supply chain.

Similarly, with blockchain-based digitized global trade information, customs and border agencies could speed invoice and bill-of-lading reviews, more effectively target inspections to only those items of most concern, and include blockchain-based trade in Authorized Economic Operator programs like C-TPAT, or Canada's Partners in Protection (PIP), and fast-lane programs such as FAST, to incentivize adoption of blockchain-based digitization, automation, and payment systems. However, to realize these benefits, blockchain and distributed ledger technology must continue to mature, and challenges in governance, standards, and interoperability must be addressed.

How does CBP define success for blockchain and customs? "For us, we define success in the trade facilitation space by improving the user experience of our trade partners and increasing enforcement actions on illicit goods," explained McAleenan. "Any technologies that can help us in these goals are ones we will pursue."[283]

GLOBAL GOVERNANCE: A NATIONAL CHALLENGE, AN INTERNATIONAL OPPORTUNITY

Challenges to broader adoption face all entities attempting to use blockchain to advance global trade. These challenges include the maturity of the technology, lack of global standards and governance, and lack of interoperability across blockchain platforms.

Despite these differences in technology platforms, all the approaches share one similar problem set: at some point, they have to intersect with national borders. This is a challenge, but it is also an enormous opportunity for customs and border authorities to help shape the direction that blockchain-based global trade platforms will take.

McAleenan explained, "A key driver for blockchain to be integrated into the international customs arena is a good governance structure. The technology is important, but both customs agencies and the various research groups working with blockchain need to be considering the governance aspect as well to facilitate adoption." McAleenan also noted the interoperability challenge:

> One issue we are particularly engaged on is ensuring that the technology community is focusing on interoperability. There are a number of different ledger protocols, alliances, and vendors working in the space. It is critical that these different solutions be able to talk to one another. If the industry ends up with a number of siloed approaches that cannot easily integrate with one another, I am concerned about the pace of adoption of the technology as a whole.[284]

For example, Microsoft's blockchain-as-a-service offering is based on an Enterprise Ethereum blockchain in the Microsoft Azure cloud, while R3CEV's pilots largely use its own Corda platform, and IBM's supply-chain pilot (e.g., pork) uses the Hyperledger Fabric.[285] While each of these pilots represents a promising use of blockchain or distributed ledger technology, there currently are no effective ways of moving data and information and automating processes across blockchain platforms. Moreover, there is no consensus over whether open-consensus blockchains such as the Bitcoin blockchain or Ethereum, or permissioned or private blockchains, represent the better model for global trade, or whether the right model is a combination of open-consensus and private or permissioned blockchains. The combination of technology and governance challenges will continue to make interoperability a challenge.

While blockchain technology can also advance both the efficiency and the effectiveness of customs and trade enforcement, government must have the ability to interact with blockchain-enabled trade finance platforms and supply chains to realize these benefits fully. Government must have the ability to interact with the range of blockchain and distributed ledger-based global trade platforms and to ingest associated records and documentation. Government can also utilize smart contracts and other aspects of blockchain and distributed ledger technology to help automate current processes for review and inspection, customs duty collection, and related processes.

Another proof of concept is the protection of *personally identifiable information* (PII) and proprietary data. CBP is investing significant time and resources into researching architecture and design options that ensure that PII or other sensitive data is not placed directly on the blockchain in any implementation.

DHS S&T also noted several other technology challenges. As DHS S&T's John explained:

> We have been making R&D investments over the last two to three years in blockchain security and privacy and have discovered that, while there are a great many interesting possibilities, there remain some fundamental gaps that need to be closed in order for this to operate at scale. Two in particular are critical to resolve.

1. Distributed key management (the issuance, management, revocation, and more of the public-private keys that are in effect a blockchain wallet) at scale is not a solved problem.
2. Given that there is no one-size-fits-all ledger data format, standards for how to create the "data payload" that is written to a ledger are critical to interoperability across blockchain implementations. We have active work going on in both to address these critical capability gaps.

John described DHS S&T's perspective on blockchain: "It is too early to determine whether blockchain technology is in any way superior to current technologies, but we believe it is the right time to create the metrics that will allow us make that determination and move out on proofs of concepts and pilots that will provide those metrics."[286]

CBP's Smith remains optimistic, while recognizing the various challenges: "We've seen some exciting results from our work with R&D projects and pilot evaluations [in areas such as IoT security], but also recognize that deploying blockchain successfully will require investment and successful management of complexity."[287]

 KEY TAKEAWAYS ON CUSTOMS AND BORDER PROTECTION

Because of CBP's role in the global trade system as the national customs and border authority for the world's largest economy, and CBP's prominent voice in the WCO, the agency has an opportunity to champion blockchain-based global trade processes and help advance and mature the technology generally. To take on this role, CBP can follow its own past successes, working together with private-sector partners and helping to develop overall governance by playing a leadership role in regional and global international organizations.

- **Resist the urge to react to an incident.** In October 2010, terrorists in Yemen tried to ship packages containing bombs into the United States using express consignment air couriers (e.g., FedEx, UPS, DHL, and others, referred to as "express couriers"). Although the work of intelligence and law-enforcement services around the world foiled these attacks, the attempt highlighted a gap in the US cargo security regime. The CBP, together with another DHS agency, the Transportation Security Administration, took steps to close this gap.[288]

- **Examine systems in place before acting.** Law and regulation already required inbound air carriers to provide electronic cargo information through a CBP-approved electronic data interchange to CBP prior to an aircraft's US arrival. Rather than create a new regulatory framework or a new system for electronic data interchange, CBP collaborated with stakeholders to develop a mechanism for collecting information necessary to identify high-risk shipments at the earliest point practicable in the supply chain.[289]

- **Prototype and test possible solutions.** Four express couriers "volunteered to provide CBP with a subset of the data elements required by [CBP regulations] as early as possible before cargo is loaded on the aircraft so that the requisite targeting could occur in the pre-loading air cargo environment."[290] Based on the success of this pilot program, CBP later formalized and expanded the pilot to include other express couriers as well as passenger airlines, all-cargo airlines, and freight forwarders.[291]

- **Identify shared interests.** CBP's collaborative approach with industry and later with other governments focused on identifying their shared interests to find the most efficient and effective operational and regulatory means to integrate new practices into existing programs. Through such collaboration, governance, and a light touch on operational, technological, and regulatory changes, CBP and other customs and border agencies around the world can advance their use of blockchain as well.

- **Resist proprietary systems.** The challenge for CBP—as for any agency in its position of prominence on the global stage—is to resist the urge to develop its own blockchain or distributed ledger for global trade. Air Cargo Advance Screening would not have been a success had CBP tried to create an entirely new program on the fly. Instead, it worked within the existing operational and regulatory framework to find solutions that enhanced security and efficiency for the government and for industry. Blockchain is best seen as a better way to achieve shared goals, not a technology science project.

- **Take a proactive approach.** Rather than waiting until this new technology fully matures, or contracting for the development of a proprietary blockchain system, CBP can harness the innovation underway in the private sector. For example, Everledger has focused on building a blockchain-based registry for diamonds moving in the global supply chain.[292] Provenance has focused on the challenge of tracing and proving food provenance from farm to table.[293] Each of these pilots enables the digitization of global trade processes on a decentralized, peer-to-peer platform, increasing data visibility and data integrity while reducing fraud and false or inaccurate invoicing and documentation. Working with companies (e.g., Digital Bazaar, Evernym, and Factom) already partnering with CBP, as well as with a range of companies active in the enterprise blockchain, supply-chain, and trade finance space, CBP can help drive innovation without becoming a technology developer itself.

- **Look for potential applications within existing programs.** CBP's Smith sees blockchain "as a complement to CBP's Automated Commercial Environment, which collects large amounts of transactional data about the shipments crossing our borders."[294] She thinks that a blockchain system could replace ACE and allow the government to collect transactional-level data at an even more granular level, potentially further back in the supply chain. However, CBP learned from its implementation of ACE not to underestimate the challenges of investing in new technology and managing the change that accompanies technology deployment. Likewise, CBP could realize major benefits as part of its mission to expand the single-window process, simply by further supporting and integrating blockchain into current initiatives. The technology burdens are low, and the shared interests among government and industry are already understood.

- **Choose pilots that lend themselves to measurement and comparison.** That means identifying metrics that matter. According to DHS S&T's John, the proofs of concepts that his team are launching "will incorporate some combination of analysis of alternatives specific to that environment, A/B testing to understand" whether the technology delivers measurably superior results than DHS's current processes. The pilots will also give DHS an understanding of what John calls "the *gain-to-pain ratio* involved in integrating the new approach with the existing technology stack and business processes."[295] Pilots can focus on real-world problems and can be tested side by side with existing programs.

- **Leverage existing roles and relationships.** CBP's partnerships with industry, foreign partners, and international organizations are critical. Said CBP's Smith, "We have great relationships with foreign governments and international organizations such as the WCO and could use our relationships to understand, share best practices, and collaborate if a specific technology proves to be a valuable solution for driving cargo security, trade facilitation, and trade enforcement."[296] The movement of cargo is inherently global, and CBP can best identify and implement new initiatives with the collaboration and support of its industry, government, and international organization partners.

- **Focus on broader governance issues.** Ultimately, global adoption of blockchain technology will require global standards for doing business. CBP can leverage the government's ability to help advance the development and governance of global standards,

interoperability of delivery systems, advocacy
initiatives, global policies, education and training
programs, and oversight efforts. For example, CBP
has such mechanisms as the Commercial Customs
Operations Advisory Committee to develop
potential approaches and can use its leadership role
in the WCO to drive global experimentation, to
create and drive standards and mechanisms for how
blockchain-based trade finance and supply-chain
platforms interact with national customs and border
authorities.

By participating in standards governance, CBP can
help drive forward global approaches to blockchain
governance generally, since standards development
is often best advanced by linking directly to solving
real-world problems. This governance layer for
blockchain adoption with respect to global travel
and trade—digital identity, secure ledger, regulatory
oversight of global supply-chain systems and trade
finance—may be the most significant contribution
CBP could make to the adoption of blockchain
technology in the global trade system, and to the
safety and security of global supply chains.

CHAPTER 7

THE EMERGING PLATFORM FOR MANUFACTURING 4.0

Major Blockchain Use Cases and Implementation Challenges

Stefan Hopf

 MANUFACTURING 4.0 IN BRIEF

- As organizations start to embrace manufacturing 4.0, the focus shifts to the integration of heterogeneous participants across the manufacturing ecosystem to enable fine-grained and responsive networks of distributed manufacturing activities. What is missing is a common and trusted platform that facilitates relationships between companies of different sizes across the value chain to build harmonized applications on an ecosystem level.

- Breaking informational silos, blockchain facilitates the transparent, secure, and controlled exchange of data across organizational boundaries. It could thereby serve as a trusted industry-wide platform for collaborative value-creation activities to orchestrate and manage local or geographically dispersed manufacturing activities.

- Illustrating the potential impact of blockchain in manufacturing, this chapter discusses four use cases that have been the focus of attention in the manufacturing industry:

  - *Connecting distributed manufacturing resources:* A blockchain-based platform facilitates interactions between buyers and manufacturers with smart contracts to streamline production processes and tokens to provide incentives for participants

- *Securing the end-to-end additive manufacturing (AM) process:* Blockchain and smart contracts serve as security layer and middleware to integrate the digital thread, underpinning all transactions for AM
- *Enabling asset life-cycle management:* Blockchain facilitates a shared and immutable product memory and provides a trail of actionable data over an asset life cycle between multiple parties
- *Increasing supply-chain visibility:* Blockchain provides near real-time deep-tier supply-chain visibility by onboarding all parties and their transactions in a supply chain on a single shared ledger

- These use cases provide only a glimpse of the transformative changes of established business models in the manufacturing ecosystem, as real-time access to actionable data and control unleashes a new era of decentralized and software-defined manufacturing.

- Despite great potential, the application of blockchain technology in the manufacturing industry is still in its infancy. This research studies major implementation challenges related to choosing a suitable blockchain protocol, safeguarding the physical-digital interface, guaranteeing network and user interface security, and evaluating the application scope for smart contacts. Go-forward recommendations provide companies with advice on where to start with blockchain innovation.

INTRODUCTION TO MANUFACTURING 4.0

Manufacturing forms the backbone of today's leading economies. Transforming raw materials into final products, the manufacturing sector accounts for roughly 30 percent value added of global gross domestic product.[297] As such, it is instrumental to the existence of many SMEs, and to a significant share of employment. Yet with globalization, increasing competition, and high pressure on margins, the manufacturing industry faces a reduction of competitive economies of scale and is forced to focus on efficiency and new revenue opportunities.

Technological advances in fields such as advanced robotics, AM, augmented reality, and artificial intelligence have fueled the grand vision of manufacturing 4.0. Promising more efficient resource use and an economically feasible mass customization of production up to lot size of one, manufacturing 4.0 aims at a horizontal integration through value networks, end-to-end digital integration of engineering across the entire value chain, vertical integration and networked manufacturing systems, and customer-oriented business model innovation.[298] Although isolated implementations have demonstrated the potential of future manufacturing on a small scale, so far no dominant platform has emerged that broadly facilitates the integration of distributed manufacturing activities and the interaction along the global value chain.

Blockchain technology could prove to be the missing link.[299] As a shared and potentially open platform, blockchain facilitates the transparent and secure exchange of information on a global scale. Breaking informational silos, blockchain could serve as a platform to interconnect and organize local and geographically dispersed manufacturing activities.

A GRAND VISION OF MANUFACTURING 4.0

THE FIRST THREE VERSIONS

The emergence of the industrial economy in the mid-eighteenth century in Europe and North America has marked a period of rapid social and economic change with an unprecedented rise in income levels and economic growth. Until today, manufacturing has seen three major industrial revolutions, and the fourth is on its way.

The initial process of industrialization was triggered by the technical invention of the steam engine and the accompanying introduction of mechanical manufacturing equipment, such as the first mechanical loom in 1784. The automation of physical work revolutionized how goods were made.

Around the beginning of the twentieth century, the second industrial revolution was fueled by the electrification of production and the shift toward mass production, based on Henry Ford's invention of the conveyor belt and Frederick W. Taylor's improvements to the efficient division of labor. Electronics and information technology (IT) spurred the third industrial revolution in the early 1970s, leading to an advanced automation of production and an individualization of production lots.

VISION 4.0

The fourth and current industrial revolution is associated with major changes induced by the IoT and *cyber-physical systems* (CPS). The IoT consists of sensors, actuators, and devices embedded in real-world objects, such as manufacturing equipment, to create a network and control infrastructure for objects. CPS combines IoT-enabled things into a complex system of physical and virtual components controlled by computer-based algorithms. CPS will gradually enable manufacturers to automate the control of physical production processes and give rise to a new era of software-defined manufacturing.[300]

The manufacturing 4.0 vision can be summarized by goals of the German Industrie 4.0 Platform:[301]

- **Smart products:** Products are uniquely identifiable and may be located at all times. Even during production, smart products know the details of their own manufacturing process and can control the individual stages of their production semi-autonomously. Moreover, it will be possible to ensure that finished goods know the parameters within which they can function optimally and are able to recognize signs of wear and tear throughout their life cycle. This information can be pooled to optimize the smart factory in terms of logistics, deployment, and maintenance, and for integration with business management applications.

- **Smart factories:** Networks of manufacturing resources (manufacturing machinery, robots, conveyor and warehousing systems, and production facilities) that are autonomous, capable of controlling themselves in response to different situations, self-configuring, knowledge-based, sensor equipped, and spatially dispersed.

- **Digital end-to-end engineering:** CPS enable the development of digital models that cover every aspect and interdependency of the manufacturing process, from customer requirements to product architecture and manufacturing of the finished product.

- **Mass customization:** It will be possible to incorporate individual customer and product-specific features into the design, configuration, ordering, planning, production, operation, and recycling phases. It will even be possible to incorporate last-minute requests for changes immediately before or even during manufacturing, and potentially also during operation. This allows businesses to manufacture one-off items and very small quantities of goods economically—even for SMEs that are unable to afford production under current licensing and business models.

Realizing the vision of manufacturing 4.0, industrial powerhouses worldwide have launched initiatives, such as Industrie 4.0 in Germany, the Industrial Internet in the United States, and the Industrial Value Chain Initiative in Japan. These initiatives pursue two different yet complementary approaches to achieve the vision of manufacturing 4.0: a vertical integration of manufacturing systems on a factory level and a horizontal integration across the manufacturing value chain.[302]

Germany and Japan mainly focus on the vertical integration of manufacturing systems on a factory level to reduce costs and increase efficiency and productivity. The vision is to create a smart factory with flexible CPS-based manufacturing structures that can be automatically reconfigured according to individual production requirements based on virtual simulations, data, communication, and software-based algorithms. The United States has mainly focused on the horizontal integration between different companies across the value chain. It aims at a harmonization of various IT systems and information at different stages of the manufacturing value chain (e.g., inbound logistics, production, outbound logistics, service) to enable an end-to-end digital engineering of products and services.[303]

THE MISSING LINK

With the implementation of IoT and CPS within the factory and across value chains, information becomes the single most important resource to orchestrate and manage software-defined manufacturing processes.

During the third industrial revolution, systems focused on information and processes of isolated functions within a company, such as the control of elements of the production process based on a *manufacturing execution system* (MES) or order requirements and production planning in an ERP system. Working with vendors like SAP and Oracle to implement customized software with on-premise data centers, large manufacturing companies managed to streamline basic internal business processes. Only recently have cloud service providers made similar tools available for SMEs, based on affordable *infrastructure-as-a-service* (IaaS) solutions. Overall, these implementations were mainly operated by single participants focusing on data and processes within the corporate boundaries (i.e., vertical integration).[304]

As organizations start to embrace manufacturing 4.0, the focus shifts to data-based and process integration of heterogeneous participants across the manufacturing ecosystem (horizontal integration).

On an ecosystem level, applications seek to automate processes across the value chain to facilitate fine-grained and responsive networks of manufacturing activities that center on problems and reconfigure themselves when done.[305]

What is missing is a common and trusted platform that facilitates relationships between companies of different sizes across the value chain to build harmonized applications that operate on an ecosystem level.[306] According to a recent survey of 210 German companies, the major hurdles in exchanging data on an ecosystem level are seen as revealing trade secrets, insufficient control over data access permissions, unclear liability for violations, proprietary standards, fear over losing competitive advantage, and the limited scope of participants.[307]

Realizing this limitation, the Industrial Data Space Association (IDSA) was formed in Germany in 2016 as "a virtual data space which supports the secure exchange and simple linking of data in business ecosystems on the basis of standards and by using collaborative governance models."[308]

Managing the flow of information in industrial ecosystems, the IDSA focuses on data as the most crucial element in emerging manufacturing 4.0 ecosystems. While the initiative has published an extensive reference model to facilitate the secure exchange and easy linkage of data in a trusted business ecosystem, it remains an open question how to secure the exchange of data and business relationships in a dynamic environment of untrusted participants on a global scale.

BLOCKCHAIN AS AN EMERGING PLATFORM FOR MANUFACTURING 4.0

BLOCKCHAIN AND MANUFACTURING 4.0

Blockchain technology provides a missing link for manufacturing 4.0. As a shared platform, blockchain facilitates the transparent, secure, and controlled exchange of information on a global scale. Breaking informational silos, blockchain could serve as a trusted platform to orchestrate and manage software-defined manufacturing processes for local and geographically dispersed manufacturing activities. Moreover, blockchain-embedded business logic could provide a functional layer for over-the-top services, unleashing vast business opportunities for manufacturers worldwide. Enabling interactions along the entire value chain, blockchain is thereby poised to emerge as a platform for manufacturing 4.0.[309]

Based on the original architecture of the Bitcoin blockchain, several special-purpose blockchains (also more broadly referred to as distributed ledger technology) exist today that cater to different application requirements. Most implementations are built around three key elements—blockchain databases, smart contracts, and tokens—that enable companies to manage essential data and processes for manufacturing 4.0 ecosystem applications (Table 7-1).[310]

TABLE 7-1

KEY ELEMENTS OF BLOCKCHAIN TECHNOLOGY FOR MANUFACTURING 4.0 PLATFORM

ELEMENT	PROBLEM IT SOLVES	TECHNICAL TERM
Blockchain	Who did what when	Attributable data
Smart contract	Computation that happens in an agreed manner	Deterministic computation
Token	Digital resources tied to some utility	Cryptographic tokens

Source: Monax Explainers, "Ecosystem Applications," monax.io, n.d.

At its core, blockchain technology consists of a distributed database that groups events (i.e., transactions) into a chain of blocks (i.e., blockchain) using complex cryptography. For an event, the blockchain database effectively verifies if the sender (i.e., keyholder) of a message has the title over an object (i.e., the right to transfer the ownership of an object) and then transfers the title to the receiver.

Since the blockchain database is shared among all network participants, it solves the problem of attribution and ordering of events at an ecosystem level in a resilient and reliable manner. In a manufacturing environment, a blockchain database facilitates the exchange of any kind of digital assets with transactions triggered by machines or humans.

Most important, blockchain can link a manufacturing enterprise's internal environment with established systems, such as MES and ERP, to the external environment.[311] This enables the controlled exchange of information at enterprise boundaries—a major barrier to overcome in order to realize an end-to-end horizontal integration in collaborative manufacturing 4.0 business models.

Smart contracts can be coded to reflect any kind of data-driven transactional business logic and ensure that computation happens in an agreed manner. Originally defined by Nick Szabo as "computerized transaction protocol that executes the terms of a contract," smart contracts are programs stored on a blockchain that follow instructions as specified without the possibility of outside interference.[312] Thus, they provide an unprecedented degree of certainty in a distributed setting. For manufacturing, smart contracts can be used, for instance, to monitor inventory levels and automatically restock by negotiating prices in a given range with ecosystem suppliers.

Tokens are asset-backed or native digital resources within an ecosystem.[313] Asset-backed tokens resemble a claim to an underlying asset (e.g., diamonds). Native tokens, such as ether (ETH) on the Ethereum blockchain, are intrinsic to a network and resemble some kind of value within the ecosystem (e.g., computing power on the Ethereum network). These tokens are typically the fuel of the network to reward stakeholders for their contribution (e.g., operating the network or providing over-the-top services).

Most important, native tokens represent a stake in the network that grows in value as the network grows. This incentivizes all network participants to contribute to the network. In collaborative manufacturing 4.0 networks, native tokens may provide a mechanism to incentivize the contribution of heterogeneous partners and even customers or competitors without individually specifying revenue-sharing terms up front.

Combining the transaction certainty of a blockchain database, the execution certainty of smart contracts, and the economic incentives of tokens, blockchain technology provides a shared platform for companies to manage data and processes in a software-defined manufacturing environment.

The shared autonomous factory model illustrates the potential of blockchain and smart contracts as platform for manufacturing 4.0.[314] The model depicts an end-to-end build-to-order process that starts at the customer and ends with a shipment of the final product:

- Once a customer configures an order, a unique product identification is created on the blockchain, and a bill of process is issued as a smart contract that details the manufacturing process.

- Accessing a marketplace for 3D design files, a suitable design is sourced using end-to-end blockchain-based encryption to protect a design file from its creation to its transmission and its use in a 3D printer.

- A standardized smart contract ensures the automated royalty accounting for designers.

- Based on the bill of process and the design file, a smart contract autonomously sources material and services required for production.

- Subsequently, the product is made in a local shared factory with current overcapacities.

- The product life-cycle information—with reliable data about materials used, production processes, manufacturing location, and date—is associated with the product ID and stored on the blockchain.

- The information can then be individually shared on demand for quality control, regulatory compliance, warranty, or recall actions.

- The final product is associated with the product ID using a crypto chip to establish a tamper-proof link between the physical object and the blockchain. Subsequently, the product is packaged, stored, shipped, and tracked by service providers.[315]

The shared autonomous factory model touches upon the vertical integration on a factory level and the horizontal integration between different actors across the value chain; it illustrates how we can achieve the manufacturing 4.0 vision of a smart factory, smart products, and mass customization on a blockchain-enabled platform.

As a general-purpose technology for transaction processing and process automation, smart-contract-enabled blockchains have the potential to become platforms for manufacturing 4.0. Yet, practical implementations of blockchain in manufacturing remain in an early stage and focus mostly on small aspects of the bigger manufacturing 4.0 picture.

While the benefits may seem very clear, we still have many challenges to overcome before we can unlock the full potential of blockchain. Subsequently, this research centers on major use cases that are gaining traction and details how manufacturing companies can benefit. We then turn to the key challenges to overcome, dominant modes of implementation, and go-forward recommendations.

MAJOR USE CASES

The application of blockchain technology in the manufacturing industry is still in its infancy. After exploring blockchain as a technology itself, companies are starting to hone in on four focused use cases (Table 7-2).

The first use case aims at a blockchain-based coordination and integration of all parties involved in future distributed manufacturing networks—from the buyer to the manufacturer and the final logistics provider.

TABLE 7-2

OVERVIEW OF MAJOR USE CASES IN THE MANUFACTURING INDUSTRY

USE CASE	CORE ELEMENTS	DESCRIPTION	EXAMPLES
Distributed manufacturing networks	Blockchain, smart contract, token	Blockchain-based platform facilitates interactions between buyers and manufacturers with smart contracts to streamline production processes and tokens to provide incentives for participants	SyncFab
Additive manufacturing	Blockchain, smart contract	Blockchain and smart contracts serve as security layer and middleware to integrate and connect the digital thread, underpinning all transactions for AM	Cubichain (consortium), Genesis of Things (consortium), Moog
Asset life-cycle management	Blockchain	Blockchain facilitates a shared and immutable product memory and provides a trail of actionable data over an asset life cycle between multiple parties	Air France, Boeing, General Electric, Lufthansa, Volkswagen
Supply-chain visibility	Blockchain	Blockchain provides near real-time deep-tier supply-chain visibility by onboarding all parties and their transactions in a supply chain on a single shared ledger	Bosch, Dianrong and Foxconn; Mahindra Group, Sichuan Hejia, Pfizer, Genentech

The second use case then focuses on the manufacturing process for AM, which is highly susceptible for a blockchain-based implementation because of its digital nature. With manufacturing processes becoming increasingly software-defined, this use case illustrates the potential of blockchain and smart contracts to secure and automate any kind of manufacturing process that requires an integration across firm boundaries.

The third use case then describes how a digital twin can be created on a blockchain to manage the life cycle of an asset after production. This is particularly relevant for high-capital-cost assets that remain in the market for decades and require multiple parties to operate and maintain. The last use case highlights the role of blockchain in increasing supply-chain visibility. Onboarding all parties in a supply chain on a single shared ledger promises end-to-end visibility of supply-chain processes. Among others, this enables efficiency increases in supply-chain finance and provides transparency for the provenance of parts to combat counterfeits.

While we can classify each use case according to its primary scope, we should note that the use cases are not mutually exclusive, and none expands across the holistic manufacturing 4.0 vision. Rather, the use cases represent small building blocks that, when combined, illustrate the broader potential of blockchain technology as a broader platform for manufacturing 4.0.

Connecting distributed manufacturing resources

Globalization and volatility in demand require an increasingly flexible production of equipment at the point of sale. To handle global demand more efficiently, manufacturing companies—many (95% in US) of which are independent small- to medium-size and so-called hidden champions in highly specialized fields—must therefore find ways to make manufacturing resources more accessible.[316] Based on significant technological advances, such as advanced robotics and data-processing capabilities, distributed manufacturing promises to connect geographically dispersed buyers and hardware manufacturers efficiently on a global scale.

While the Internet has greatly contributed to the visibility of global production capacities, transaction costs have remained prohibitively high because of a lack of digitization and integration of manufacturing processes. As a result, intermediaries and large procurement firms emerged to manage sourcing, contracting, and quality assurance. Coordinating demand and supply, these intermediaries dictate prices, lack intellectual property protection, and make it difficult for smaller innovators and companies to access manufacturing resources.

In a survey of 500 procurement professionals, 31 percent cite finding the right manufacturing suppliers as a major problem and 39 percent of respondents have experienced security breaches in the last 12 months.[317] Overall, inefficient product procurement processes account for a yearly loss of $1.5 billion in revenue for North American businesses.[318]

SyncFab, a San Francisco-based initiative, launched in 2013 "to be the first design-to-manufacturer interactive supply chain ecosystem."[319] SyncFab facilitates manufacturing processes by connecting physically dispersed enterprises and individuals with machine shops. Since 2013, SyncFab managed to onboard over 77 computer numerical control machining capabilities at machine shops in California.

Envisioning an efficient and highly automated peer-to-peer buyer-to-manufacturer platform, SyncFab currently establishes a smart manufacturing blockchain that "aggregates all orders and sends requests directly to manufacturers that match the buyer's requirements … utilizing our smart contracts to streamline procurement processes, eliminating wasted labor-hours on miscommunication that lead to manufacturing mistakes or delays."[320]

Contrary to today's siloed solutions, blockchain technology promotes horizontal integration. As information is stored, verified, and agreed upon simultaneously across the entire value chain, it creates "an ideal ecosystem for manufacturing companies concerned with security and intellectual property."[321]

Migrating its current platform to a blockchain-based solution, SyncFab has initiated a private token presale in mid-November 2017, with the public main sale to start on in mid-February 2018. The platform is intended to work as a decentralized application with what

SyncFab is calling an MFG utility token to facilitate a value-sharing system within the decentralized manufacturing ecosystem.[322]

Most important, the blockchain-based SyncFab platform facilitates the interaction between purchasers and manufacturers. Depending on a manufacturer's order history, machine capacities, and earlier product designs related to a purchaser's requirements, the platform will directly link purchasers to manufacturers, speeding up procurement and production without brokers.

Completed purchase orders are recorded on the blockchain, helping users to build an immutable history, providing information about past performance, reliability, and on-time delivery. We could thereby certify and make available entire parts of the supply chain to potential purchasers without the need to renegotiate. This creates trust that orders placed will be fulfilled according to specific requirements.[323]

SyncFab intends to codify transactional relationships between interacting parties in smart contracts. These contracts can store encrypted intellectual properties with limited access rights or *requests for quotations* (RFQ) inviting manufacturers to bid for a manufacturing project. Moreover, we can also create smart contracts for purchase orders, documenting bidder and quote amount, production criteria, design files or any other sharable IP, inspection reports, and payment terms.[324] Smart contracts are primarily suitable when the involved parties can define the terms of a transaction without ambiguity and objectively measure and verify the success of a transaction.[325]

SyncFab uses blockchain-based MFG tokens to align incentives in the ecosystem, potentially to reward manufacturers who place faster bids and competitive quotes in response to RFQs. Upon submitting a quote to a purchaser, manufacturers can also attach MFG tokens on top of their quote as a form of discount. Moreover, SyncFab adds an MFG token-based transaction fee on any final purchase order to finance the development and operation of its platform.[326]

Overall, the SyncFab platform coordinates actors along the manufacturing value chain and therewith facilitates horizontal integration—a key goal of manufacturing 4.0 initiatives. Similar to other platforms, it aims at *uberization*, the deployment of under-utilized manufacturing capacities. By eliminating intermediaries such as brokers, outdated software, and inefficient procurement processes, the platform significantly reduces transaction costs. It thus lowers the barrier of entry for purchasers as well as manufacturers and creates a transparent distributed-manufacturing network on a global scale. As sourcing processes and manufacturing equipment are increasingly software-defined, blockchain-based smart contracts broaden the scope of automation, fueling the previously illustrated vision of shared autonomous factories.

Securing end-to-end additive manufacturing

Additive manufacturing represents a paradigm shift in manufacturing, as it allows producers to flexibly create individual objects by adding layer upon layer of material (e.g., plastic or metal) on a general-purpose manufacturing device (sometimes referred to as a "3D printer"). Thereby, AM facilitates the manufacturing 4.0 promise of mass customization, as the manufacturing process is entirely computer controlled and can simply be customized by feeding different *computer-aided design* (CAD) based files without the need for expensive retooling.

Today, individuals and groups within the maker movement or in industrial settings use AM for prototyping in the design and preproduction phase to produce small-batch parts. Even though the benefits of AM appear clear-cut, AM has so far struggled to move into industrial serial production because of a lack of economies of scale. Producing small-batch parts in the design or preproduction phase is vastly different from an economically feasible mass production of parts.

A major challenge in scaling AM is seen in silos of information and disparate software systems that prevent full visibility and automation across the AM manufacturing process. Realizing this challenge, the

National Institute of Standards and Technology (NIST) and others are working on integrating software design platforms, multiple AM technologies, and disparate physical manufacturing locations to create an integrated end-to-end digital thread as "a single, seamless strand of data that stretches from the initial design to the finished part."[327]

Industry experts view blockchain technology as a major enabler for an integrated digital thread for AM. As such, blockchain technology provides a "security layer and middleware to integrate and connect the digital thread, underpinning all of the transactions that occur throughout the digital and physical life cycle for AM."[328] Changes to a design, for instance, are made instantly and across all involved parties. Moreover, the blockchain provides an indelible and traceable record of changes and protects intellectual property against unauthorized access.[329] Taking a greenfield approach, the aerospace precision parts manufacturer Moog, as well as manufacturing industry consortia Cubichain and Genesis of Things, have demonstrated the feasibility of blockchain to enforce a reliable digital thread in AM.[330] Cubichain illustrates the use and value of blockchain along the AM process.[331]

The AM process starts with a design phase by creating a *digital product definition* (DPD). A hash ID of the original DPD is pushed as metadata on the blockchain to ensure data integrity in the form of an indelible and secure record. During the design phase, several handoffs occur as the DPD gets modified in different design software from various engineers, departments, and even across companies. These changes are tracked by often disparate *product life–cycle management* (PLM) systems requiring significant configuration effort and centralized governance.

During this stage, blockchain can facilitate a near real-time synchronization of DPD data among different companies and departments. As a shared ledger, blockchain provides a secure transaction layer to track DPD version changes across different file formats and maintain traceability across the entire design phase.

In addition to the actual design, related metadata, such as the proper calibration of a 3D scanner or the correct version of CAD software, can also be stored with the DPD file. As most blockchain implementations rely on an append-only mechanism, this facilitates iterative feedback and simulation loops in a distributed setting. The design phase is particularly suitable for blockchain-facilitated implementations, as its value-creation processes are almost entirely digital and can therefore directly interface with the blockchain.

At the beginning of the build phase, the final DPD is transferred to the manufacturer. The manufacturer then compares the hash ID with the hash ID provided by the DPD designer to ensure that the file has not been tampered with. This transfer and verification can also work fully automated, using smart contracts to "locate the most appropriate printer (based on attributes such as availability, price, quality, and location) and automatically negotiate terms, such as price, quality level and delivery date."[332] The DPD is then directly transferred to a 3D printer with zero human access or interference.

No risk of human interference is particularly important in mission-critical components, such as replacement parts for an airplane. Airbus, for instance, explored how "sensitive design data could be sent to any 3D printer in any country that wants to build Airbus' 3D-printed parts, as long as it guarantees the quality and security standards as verified by the embedded smart contract. The same contract could enforce the immediate deletion of the data upon printing."[333]

Once a part is produced and its build quality is verified based on in-situ machine vision, the design metadata is updated with provenance data and a time stamp. As complex parts may require manufacturing audit trails for certification, the machine control and sensor data from the entire manufacturing process can also be added to the metadata of the part.

In addition to an explicit identifier (e.g., a serial number) embedded during the manufacturing process, an identifier of a part can be generated and included on the blockchain by using an *ultra-high-definition*

(UHD) 3D scanner for digital metrology certification and *X-ray fluorescence* (XRF) digital material signatures to proof authenticity. This ensures attribution and provides a way to record the chain of custody of parts.

Because of the digital nature as well as the requirements for connectedness and security, the AM process lends itself to an application of blockchain technology. A blockchain-based and smart-contract-enabled digital thread promises a massive reduction in transaction costs. Altering fundamental economic trade-offs, this may fuel manufacturing 4.0-envisioned mass customization. AM-based manufacturing lowers the capital required to reach a minimum efficient scale for production, thus reducing the manufacturing barriers to entry. Moreover, economies of scope are lowered as AM facilitates an increase in the variety of products per unit capital by reducing production changeovers and manual customization.[334]

These changes point toward a democratization of manufacturing at point of use, supply-chain disintermediation, and an empowerment of customers, as well as small and medium-sized enterprises. Yet, early implementations appear to be driven by manufacturing giants joining forces in consortia, such as Boeing and Northrop Grumman as part of Cubichain Technologies in the United States. In Germany, EOS, a world leader in the field of industrial printing technologies and a driving force behind the Genesis of Things project, has recently announced the joint development for serial AM together with Premium Aerotech and Daimler—it remains to be seen if blockchain technology will facilitate parts of the solution.[335]

Enabling asset life-cycle management

Any industry with complex pieces of equipment, such as aircrafts or cars, needs to keep track of an asset over its life cycle. A plane, for instance, often operates for 10 to 30 years before it gets disposed of. Over its lifetime, a plane typically has multiple owners and is maintained by different service providers.

As an asset changes owners over its life cycle, a credible proof that it was assembled, operated, and maintained according to the specifications becomes an issue of trust—even more so for life-critical equipment, such as an aircraft. Are the parts of an aircraft genuine and in good working order? How to prove that a certificate has not been tampered with?[336] With multiple parties, such as suppliers, OEMs, airlines, MROs, and regulatory agencies involved, information asymmetries are common. The documentation frequently consists of disparate paper files and provides only a fragmented history of an asset.

A blockchain, as a shared ledger, could provide a single and indisputable source of truth for the history of an asset. This may include the history and provenance of parts with unique identities, which can be provided by suppliers as described in the previous AM use case. During the assembly, the OEM then creates a digital twin of a complex piece of equipment on the blockchain that is associated with various parts. Once in operation, the maintenance and repair history can be updated on the blockchain. An asset's use and damage events can be added by secure IoT sensors. Finally, a blockchain also enables the transfer of ownership of an asset, including its entire history.

We see early implementations and *proofs of concepts* (POCs) in the automotive and aviation industries (mainly the latter). In the automotive industry, Bosch and TÜV Rheinland, for instance, secured the car odometer by writing and continuously updating the mileage for a particular car on a blockchain.[337] General Electric has recently patented a concept for a "dynamic optimization" system that includes multiple aspects of managing, operating, and maintaining an aircraft.[338]

Taking a similar approach, Volkswagen and BigchainDB have tested a car passport that records fuel consumption, mileage, and damage data of cars; Air France has trialed blockchain for MRO; and Lufthansa Industry Solutions has recently launched the Blockchain for Aviation (BC4A) initiative to explore use case along transparency in flight maintenance.[339]

Boeing has taken a holistic approach by piloting the use of block-chain for the management of an entire aircraft life cycle.[340] The life cycle of an aircraft can be distinguished in four key phases: design and build, schedule and operate, monitor and maintain, and dispose.[341] Each phase is supported by various systems, such as *manufacturing operations management* (MOM) in the design and build phase, *airline operations center* (AOC) in the schedule and operate phase, *aircraft maintenance systems* (AMS) in the monitor and maintain phase, and *aircraft demolition management* (ADM) in the dispose phase. To date, these systems are mostly silos within different organizations. By creating a shared IoT-enabled blockchain platform, data from these silos can be combined as an asset moves across the phases of its life cycle and can be shared among various stakeholders in the aircraft ecosystem.[342]

A blockchain-based digital twin of an aircraft is created at the beginning of the design phase. The information associated with the digital twin then gets updated as the aircraft is manufactured, delivered, operated, maintained, and disposed of. During each phase, state changes and relevant data of the aircraft are transferred to a blockchain platform. For example, in the operation phase, a Boeing 787 generates roughly half a terabyte of data for each flight.[343]

At the end of each flight, relevant data (such as those collected during a landing) can be associated with the digital twin of an aircraft. IoT sensors can provide a g-force value that indicates whether a landing was soft or hard. Depending on the landing type, a number of consumed landing cycles can be calculated. Based on historic data on consumed cycles, a predictive maintenance model forecasts the next inspection date. This information, including augmented data, such as weather conditions during the flight and at the time of landing, is then pushed to the blockchain. Clients who rely on information associated with a particular aircraft ID then receive an update of the landing event, which can trigger subsequent actions, such as MRO services for the forecasted date of inspection.

Asset life-cycle management on the blockchain reduces information asymmetries between multiple parties, as it provides an immutable history of an asset. As Nobel laureate George Akerlof argued in his work "The Market for 'Lemons'," this will lead to more efficient asset markets with reduced adverse selection, as buyers will be able to more accurately assess the value of an asset prior to sale or operation.[344]

Blockchain-based near real-time transparency on asset history and utilization will also fuel business-model innovation for manufacturers. In an asset context, manufacturing business models can evolve along four categories: transaction, service contract, product-service system, and product-as-a-service.[345]

Today, most manufacturers pursue transactional business models by selling a piece of equipment. The interaction with a buyer is limited to a single interaction—for instance, the sale of a car. Service contracts are also widespread in the manufacturing industry and require an additional interaction in case of a service incident—for example, a 24-hour repair service in case of a car breakdown. This typically requires some information on the past asset utilization, such as previous maintenance work.

A product-service system, in contrast, requires an integrated product and service offering to deliver additional value as the product is used, such as predictive maintenance services. This offering requires the continuous monitoring of asset utilization by tapping operational sensor and supplemental data in near real-time. For an aircraft, predictive maintenance services are based on a secure and shared audit trail of data provided by suppliers on the parts, by OEMs on the assembly, by airlines on the operation, and by MROs on maintenance services.

In a product-as-a-service business model, a manufacturer only sells the function of a piece of equipment on a usage basis while retaining the actual ownership of the asset—a model pioneered by Rolls-Royce in selling engine hours on a fixed-cost-per-flying-hour basis.[346]

Most interestingly, the business model aligns interests between a manufacturer and customer, as both parties are incentivized to maintain an operational asset, minimize downtime, and reduce waste. Part of the operational risk thereby shifts to the manufacturer. A product-as-a-service business model also alters the cost structure, as customers do not incur fixed capital costs for buying a piece of equipment, but only operating expenses with the opportunity to optimize capital expenditures.

The shift to product-as-a-service business models will occur for high-complexity and high-capital-cost assets in the business-to-business (B2B) domain at first. Cumulative learning effects will extend the scope to the business-to-consumer (B2C) segment for lower-cost assets.

From a manufacturing 4.0 perspective, product-service-system and product-as-a-service business models require *smart products* that know the parameters within which they function optimally and can recognize signs of wear and tear throughout their life cycles. This requires the combination of various emerging technologies, such as IoT, 5G (the next-generation wireless system), machine learning, and edge computing. As illustrated in the Boeing use case, blockchain technology provides another critical component, as it facilitates a shared and immutable trail of actionable data over an asset life cycle between multiple parties.

Increasing supply-chain visibility

A supply chain represents all links between parties involved in creating and distributing goods, starting with suppliers of unprocessed raw materials and ending with the delivery of a finished product to the consumer.[347] Today, complex supply chains frequently span hundreds of stages and dozens of geographical locations.[348]

More than ever, the accelerating pace of innovation and the manufacturing 4.0–fueled race for mass customization require manufacturers to efficiently manage, adapt, and continuously optimize their supply chains. Yet, a survey of 360 international senior executives in the manufacturing sector shows that fewer than 82 percent of companies have limited visibility beyond their tier-one suppliers.[349] As a result, manufacturers frequently run the risk of supply-chain failures, and customers lack a reliable way to verify the provenance of purchased products and services.

Blockchain technology is expected to drastically enhance supply chains by providing near real-time deep-tier visibility based on a trusted ledger that is shared across all parties. Depending on the stage within a supply chain and the focal industry, increased visibility provides various benefits. As a raw-material supplier, mining giant BHP Billiton, for instance, is using blockchain to record and secure mineral analysis provided by heterogeneous outside partners.[350]

On the other end of supply chains, the retail company Walmart is experimenting how to improve food traceability by providing trusted information on the origin and delivery of food such as pork.[351] Focusing on production, manufacturing companies currently explore leveraging visibility for two applications: supply-chain finance and provenance.

The application of blockchain in supply-chain finance aims at onboarding all parties in a supply chain on a single shared ledger to automate and accelerate cash flows throughout the supply chain. An improved or even end-to-end visibility of supply-chain processes provides the trust required for manufacturing companies to engage in reverse factoring with smaller or low-trust suppliers. Manufacturers, as the ordering parties, thereby provide direct financing to their suppliers—typically at a lower interest rate than with basic factoring.

The first pilot use cases have been advanced by Dianrong and Foxconn, the multinational conglomerate Mahindra Group, and the Chinese agricultural production company Sichuan Hejia.[352] While all pilots aim at facilitating supplier-to-manufacturer trade-finance transactions—particularly for small and mid-sized enterprises in deep-tier supply chains—Dianrong and Foxconn also focus on onboarding nonbank lenders to their Chained Finance platform. They intend to focus on suppliers from the tech, auto, and garment industries at first, because of the relatively shallow pool of suppliers.[353]

The application of blockchain for provenance in supply chains aims at providing visibility into the origin of a product. In manufacturing, provenance plays a key role in combatting counterfeit goods. For several industries, counterfeit goods are not only a major economic threat but may even be life-critical.

Fake pharmaceuticals, for instance, constitute up to 15 percent of global supply and can cause hundreds of thousands of deaths annually.[354] To thwart counterfeiters, Pfizer and Genentech (a biotechnology subsidiary of Roche) have launched the Ethereum-based MediLedger project to enable manufacturers to track and trace prescription medicines according to the requirements set by the US Drug Supply Chain Security Act (DSCSA).[355]

Similarly, Bosch, a German multinational engineering company, is facing the problem of fake automotive spare parts that are frequently returned to Bosch with quality complaints. Bosch has developed a Hyperledger-based proof of concept for tracking the provenance of an automotive part from its creation in one of the Bosch plants to the consumer:

- In a first step, the Bosch plant registers the part with a secure label (e.g., an inscribed serial number or watermark code) and accompanying information on the blockchain.

- The part is then shipped with information about the logistic provider and destination to the Bosch Automotive Aftermarket division that registers the arrival.

- From there, the part is shipped to the distributor and sold to the consumer.

Each step is documented on the Hyperledger blockchain with references to the past steps in an immutable chain. Scanning the part, the consumer can verify its originality and provenance; and Bosch can detect fakes on an individual part level, identify gray-market imports, and greatly reduce its costs incurred through counterfeits.[356]

Blockchain has the potential to provide unprecedented deep-tier supply-chain visibility in near real time. This will enable manufacturing companies to engage in reverse factoring by directly financing smaller or low-trust suppliers. Manufacturing companies can also report the provenance of their products to increase the trust of buyers and combat counterfeit goods. While these are two transformative applications of blockchain technology in the manufacturing industry, increasing supply-chain visibility will spawn efficiency increases and new business models in the entire supply-chain ecosystem and adjacent industries.

IMPLEMENTATION CHALLENGES

Early implementations face several challenges. Foremost, the selection of a suitable blockchain protocol requires an extensive assessment of requirements and available feature sets, as well as maturity of the respective protocol. Second, blockchain implementations that require a link to the physical world have to safeguard the digital-physical interface. Third, the network and user-interface security must be provided at all times. Fourth, the implementation of smart contracts requires an understanding and evaluation of the suitable application scope.

CHOOSING A SUITABLE BLOCKCHAIN PROTOCOL

With a broadening availability of various blockchain protocols (e.g., Bitcoin, Ethereum, Hyperledger), the protocol choice requires a comprehensive analysis of advantages and disadvantages. In the manufacturing context, decision-makers should evaluate a blockchain protocol along various dimensions.

- **Choice of openness.** This dimension determines some of the main protocol features (Table 7-3).[357] In some blockchain manufacturing applications, such as aircraft life-cycle management, the application scope may be limited to a pre-approved number of known participants, favoring the choice of enterprise blockchain protocols (e.g., Hyperledger). Other use cases, such as additive manufacturing, may benefit from the network effects of an open blockchain solution (e.g., Ethereum). A pre-approved number of known participants reduces the need for algorithmic trust and generally allows for faster transaction throughput, more holistic access level controls, and potentially more cost-effective operations.

- **Protocol governance.** Blockchain protocols are typically governed by developer communities (e.g., Bitcoin or Ethereum), by consortia (e.g., Hyperledger or R3), or by companies (e.g., Ripple or Chain). While consortia and companies generally provide a clearly defined and transparent protocol governance, developer community-governed protocols have frequently seen governance disruptions and unexpected changes to protocols. As manufacturing blockchain applications oftentimes run in B2B environments with life-critical processes, governance and protocol changes can become a major issue. As opposed to platforms (e.g., Ethereum), several blockchains (e.g., Hyperledger or Monax) can also be run as software within a company or network of companies, mitigating the risk of unexpected protocol changes.

- **Application scope.** A final dimension concerns the intended application scope of a blockchain protocol. While early blockchain protocols (e.g., Ethereum, Hyperledger) have generally focused on providing industry-agnostic functionality (e.g., smart contracts, chain code), there is an increasing number of special-purpose blockchains to consider. Instead of building features for the lowest common denominator, special-purpose blockchains aim at implementing superior industry-specific feature sets.

Manufacturing use cases frequently require the management of physical assets in operation within milliseconds and on a highly granular level—transaction requirements that general-purpose blockchains largely fail to provide (i.e., low transaction throughput per second and high transaction fees).

In contrast, new protocols such as IOTA promise highly scalable *machine-to-machine* (M2M) transactions in real time with no fees. Even though new protocols may require time to mature until large-scale implementations can be rolled out in a production environment, special-purpose blockchains should be embraced and carefully evaluated for each use case.

TABLE 7-3

GENERALIZED FEATURE COMPARISON OF ENTERPRISE AND PUBLIC BLOCKCHAINS

FEATURES	ENTERPRISE (PERMISSIONED)	PUBLIC (PERMISSIONLESS)
Access	Permissioned read and/or write access to database	Open read/write access to database
Speed	Faster	Slower
Security	Pre-approved participants ("trusted")	Open network ("trustless")
Identity	Known identities	Anonymous/pseudonymous
Asset	Any asset	Native assets

SAFEGUARDING THE PHYSICAL-DIGITAL INTERFACE

Another challenge relates to the physical-digital interface of manufacturing equipment, input material or products, and the blockchain as a digital ledger. The interface requires a unique identification of physical goods and their current state. For high-value items, sophisticated tagging or measuring techniques (e.g., UHD-3D scanners) could offer a solution. These approaches may, however, not be economically feasible for low-value and high-volume produce. Therefore, we must understand that if the trust issue of the physical-digital interface is not controlled through supplementary technologies or any other way, blockchain will probably not provide a solution. There are currently three major approaches to secure the physical-digital interface.

First, objects can be identified based on their physical properties as passive identifiers. Everledger was one of the first companies to use this approach to secure diamonds on a blockchain. Creating an immutable digital footprint, Everledger uses the four Cs (cut, clarity, color, and carat weight) and measures more than 40 attributes to identify a diamond uniquely. As the diamond moves from an uncut raw stage to a polished diamond, the digital fingerprint is updated by certified partners as its physical properties are transformed.

Second, there are active identifiers, such as serial numbers, QR codes, or embedded IoT-devices. These can be integrated during production (e.g., adding a serial number to a car replacement part during production) or at a later stage (e.g., by adding a QR code that is statically linked to blockchain identifiers using a secure hash). Yet most of these identifiers run the risk of being easily cloned or becoming detached from the physical object.

Third, an increasing number of companies are focusing on creating active crypto identifiers. These new sorts of identifiers combine established technologies, such as near-field communication devices and public key cryptography to facilitate the direct interaction of a physical object and a blockchain. The object thereby receives an unforgeable identity to interact autonomously with a blockchain and with other connected devices on a blockchain platform.

While this creates an ID native to the blockchain authentication system that cannot be cloned or copied, it does not prevent IDs from being physically tampered with. Vendors in this space therefore focus on making a tampering attempt immediately visible (e.g., a CryptoSeal sticker provided by Chronicled that creates a permanent damage of the embedded circuitry upon sticker removal) and prohibitively costly (e.g., crypto chips provided by Riddle&Code that are susceptible to manipulation, such as memory remanence, frozen RAM, or monitoring electromagnetic signals).[358]

GUARANTEEING NETWORK AND USER INTERFACE SECURITY

Besides safeguarding the physical-digital interface that is important for any industry dealing with non-purely digital products or services, such as manufacturing, it is equally important to guarantee the security of the blockchain network itself and the interface to the user.

Bitcoin has so far demonstrated the network security of blockchain technology. Being the first public blockchain implementation, it provided a maximum surface of attack and has withstood major hacking attempts. Thereby, the consensus mechanism provides a major element of blockchain network security. With established consensus mechanisms (such as proof of work in the case of Bitcoin) becoming increasingly costly, new approaches are proposed (e.g., proof of stake).[359]

Protocol changes not only affect consensus mechanisms but also how data are organized. Instead of using blocks, IOTA, for example, makes use of directed acyclic graph chains. While new mechanisms promise greater efficiency and better performance, it remains to be seen if they match the original Bitcoin blockchain protocol in terms of network security.

The security of a system is only as strong as its weakest link, which in many cases is the actual user. Contrary to the common misconception, most blockchain hacks did not occur at a network protocol level, but at the user interface to the blockchain network—mostly wallets, exchanges, and Dapps built on the protocol.[360] Consequently, the blockchain user interface is a key element to secure. In a manufacturing environment, this concerns human users and machines that have to identify themselves on the blockchain network using a private key. Keeping the private key secret and in a safe—physical or digital—place constitutes a major challenge.

Moreover, sophisticated Turing complete scripting languages, such as Ethereum, allow users to write complex applications that oftentimes cannot be guaranteed to be error-free. For mission-critical blockchain-based smart-contract applications that may power an aircraft, this becomes a prerequisite. Mechanisms to verify formally the intended functionality of an application are thus currently a major research priority and should be a major concern for blockchain users.[361]

EVALUATING THE APPLICATION SCOPE FOR SMART CONTRACTS

Smart contracts contain the promise that a computation happens in an agreed manner. As such, they are at the heart of any application focusing on the automation of business processes. Yet, the suitable application scope of smart contracts remains fuzzy. In practice, at least two criteria must be fulfilled for smart contracts to create significant value.

First, the terms of a contract need to be defined without any ambiguity by the involved parties. This requires a clear and explicit understanding of the performance and execution criteria of a contract. Data-driven transactional (close to discrete) contracts—for example, a purchase of a standardized car part (i.e., a search good with clearly defined features and characteristics)—may largely facilitate this condition, as the product and conditions for a transaction can clearly be defined up front. Relational contracts, in contrast, are placed in a broader social context with implicit understandings embedded in behavioral aspects, such as an employment contract.[362]

Second, the successful execution of a contract needs to be objectively and easily measurable. While this can generally be achieved for digital or digitized assets (e.g., the virtual transfer of money), it is more difficult for physical output (e.g., the automated production of a car part)—even more so if the value creation process involves any kind of human performance that can induce unexpected variation in the output quality (e.g., the assembly of a car). Measuring the conformance of physical products and services to previously specified objectively measurable quality criteria thus requires sophisticated physical-digital interfaces (e.g., sensors, scanners).

While some highly transactional business processes may be susceptible for smart-contract implementations (e.g., automated bidding
processes for standardized parts), many applications will not entirely
fulfill both criteria and require a significant amount of subjective
human judgment (e.g., evaluation of an RFQ for a complex piece of
equipment). Instead of purely smart contracts, many applications will
therefore require blended contracts with automated smart elements
and some elements requiring human judgment or interaction.[363]

KEY TAKEAWAYS ON MANUFACTURING 4.0

Blockchain technology provides an integral
component in the vision of manufacturing 4.0. As a
shared ledger, blockchain can give rise to industry-
wide shared platforms for the secure exchange
of data. Connecting manufacturer, upstream
suppliers, downstream customers, and consumers,
blockchain as a platform can enable end-to-end
engineering processes and economically feasible mass
customization at scale.

- **The immutability of blockchain will be crucial.**
  We need a permanent record to establish a digital
  product memory over the life cycle of an asset with
  shared ownership, operation, and maintenance
  processes. Combined with sophisticated machine
  learning algorithms, information on provenance
  as well as wear and tear will be the basis for smart
  products that anticipate technical failures or
  opportunities for optimization.

- **Real-time access to data and control becomes a commodity.** As manufacturing equipment and supply chains are increasingly equipped with sensors and connectivity, data will become an asset class. In combination with blockchain as a secure data-sharing infrastructure and smart contracts as means to automate processes, industry-wide data-driven and software-defined manufacturing activities appear within reach.

- **Our four use cases share a high feasibility for blockchain-based implementations.** Each demonstrates the potential of blockchain technology in the manufacturing sector. While these use cases (Table 7-4) appear to be the low-hanging fruit and are the current focus of industry attention, they will also provide the basis and inspiration for a plethora of new blockchain-based products, services, and business models in the manufacturing industry, such as marketplaces for validated machine data, smart-contract-based product and service liability insurance, automated predictive micro-maintenance contracts, pay-per-use smart-contract-based asset sharing, provenance-based marketing, or dispute management.

- **Several implementation challenges exist.** Most important, companies must carefully evaluate the use of permissioned, permissionless, or hybrid blockchain protocols according to their use-case requirements. While permissioned blockchains may offer a higher performance for some requirements (e.g., transaction throughput), they are typically restricted to a pre-approved set of participants.

- **Another crucial element to consider is the protocol governance.** Some (mostly permissioned) protocols may be implemented as stand alone software without the need to engage in or monitor protocol governance. Many permissionless protocols (e.g., Bitcoin, Ethereum), however, are governed by developer communities and network participants (e.g., users, miners, node operators) that decide upon central changes to a protocol. Stakeholders must proactively engage in shaping industry standards and delivery to ensure that protocols continue not only to support their use case but also to improve related feature sets.

- **Securing the user interface and the network is critical.** As manufacturing products and services are mostly based on physical value-creation activities, blockchain use cases require a secure physical-digital interface to identify physical goods and their current state. Another key challenge is evaluating the application scope for smart contracts.

- **The most important recommendation is to get started.** One way is to head straight for implementation with small and focused internal POCs. As illustrated in the use cases, an increasing number of smaller initiatives explore pilots and the implementation of highly focused blockchain applications. These are typically led by single manufacturing companies in support of established IT vendors or blockchain technology companies that provide the required expertise.

- **The scope of the pilots is mostly to learn about blockchain.** We need to be able to assess blockchain's business value. For publicly deployed implementations, we should focus on non-mission-critical pilots, as they provide considerable surface for attack and require a fallback plan in case someone discovers and exploits a loophole in the implementation.

- **Another option is to engage in a consortium.** Firms can join such consortia as the Trusted IoT Alliance to acquire basic knowledge, to stay up-to-date on current trends, and to establish industry standards jointly.[364] Consortia should not begin with standardization, because we have little practical experience with major blockchain implementations in productive environments yet.

- **Consortia should initially focus on gathering practical experience.** Discovering challenging edge cases will help define standards. Aiming at open standards, most consortia (e.g., Trusted IoT Alliance, Hyperledger) publish their code base and report their progress in white papers. Overall, this encourages discussion and early pilot applications to reach standard drafts that are pre-vetted and have a broad support base.

- **Leaders can evaluate use cases along various dimensions.** To assess the suitability of a blockchain-based implementation for use cases at hand, it can be helpful to follow decision trees or simple assessment criteria (Table 7-4).[365] These provide a first indication of whether or not a use case at hand actually requires a blockchain.[366]

TABLE 7-4

BLOCKCHAIN USE-CASE ASSESSMENT FRAMEWORK

	Multiple parties share data	Multiple parties update data	Parties need to verify data	Intermediaries add cost and complexity	Interactions are highly time-sensitive	Transaction depends on another
Distributed manufacturing networks	x	x	x	x	x	x
Additive manufacturing	x	x	x	x		x
Asset life-cycle management	x	x	x	x		x
Supply-chain visibility	x	x	x	x		x

Source of data: Gunther Dütsch and Neon Steinecke, "Use Cases for Blockchain Technology in Energy & Commodity Trading," PwC, July 2017.

- Use cases are generally suitable for blockchain-based implementations if multiple parties are required to share data and need a common view of the information (e.g., sharing RFQ information in a distributed manufacturing network).

- Beyond sharing data, many implementations also require network participants to update data in a coordinated manner (e.g., updating the status of production in a distributed manufacturing network). A verification is required when participants have to trust that recorded actions are valid (e.g., the status of production was updated by a particular person at a given point in time).

- Another indicator for a blockchain-suitable solution is costly intermediaries that add complexity (e.g., large procurement firms emerge to manage sourcing, contracting, and quality assurance).

- When interactions are time-sensitive, blockchain can potentially reduce delays (e.g., smart contracts can significantly speed up the manufacturing process by automating standardized manufacturing agreements).

- The last criterion refers to the interdependency of transactions that blockchain facilitates (e.g., a subsequent production process is automatically triggered once the previous process is complete).

CHAPTER 8

ADDITIVE MANUFACTURING AND BLOCKCHAIN

Creating Efficient Supply Chains for Moog, Inc.

Vineet Narula and Prema Shrikrishna

 ## ADDITIVE MANUFACTURING IN BRIEF

- Moog, an aircraft precision-part manufacturer based in New York and operating in a highly regulated industry segment, counts US Department of Defense, Airbus, Lockheed Martin, and Boeing among its customers. Because of the nature of Moog's industry, any inefficiencies and counterfeits in its products, parts, or supply chains can delay missions, compromise the integrity of critical systems, and endanger human lives.

- This case follows the development of a proof of concept that combines blockchain technology and additive manufacturing (aka three-dimensional printing) to track provenance throughout Moog's supply chain, provide greater assurance and efficiencies to its customers, and fundamentally change the economic workings of its industry.

- Additive manufacturing alone will likely not solve all supply-chain challenges. For example, even if Moog printed a part in two days, delays in tooling, audit protocols, or regulatory approval could hinder its deployment. Ancillary industries, regulatory bodies, and

165

suppliers must work in tandem, and a platform that combined 3D printing and blockchain capabilities would enable them to do that.

- To address supplier complacency in an industry with high barriers to entry, the platform could also become a marketplace and a reputation management system. Vendor performance and user experience could factor into vendor ratings, which would be visible to all internal Moog teams and could contribute to existing vendor management system scorecards.

- The case looks at the roles of customers, suppliers, and the Moog team in leveraging connectivity, 3D printing, and blockchain benefits to manage their interactions within a distributed supply chain. It follows a product through the entire process to demonstrate how this combination of technologies might transform global supply chains and forever alter the economics of precision manufacturing.

PROBLEM TO BE SOLVED

With complex supply chains spanning multiple tiers of suppliers, inability to identify origins of a product, counterfeiting issues, and shrinking operating margins that go as low as 0.07 percent, aerospace engineering businesses must continue to move away from a manufacturing strategy toward a supply-chain strategy.[367] This shift could involve catalyzing the power of a distributed network to improve efficiencies. Where legacy systems operate with a single source of truth, where each supplier has its own version of truth, changes in design data for any part and a supplier's failure to update that information could increase *notices of escape* (NOEs) or noncompliance by almost 10 percent.

Aerospace regulations, Federal Aviation Authority (FAA) audit protocols, and US Department of Defense (DOD) standards such as AS9100 *electronic historical records* (EHRs) require paper trails for all parts, maps, photographs as evidence of organization, functions, policies, decisions, procedures, and process authorizations.[368] With millions of parts manufactured from global supply chains and the average lifespan of an aircraft pegged at 30 years, the process of maintaining records can only increase in complexity.[369]

Maintaining intact supply chains and spare-part supplies over the extended lifespan of aircraft is a major challenge for manufacturers and their customers. This challenge is not unique to the aerospace industry: regulated medical and industrial industries also face increasing complexity of processes, uncertain provenance of supplies, and conflicting data.[370]

INTRODUCTION TO THE CASE

Moog began its business as a designer and a supplier of missile components and aircraft over 50 years ago.[371] From Formula One racing and commercial aircraft flight controls to power-generation turbines, its motion control technology increases performance in multiple markets and applications. Headquartered in East Aurora, New York, it has over 11,000 employees globally, with presence in over 28 countries and over $2.4 billion in revenue.

Moog aspires to be a part of Industry 4.0 by leveraging its core competencies and emerging technologies to become the recognized leader in digital manufacturing and networked digital supply chains.[372] Additive manufacturing creates unique opportunities in aircraft manufacturing; and blockchain architecture can contribute to improving economic, social, and environmental models of supply chains.[373]

Jim Regenor, Moog's business unit director of transformative technologies, and George Small, chief technology officer, were the first to explore the convergence of 3D printing and blockchain applications that did not otherwise have precedence in the industry.[374] The team at Moog believed that executives who focused solely on financial metrics were missing the point because a company could derive exponential first- and second-order benefits from using new technology.[375] However, when making the case for a pilot project that proved a particular business concept, Regenor and Small understood that they could not tell their executive management team that such a technology would improve Moog's bottom line by a certain percentage, because roll out would be an iterative process—launch it, learn from it, and adjust it—and so they would continue to economize scope and scale as they went down the path of proving their concept.

Not participating in the process of this advancement was not an option. "You can't control the advancement of technology; history has shown that time and time again," said Regenor. "A couple of years back, it was hard to find a publication that showed any details of how supply chain can benefit from blockchain. Now it's everywhere."[376] He was referring to how quickly researchers and business have seen value and industry applications have gained momentum.

PLANNING THE PILOT TO PROVE THE CONCEPT

In developing its POC, Moog was cautious in defining an MVP timeline. The company risked sticking to the drawing board and continually adapting its model to changes in technology rather than launching a pilot and learning from implementation. Instead, it had to keep the architecture dynamic to accommodate interoperability standards.

Currently in its VeriPart blockchain solution, Moog is experimenting with algorithms that could replace middlemen. "With a natural bias toward using middlemen in operations, we need to eliminate middlemen or dependencies that do not add value," said Regenor.[377]

Moog is working to remove deadwood from its processes and the opacity that comes with it. With the freedom to develop solutions for customer problems, Regenor and Small want to divert the debate from quarter-to-quarter financial pressure to a vision about innovation.

At a recent conference, Moog's CEO, John Scannell, spoke about blockchain as core to Moog's future. Moog was founded on an entrepreneurial spirit. "We are back to the future by going to our roots," said Regenor.[378]

GOING FROM PRODUCT PILOT TO PLATFORM

With an objective to be a leader in this space, Moog wants to create a blockchain platform where consumers and producers can exchange value. The metrics will involve measuring number of adopters, integration with upstream and downstream clients, number of exchanges of intellectual property (IP) value, and numbers of schematics downloaded and printed per unit time. As this phase progresses, Moog moves from a proof of concept to a minimal viable product in additive manufacturing and eventually to a platform that exchanges IP assets and value. Finally, Moog sees the future as a blockchain-enabled platform that creates a "point of use, time of need" networked digital supply chain. Moog will realize the value as the platform forces the non-value-adding steps (e.g., warehousing, transportation, inventory, and customs brokerage fees) out of the supply chain.

Establishing trust will be paramount. Innovators and developers will need to know that, if they make their designs and data available for others to use, the platform's cryptosecurity will prevent piracy or tampering, and through smart contracts, they will receive almost instantaneous payment for every design downloaded.[379] They need to be sure that their intellectual property is protected and that they will be the beneficiaries of the value they are creating within a supply chain.

Blockchain architecture presents interesting solutions to these challenges. However, since the technology is nascent, there are few end-to-end solution providers. Also, with varied levels of ERP and technology systems across the supply chain, interoperability between the blockchain platform at Moog and those of its suppliers will take time to achieve.

ANALYSIS OF THE CASE

The spur in additive manufacturing indicates the industry's faith in the power of digital. For these processes to scale at the industrial level, a series of complex, connected, and data-driven events must occur. Deploying 3D printers is less a physical- or hardware-associated production challenge and more a data- or records-management one. Data availability and interconnectivity can help drive the adoption of additive manufacturing in the supply chain by changing the paradigm from shipping parts to exchanging data.

By utilizing sensors and connectivity to increase in-transit visibility and moving toward IoT, blockchain potentially serves as the data or transaction layer for all this information, encrypted and moving within and among organizations.[380] With additive manufacturing, Moog foresees new business models, myriad new options for how, when, and where products are fabricated. Businesses need to decide which network of supply-chain assets and which mix of old and new processes will be optimal. We expect high-value, high-risk segments such as aerospace to make the shift sooner, and Moog is ahead of the curve.

LEVERAGING TECHNOLOGY AND INNOVATION

Let's look at a blockchain transaction on Moog's proposed new platform. Let's suppose an airframe manufacturer has a requirement for an airplane part or system and has identified Moog to help furnish that requirement through a *request for proposal* (RFP) process. The RFP process involves extensive internal cross-team collaboration that will be "off the blockchain." In this POC, the assumption is that the manufacturer and Moog share a blockchain platform or have interoperable systems to secure their exchanges of information and value.

The customer's part

In the development phase, the customer engages with Moog and collaboratively details requirements: part specifications, quality standards, testing protocols, audit requirements, cost, and delivery time. The customer establishes a standard business contract in the system (*master service level agreement* or MSLA) that governs the relationship between the customer and Moog. In accordance with standard protocol, if Moog's proposal has been accepted, a smart contract is created in the system thereafter. Since this is a permissioned blockchain ledger, Moog's administrative access enables it to query and update the ledger whereas suppliers only have query rights. Each transaction triggered by the customer generates a private key, which is authenticated with Moog or a certified on the blockchain.

In production phase, the customer triggers a smart contract on a permissioned blockchain platform. The contract selects Moog as a supplier and generates multiple *purchase orders* (POs) for various parts to Moog. These POs contain several shipsets per month, which detail the parts and the assembly components Moog must build.[381] The contract also contains information on assets such as IP, CAD data, and other requirements. Assets in any smart contract can range from the tangible (machines and hardware) to the intangible (trademarks or licenses).

For example, a single shipset for an aircraft flight control hardware can include 50 to 100 assemblies, each made of tens and hundreds of subparts and subassemblies. The blockchain aggregates these POs and time-stamps them as an acknowledgment of receipt. Each time a transaction is triggered, a block is created; and when the transaction is processed, the block is hashed by the blockchain. A version check is performed prior to appending a block to ensure that states for assets have not changed since the execution of the code.

Moog's part

Moog receives a PO embedded in a smart contract and transfers it to its existing ERP system for internal tracking through its production line. The ERP generates an order, and then Moog assesses which suppliers might be best capable of delivering the required parts. These suppliers are *approved* and *qualified*, meaning that they have met the requirements of an airframe customer, DOD, FAA, and others. Given the regulatory environment and the risk to people's lives, both DOD and commercial aerospace industries have stringent requirements for empaneling a supplier. Both industries can have additional flow downs because of security, quality requirements, government acquisition regulations, and so forth. The suppliers are pre-authenticated and, therefore, trusted parties on the platform. In a scenario of multiple peers, the transactions among suppliers and Moog will contain signatures of every endorsing peer on the ledger. With CAD data and manufacturing updated within Moog, the smart contract automatically updates itself with the latest version of the data.

The supplier's part

Once Moog places the new PO on the platform, it triggers another smart contract for the supplier to review the PO details and confirm acceptance. The new smart contract carries forward the hash from the previous transaction and has clearly spelled-out instructions concerning part specifications, quality standards, testing protocols, and audit requirements. Suppliers do not have permissions to edit the Moog-generated smart contract. They have read-only query rights: they can trigger queries for clarification but not edit them.

The real-time transmission of data creates efficiencies that are otherwise impossible with paper documentation. Every subsequent audit can use these digital trails as sources of truth and as indicators of part maintenance and obsolescence, since these trails include time stamps. With known identities, the blockchain holds each party accountable at every stage.

TRANSFORMING SUPPLY CHAINS

Supply chains are strategic levers optimized to extract more value and lessen costs. At a meta-level, supply-chain optimizations contribute substantially to globalization and offshore manufacturing. The optimization of the supply chain through *just-in-time* (JIT) methods of, or reducing spend on, inventory management aims to rationalize the expenses that can make or break market leadership.

With blockchain technology, supply chains will move from competitive to collaborative: large firms will place RFPs on an open, trusted platform (i.e., public-permissioned distributed ledger) and invite suppliers to bid.

The suppliers with relevant production capabilities will belong to a consortium that is a value-chain network with membership prerequisites. These prerequisites may involve identity (name, proof of existence, tax identification number), governance (audits, human rights protections, environmental certifications, FAA approvals), and legal frameworks in addition to their ability to manufacture per the client's requirements shared on a public-permissioned blockchain.

In a plug-and-play model of a consortium, pre-approved global suppliers of additive manufacturing bid for an order depending on the geographical location.[382] Let's say the US business owners have a requirement for 3D parts for a Brazilian client; hence, a supplier in Brazil wins the order and supplies the part. For each download of the design, for which a business owner has claimed IP rights, that business owner receives a royalty. The consortium realizes not only protection of each member's IP but also efficiencies in manufacturing time, shipping, and insurance, and instantaneous recognition of revenues. The neutrality of the platform creates trust that encourages supplier participation.

With the global supply-chain market estimated to have a market value approximating $40 trillion, blockchain has the potential to redefine economic structures and value flows that underpin supply-chain decision-making.

RESHAPING—PERHAPS REVERSING—GLOBAL TRADE

Around the world, politicians are debating whether to impose trade barriers to curb skilled job loss in a range of industries.[383] Perhaps they should instead be exploring how 3D printing could reshape manufacturing, thereby reversing globalization.[384]

Technological advancements alter the ratio of capital-to-labor costs in production so that companies can afford to manufacture products closer to consumers. The proximity to customer increases speed of order fulfillment and reduces exposure to currency fluctuations and other risks.[385] Additive manufacturing also decreases the cost variance between manufacturing locally and offshoring to inexpensive labor. If manufacturing costs for printing an item locally or overseas are the same, then the locally printed item will be cheaper because of lower transportation costs from printer to end customer or assembly factory.[386]

Owning 3D printing equipment, joining a consortium, and paying a licensing or subscription fee are the prerequisites to participating in what we see as the "additive economy." We expect fresh entrepreneurship to take the reins, blockchain-based trade finance to unlock and convert inventory value into capital financing, and entry barriers to drop.

However, we must remember that low-end manufacturing is traditionally the first rung on the economic ladder: developing countries use their newly gained industrial expertise to move into higher value-added manufacturing and services. Removing this first rung could stunt emerging markets such as Indonesia, India, and Vietnam, which have just begun their climb.[387]

KEY TAKEAWAYS OF ADDITIVE MANUFACTURING

- **Blockchain is in a fledgling state.** Transitioning from existing ERP systems to a blockchain depends on the platform demonstrating its ability to solve complex problems at scale, and it hasn't done that yet. The blockchain fabric must provide for a micro granularity to gain access into every participant across multiple tiers on a supply-chain network, track provenance of goods, and maintain immutable records of all aspects of the production and storage of a finished good through to sale and after sale.

- **The manufacturing industry needs clarity.** Unlike the information technology industry, the manufacturing industry needs to understand the capital, operational, and recurring expenses associated with selecting a blockchain platform. Global ancillary industries such as banking, customs, shipping, logistics, and insurance must evolve simultaneously for this technology to go mainstream.

- **Businesses will need a new product strategy.** To adopt this technology, businesses must answer a very different question with their product strategy: not "How do we sell?" but "What do we sell?" Companies must also imagine how they can maintain or improve their value proposition and customer delight in an era of additive manufacturing orchestrated on the blockchain. They must answer, "How can customization give us first-mover advantage?" and "What aspects can we improve, now that we have eliminated restrictions or delivery delays?"[388]

- **Businesses must tie proofs of concepts to growth.** Reflecting on their pilot, Jim Regenor and George Small emphasized the need to tie the POC to core growth vectors in the business. If businesses operate with a quarterly perspective, they should use blockchain to solve issues related to core business propositions such as better, leaner, lesser, or cheaper. Regenor and Small also suggested starting small, creating resonance within the business, getting stakeholder buy-in, and understanding how to create future competitive advantage.[389]

- **Blockchain enables point-of-use manufacturing.** The digital freedom accorded by an additive manufacturing-based supply chain may break down disparate geographic locations for production closer to the point of use. The transmission of additive manufacturing data and the comparative convenience of printing parts on or near location should reduce dependence on offshore manufacturing. To mitigate the downside of this global reversal, every country should vastly improve access to infrastructure and education, cultivate its scientific talent, foster a culture of technology adoption, and respond quickly with appropriate economic and trade policies.

CHAPTER 9

BELT AND ROAD BLOCKCHAIN CONSORTIUM

Building Digital Trust for Cross-Border Trade

Prema Shrikrishna and Vineet Narula

 BELT AND ROAD IN BRIEF

- The Belt and Road Initiative represents the largest global collaboration on infrastructure development since the post-World War II era. It aims to minimize the current friction in cross-border trade and global supply chains.

- The Belt and Road Blockchain Consortium is building out the digital infrastructure, creating necessary layers of legal, identity, and governance protocols, which will provide speed, security, and transparency in transactions.

- The consortium is an inclusive and multistakeholder model. It helps to align economic and diplomatic interests and incentives, harmonize local rules and regulations, share best practices and intellectual property, and provide ongoing governance. As a staging ground, Hong Kong is ideally situated and conducive to business and innovation, with modern municipal systems, a highly skilled workforce, a strong service sector, and laws governing electronic transactions.

- Verifiable digital identification of people, devices, and organizations is critical to the initiative. Hongkong Post, InvestHK, and HSBC are among those working on technology and processes for knowing each customer, machine, and business that will be conducting transactions within the Belt and Road member countries.

- Stakeholders bring core capabilities to the table, including expertise in digital certification, logistics, trade finance, supply-chain optimization, standards setting, incubating start-ups, consulting, and auditing.

- Stakeholders also participate in governance to ensure, for example, Sharia-compliant provenance and financing, green financing for sustainable development, and enforcement of the trade arbitration framework, alternative dispute resolution process, and a patent nonaggression pact.

INTRODUCTION TO ONE BELT ONE ROAD

In October 2017, the 19th National Congress of the Communist Party of China approved and incorporated the Belt and Road Initiative into its constitution.[390] In the last two centuries, we cannot think of infrastructure projects that a government has etched in the constitution of its country. This was a historic moment for Xi Jinping, who proposed the Belt and Road Initiative in 2013. The Belt and Road Initiative seeks to create a Silk Road Economic Belt and the 21st Century Maritime Silk Road by increasing connectivity among the original 65 countries across Asia, Africa, and Europe.[391]

Some have compared the initiative to the Marshall Plan—without the war—involving over 65 percent of the world's population, generating one-third of its gross domestic product, and moving a quarter of all its goods and services.[392] Others have described President Xi Jinping's initiative as the biggest development push in history.

Chinese acquisitions in the countries involved officially link to Belt and Road. President Xi Jinping's signature foreign policy totaled $33 billion, surpassing the $31 billion tally for all of 2016.[393] Moreover, the rise of digital platforms has enabled consumers to transact in any part of the world. According to Forrester Research, worldwide B2C cross-border e-commerce may reach $424 billion by 2021, making up 15 percent of all online commerce.[394] China's Belt and Road Initiative is a project "too big to ignore," with the potential to transform global trade if its participants execute its digitization in an equally transformative manner.

However, they face fundamental challenges with physical and digital trade infrastructure that they will need to address for more effective and efficient supply chains. These include but aren't restricted to verifying the identities of parties in a transaction, advancing safety and security protocols, expediting customs settlement, and facilitating border controls. The future architecture of digital trade must take into account the need for aligning social, economic, and environmental interests between public and private sectors. This initiative is a mammoth undertaking, one that will define standards for world trade for generations to come.

Blockchain is a global peer-to-peer network, the protocols of which ensure transparency, security, and reliability. When one party transfers a piece of digital property to another party over the blockchain, all participants in the network can see the transfer. Moreover, the transaction is time-stamped and secure, and everyone can see when it is completed. Global supply chains can seek to leverage blockchain for the provenance of goods and services.

The future of trade has been surfacing regularly in international discussions of such agreements as the North American Free Trade Agreement (NAFTA) and Trans-Pacific Partnership (TPP), which were designed to open trading borders, help large businesses access newer markets, lower trade barriers, and ultimately benefit small businesses and customers. Bilateral or multilateral trade governance models are great but may not be good enough to exploit the opportunities in trade along the Belt and Road. While governments create circumferences around the economics of these agreements, they often set aside such issues as intellectual property (IP) protection, human rights, environmental standards, and, above all, equitable growth.

The Belt and Road Blockchain Consortium (BRBC) seeks to add another dimension to the element of trade, that of digital identity, so that we can move toward a future where strategy revolves around IP trading, commissioning, and protection. Enabling an alternate vision of the consortium involves bringing stakeholders such as banks, customs and port authorities, audit agencies, postal authorities, and public key infrastructure authorities not only to understand each other's concerns but also to enforce greater trust through blockchain technology. The emphasis now is more on architecture and governance than on the choice of technology.

Hong Kong is at the forefront of leading this change as it enjoys a vantage point geographically as well as through the strength imposed in its legal and financial systems. Its Electronic Transactions Ordinance of 2000, which recognizes digital signatures, serves as a precursor to the BRBC.[395] With all stakeholders solving for trust, the faith bestowed on platforms by consumers, and the need to create equitable economic opportunities, the BRBC has set out to transform global trade.

HOW TO TAKE THE FRICTION OUT OF TRADE

Imagine markets where buyers and sellers across borders find one another almost immediately without cost and have access to information about the reputation of their vendors—where cross-border trade is primarily digital with enhanced emphasis on trust, instant settlements, and open borders to trade.

To realize such friction-free trade, policymakers and business leaders everywhere should make harnessing the power of digital technology a top priority. On the supply side, cultivating local ecosystems with tech start-ups, universities, and companies, and developing talent able to code or manage big data can give birth to a new generation of business globally. Coupled with new technologies around manufacturing such as 3D printing, AI, and robotic automation, these shifts eventually have a potency to disrupt the "distance increases costs" conundrum.

Pindar Wong, chair of VeriFi and the chief architect of BRBC, believes that *push-based* supply chains—often driven by seasonal forecasts based on aggregate demand—and the existing trade governance provided under the World Trade Organization, may be unable to handle the evolutionary complexity of digitally designed manufacturing and trading processes. To prepare for this complexity, Wong suggested that we need to pivot to *demand chains* that are *pull-based*— that is, driven by real-time forecasts based on daily consumption at the store level—and evolve a multistakeholder governance model, just as the stewards of the Internet did.[396]

Creating a process for finding new markets is altogether different from developing a new product or service; it requires convincing governments, industry, and other constituencies to see the future in a different light. The effects can be far-reaching, as such ideas are capable of taking on lives of their own.

HOW IS BELT AND ROAD BLOCKCHAIN CONSORTIUM SEEKING A SOLUTION?

How does blockchain solve the "distance equals cost" conundrum? Because it enables digital identities for entities (i.e., people, businesses, governments, and both physical and digital assets) and supports single payments systems, coordination of tax issues, data privacy, and integrated logistics, it significantly reduces the cost of authenticating the transactions. Instead, flow of information will allow for real-time interventions—legally and otherwise—rather than retrospectively, resulting in enhanced trust.

Instead of working within the confines of competition, this ambitious cohort seeks to systematically dissect norms and create layers of legal, identity, and governance protocols by looking across the conventionally defined boundaries of competition—across industries, across strategic groups, across the functional-emotional orientation of an industry, and even across time.

Under the consortium's motto of "Public Governance, Private Business," the BRBC's designers are developing the Belt and Road Blockchain by

- "Containerizing risk," whereby parties run their businesses through code in a self-contained and more predictable environment, thus minimizing risk
- "Automating capital," that is, programming capital through smart contracts, in which code governs the flow of capital (e.g., automatically paying suppliers upon the delivery and verification of goods), thereby minimizing human intervention and other exigencies. ·

With such complex workings and the need to be realistic about achievements, development moves at a pace with which each member is comfortable.

The overall desired goal is to deploy a different kind of infrastructure that can achieve exponential efficiencies over marginal efficiencies. The design goals include an ambitious new capital accounting model that supports financial stability, human success, social trust, natural resources, and ability to monetize data for everyone.

When in operation, BRBC would challenge the concepts of small-volume manufacturing by creating a new architecture that would stand the test of time. With remote sensors associating factory emissions data with a factory's identity, it could open up avenues for green financing, that is, "the financing of investments that generate environmental benefits as part of the broader strategy to achieve inclusive, resilient, and sustainable development."[397]

Such an architecture could also push for elaborate measures on energy conservation with bullish growth and create a circular economy, described by the nonprofit Waste and Resources Action Programme as "an alternative to a traditional linear economy (make, use, dispose) in which we keep resources in use for as long as possible, extract the maximum value from them while in use, then recover and regenerate products and materials at the end of each service life."[398]

For the BRBC, success would imply functionality of the platform taking precedence over politics. A platform that allows for arbitration, IP protection, and trade, calling for cooperation, and looking beyond geopolitics. Monetizing the intellectual property used to assemble products and services, on demand, for the "Just Click It" economy is the transformative design goal.

THE BRBC MODEL FOR SOLVING BIG GLOBAL CHALLENGES

WHY USE THE CONSORTIUM MODEL?

Global consortia are run like cooperatives, with equity and interests that work toward a mutually beneficial goal. According to Deloitte, over 40 consortia have formed globally to explore DLT and blockchain in financial services, healthcare, and energy, to name a few areas of interest.[399]

Belt and Road now spans over 130 economies, the breadth of which makes it extremely complex from an infrastructure and global supply-chain perspective.[400] BRBC's participants represent strategic partners across the value chain such as liquidity providers, strategic consulting firms, regulators, global supply-chain experts, and so forth. These participants with different business incentives are aligned on exploring the premise that institutional trust may diminish over the years as DLT becomes more prevalent in establishing proof of work as a trust mechanism.

The consortium participants must also carefully represent their regulatory compliance, which the BRBC would also need to meet, especially those regulations relating to IP protection.

The Belt and Road Initiative aims to connect Asia, Europe, and Africa along five routes. The Silk Road Economic Belt focuses on:

- Linking China to Europe through Central Asia and Russia

- Connecting China with the Middle East through Central Asia
- Bringing together China and Southeast Asia, South Asia, and the Indian Ocean.

Meanwhile, the 21st Century Maritime Silk Road focuses on using Chinese coastal ports to:

- Link China with Europe through the South China Sea and Indian Ocean
- Connect China with the South Pacific Ocean through the South China Sea.

Consortia make sense because the success of DLT requires significant levels of market presence, market participation, collaboration, and investment.

The consortium is less about a technology solution or a particular business model. It is more about how companies, which have not been able to trust each other in the past, can come together and collaborate and share information. The trust shifts to the shared ledger/technology solution. The participants just need to have similar incentives in terms of:

- The mix of confidentiality and transparency (as captured in the design choices and operating rules for the shared ledger platform)
- Functionality and processes
- The approach to governance
- A shared view of regulation and compliance

A consortium model that uses blockchain to establish trust among parties is a renewed system in a digital world. It allows participants to collaborate and share information in a way that has not been possible before.

We have seen the rise of consortia across sectors to understand better the use of such complex systems, from options like Ethereum and *distributed autonomous communities* (DACs) to hybrids like the modular Hyperledger (Fabric) and private blockchains such as

R3 Corda, Taiwan's Amis fintech platform, and the Clearmatics utility settlement coin. Many of these private models rely heavily on industry input and engagement.

If organizations use a public model, then they need not pay to join. If they use a consortium model, then they may need to pay a fee. For example, as of May 2018, member companies of the Linux Foundation pay an additional $250,000 for premier status in the foundation's Hyperledger project. For general status in the Hyperledger project, companies pay fees on a sliding scale based on their size: firms with fewer than 50 employees pay $5,000 to join Hyperledger and another $5,000 to join the Linux Foundation, whereas firms with more than 5,000 employees pay $50,000 to join Hyperledger and another $20,000 to join the foundation. Linux may waive fees for select government bodies, nonprofits, and open source ventures.[401] Companies of all shapes and sizes can join. The private model is more expensive and exclusive. Incidentally, companies like R3 are also participants in and contributors to Hyperledger through one of its main projects, Fabric.[402]

All of these models are trending toward open sourcing their code to allow developers to build on top of their platforms and form communities around the technology. The DACs are truly a new business model as they are building decentralized companies in which the network participants are part owners of the company. Centralized companies will go away and the projects are creating their own economic ecosystems. Many of these projects are raising money through ICOs and those who invest get "app coins" are owners and users of the network.[403] These are essentially decentralized software protocols that are "disrupting the disruptors."[404]

Developing the consortium beyond that of selecting a technology platform requires a sure vision of the consortium's role, its governance framework, and operational rules. The framework should be acceptable to all parties concerned.

In setting up governance structure for the consortium, an agreed group of founding members was established at launch in September 2017. These members are responsible for definitions, implementation, fostering collaboration, and providing oversight for self-governed working groups. The agenda also includes establishing the rules of an alternative dispute resolution process, a patent nonaggression pact, and oversight of their enforcement.[405]

WHAT GIVES HONG KONG ITS COMPETITIVE ADVANTAGE?

Hong Kong became part of the People's Republic of China (PRC) in 1997. Hong Kong preserved its free-enterprise economy under the 1984 Sino-British Joint Declaration on the transfer of Hong Kong's sovereignty to China. As a part of the Declaration, the PRC guaranteed that it would preserve Hong Kong's capitalist economy and its social and political system for at least fifty years.

Under the "one country, two systems" principle, Hong Kong enjoys a double advantage: Hong Kong's proximity to China ensures goods and services can enter the mainland market with preferential treatment under the Mainland and Hong Kong Closer Economic Partnership Agreement (CEPA). The two-systems advantage allows Hong Kong to retain its internationally compliant civil and political, economic, social, and cultural systems.

Strategically situated in the heart of the Asia Pacific region, with well-established land, air, and sea transport networks, Hong Kong is connected to half of the world's population within a five-hour flying time.

Conducive business environment

According to *Doing Business 2017*, Hong Kong ranks fourth out of 190 countries in business climate.[406] Hong Kong was the fourth-largest recipient of *foreign direct investment* (FDI) in the world in 2016, behind the United States, the United Kingdom, and China, according to the "2017 World Investment Report."[407] Furthermore, it is also the 11th supplier of FDI flows in the world. Hong Kong is one of nine developing countries listed in the twenty largest economies in the world.

In several dimensions, its position has actually been consolidated, not eroded, in recent years. Hong Kong has proved to be more reliable than the Mainland as a source of equity financing. Since 2012, Chinese companies have raised $43 billion in initial public offerings in the Hong Kong market, versus just $25 billion on mainland exchanges, according to Dealogic.[408] More than anywhere else in the world, Hong Kong has also provided Chinese companies with access to global capital markets for bond and loan financing. What is more, Hong Kong is the key hub for investment in and out of China. It accounted for two-thirds of FDI into China last year, up from 30 percent in 2005.[409]

Although much of this money is simply passing through Hong Kong, foreign companies also use the city as their staging post for investing in China as it offers them something that no mainland city does: a stable investment environment, protected by fair, transparent courts that enforce long-established rule of law.

Hong Kong has one of the most tax-friendly economies in the world, according to PricewaterhouseCoopers' *Paying Taxes 2016* study of 189 economies.[410] It has dramatically increased its spend over the years to retrain its workforce in information technology services. It has government-led programs such as Hong Kong Science and Technology Park's incubator, which provides subsidized office space, consultancy services, investment matching, and a small financial aid package to support R&D. The Design Incubation Programme (DIP) provides office space for design tenants and other professional support, and Cyberport helps creative digital media SMEs and start-ups to realize their ideas and build their business.

Strong services sector

Limited land and cost of real estate inhibits the presence of a large manufacturing economy; instead, Hong Kong focuses on the necessary activities for the re-export of goods produced by Hong Kong enterprises in China. The service sector has and continues to be dominant in Hong Kong and forms almost 93 percent of gross domestic product. Being the largest economic sector even prior to 1997, Hong Kong's service sector has since grown significantly in the fields of trade and transportation.

Hong Kong's considerable investment in the development of human resources can greatly work to its advantage in an increasingly digital economy. There are more than 300,000 SMEs in Hong Kong that make up 98 percent of the city's business, employing almost 50 percent of the private-sector workforce.

Innovation in emerging technologies is an opportunity for these small enterprises to improve productivity, collaborate, and expand their reach through e-commerce, potentially turning some of them into global players. These enterprises in mainland China are seen as competitors but also as opportunities because of Hong Kong's privileged relationship with China.

Electronic Transactions Ordinance

One piece of legislation in Hong Kong that allows for transitioning from physical to digital trade is the Electronic Transactions Ordinance (ETO).[411] To provide a clear legal framework for the conduct of e-business in the Hong Kong Special Administrative Region (SAR), the ETO was enacted in January 2000 and updated in June 2004. In general, the ETO is to

- Accord electronic record and electronic signature the same legal status as that of their paper-based counterparts.
- Establish a voluntary recognition scheme for certification authorities to enhance public confidence in electronic transactions.

Certification authorities (CAs) issue *digital certificates*, that is, "veri-fiable small data files that contain identity credentials to help websites, people, and devices represent their authentic online identity."[412] They are a form of electronic record that guarantees the identities of parties conducting electronic transactions. CAs also create processes for digi-tally recognizing people, machines, and businesses.[413] A commercially run CA can apply to the government chief information officer to become a recognized CA on a voluntary basis. Recognition will be granted only to those certification authorities and digital certificates that have reached a standard acceptable to the government.

Legal recognition of electronic signatures, backed by digital certif-icates, opens up newer avenues of building and enforcing trust. The crux of identity on blockchain platforms could be based on a dual-factor identification protocol with a public and a private passkey. Every authorization would be tantamount to a digital consent, which could hold legal validity in the eyes of law. This could also hasten the speed of moving transactions along the value chain and reduce the exces-sive need for audits.

"Anything in the world that has a label or a brand, or an IP address—there has to be legal arbitration rules to back those. We need to define relationship between nodes and they are working on how to make certification authority powerful with enforceable authority," said Eva Chan, vice chairperson, Hong Kong Public Key Infrastructure Forum, and chairperson of the Smart City Industrial Committee, Chinese Manufacturers' Association of Hong Kong.[414]

By providing legal certainty in mapping blockchain wallet addresses to corporations, with the blockchain itself providing evidence for efficient dispute resolution, Hong Kong will export its entrepreneurial way of life and its efficient way of doing business, said Pindar Wong of the Belt and Road Blockchain Consortium.[415]

Powered by the digital Belt and Road Blockchain and under Hong Kong's ETO, the consortium facilitates transnational digiti-zation of trade facilitation and financial services by reducing the cost of resolving cross-border *electronic identity* (E-ID) disputes along the Belt and Road.

WHY IS DIGITAL IDENTITY SO CRITICAL?

Which comes first, trust or money? What does it take to create this trust to facilitate this M2M economy? What then, can be an equation to describe the factories of the future? This formula allows businesses to insure, commission, track, trace, and trade IP:

KYC (Know your customer) + KYM (Know your machine)
= KYIP (Know your intellectual property).

This consortium can also help reduce costs of these organizations' operational processes, not just KYC but KYM (know your machine). According to Thomson Reuters, an average bank spends £40 million a year on KYC compliance; and some banks spend up to £300 million annually on KYC compliance and *customer due diligence* (CDD).[416] This will require a digital identity structure on the blockchain that all consortium members agree on and can extend to not only individuals but also businesses (KYB—*know your business*).

Hongkong Post: Solving for identity

The Hongkong Post plays an important role around creating frameworks to solve for identity (KYC, KYB, and KYM). In 2000, it established a public key infrastructure and began acting as the first public CA in Hong Kong, issuing "digital certificates, namely Hongkong Post e-Certs, to individuals and businesses to facilitate the identity verification of the subscribers over the Internet."[417] Hongkong Post is well connected: it is a member of the Asian-Pacific Postal Union, the Asia Pacific Post Cooperative, and the Universal Postal Union.[418] As a master connector, it can help member governments to set up their own CAs according to international standards. It wants to create visibility around information, money, and logistics flow, and to lower the risk of cross-border trade.

The Hongkong Post has 125 post offices.[419] When patrons want to apply for digital identity, they physically visit one of seven designated post offices to submit their e-Cert paperwork and receive an authenticated and encrypted e-Cert in the form of a smart ID card, file card, file USB, or token.[420] The role of the CA will also include generating the dual-factor authentications. Organizations can adopt similar processes along the belt, making mutual recognitions enforceable by law. For someone from China visiting Hong Kong, the CA can use the blockchain-based IDs to verify the visitor's credentials.

Public CAs like Hongkong Post are those that have established a trusted relationship with existing governments. Hong Kong has taken nearly twenty years to establish this trust and does not necessarily need to throw it away.

InvestHK: Fundraising and advocating for governance protocols

BRBC sees the future as an internet of blockchains. Why will Iran or Afghanistan accept an ID from someone else? For this blockchain of blockchains to run, we need common standards, governance protocols. As the FDI arm of the Hong Kong government, investHK plays the role of an advocate as well as a fundraiser to build the momentum around the project.

According to Charles D'Haussy, head of fintech at InvestHK, the department of the Hong Kong SAR Government responsible for FDI, "What the BRBC needs next is a road show—to build a blockchain protocol. You put assets publicly available so that people can participate."[421]

HSBC: "Knowing your customer" as a means of lowering risk

With international trade, the bank is undertaking credit risk exposure. The ability to establish trust collectively is important. This also helps to reduce the risk, as everyone can trust the same information. With trade finance solutions, we expect systems around the world to become active participants in exchanging information. HSBC is supporting the Global Trade Connectivity Network via the Hong Kong Monetary Authority and the Monetary Authority of Singapore.[422] Banks were the previous identity anchors in the global trade system and will continue to play a role. However, the ability to establish counterparty identity is now an open proposition.

Banks have had to forego relationships because of not knowing who they are dealing with. The consortium has the value proposition that the only problem to focus on is that of identity. For this consortium to work, the underpinning action will be collaboration across the value chain. The value then becomes integrated rather than isolated.

WHAT IS BRBC GOVERNANCE?

The founding members and participation members joined the BRBC with different benefits or tiers of benefits based on the consortium agreement's operating rules, which the governance board will determine. These rules govern legal and structural decisions of the consortium, as well as decisions to be implemented on the shared ledger based on a specific technology.[423]

All participants need to commit to complying with the operating rules of the consortium. The participants agree to use the BRBC blockchain as evidence to resolve ID disputes and changes of state in legal liability. Moreover, the cost of joining the consortium is the cost of KYC according to the consortium's criteria.

The smart-contract system and the rules engine help ensure consistency between real-world contracts and smart contracts in both private and public models because "code is king" does not hold up. In the Internet of Agreements, when technologists deliver machine-to-machine handling of agreements to a high enough standard, it will revolutionize business and international cooperation.[424] The blockchain is the most likely platform to give rise to that world. It is the world that the smart-contract ecosystem will create as it matures.

As part of the Smart Contracts Initiative, the consortium's founder Pindar Wong called for participation in an ICANN-like body to facilitate the digitization of trade among the 130-plus Belt and Road economies.[425] This body meets in Hong Kong on the last Thursday of each month.

A third of the Belt and Road economies adhere to the Muslim faith—and China is home to 26 million Muslims—and so the BRBC is looking to provide Sharia-compliant provenance for the trading of halal-products along the Belt and Road.[426] For example, an open halal blockchain would provide a reliable and verifiable record of food at every point in the halal process, from point of origin to point of consumption.[427] Such a supply chain would also require Sharia-compliant financing techniques, specifically a blockchain that implemented *mudaraba*, *musharaka*, *murabaha*, *ijara*, *istisna'a*, and *salam* contracts and instruments.[428]

Additionally, the consortium will assist with digital green finance to support greening of the Belt and Road Initiative. Ma Jun, chief economist at the People's Bank of China Research Bureau, said that the use of green financing in this massive undertaking "was in the long-term interests of Chinese investment institutions and much-needed for sustainable development."[429]

The consortium will also provide input to the development of a Belt and Road trade arbitration framework. For trade that originates from or terminates in one of the Belt and Road economies, the consortium is technically neutral but develops buy-side business standards for electronic-ID disputed resolution processes and standardized interoperable smart-contract standards that increase trust and transparency in cross-border trade.

While there are clear efficiency benefits and cost savings that shared ledgers can provide through collaboration and more effective information sharing, this does not mean that competitive and antitrust risks will disappear. There is no reason why consortium activity on a private shared ledger would be exempt from these laws.

WHICH CORE COMPETENCIES DOES EACH STAKEHOLDER BRING TO THE TABLE?

SCMO: Representing views of trade, supply chain, and logistics

Supply Chain Management Outsource (SCMO) is a logistics consultancy headquartered in Samoa with 40 offices in 25 countries, a number of which are Belt and Road participants. With Hong Kong as a trading hub and SCMO as an adviser to the best in logistics business, SCMO wanted to represent its stakeholders while the base architecture is in development.

According to SCMO, "We are currently in the IoT era, which will be followed by the 'sharing economy' era, and then by the AI era."[430] BRBC is fascinating because it is redrawing the global economy. A government could look at creating a single trade window system, but cheating is a common issue. The BRBC is looking at deploying blockchain as an ecosystem and developing the concept platform that sustains that ecosystem in a trustworthy manner.

Nicolas De Loisy, president of SCMO, said, "Blockchain cannot digitize the world economy. It will, however, be a critical part of the sharing economy."[431] At present, SCMO is evaluating IoT to take information from the physical to the virtual world. Members of its team attended the "Blockchain in Shipping and Logistics" event organized by Chain of Things as part of Hong Kong Maritime Week in 2017.[432] Blockchain comes in to ensure the identity of things, the interoperability of data, and the security of both.[433]

GS1: Bringing its expertise to defining industry standards

Founded in 1973, Global Specifications 1 (GS1) is a nonprofit international organization comprised of members who collaborate on the governance of global standards for supply chains.[434] Most people know it for the barcode, also known as the *universal product code* (UPC), a machine-readable pattern of parallel lines of various widths printed on a product package. Members of supply chains use them to encode information such as product numbers, serial numbers, and batch numbers.

GS1 is the gold standard of data for the retail segment. GS1 is launching a global data cloud, which will be able to combine data from its Global Electronic Party Information Registry, its Global Data Synchronization Network, and catalogues maintained by local offices.[435]

China has 50 million pieces of information per day stored locally. The global initiative is to develop a cloud that holds all pieces of information together (over 100 million daily). Currently, participants cannot certify that information. Going forward, whenever end users want more information, they will be able to access it through the barcode and authenticate it. "We are developing our own standards pool—how can you create identifiers to have some indication online and most of it offline," said Dr. Stephen Lam, chief operating officer, GS1 Hong Kong.[436]

GS1 wants to be an enabler for provenance around international trade. The BRBC decided to work pragmatically with GS1 rather than create a competing standard. BRBC involves 73 countries, 55 of which have GS1 offices. BRBC wants to enable business entities to conduct trade using GS1 standards. With such GS1 and ISO open standards as Electronic Product Code Information Services and Core Business Vocabulary, members of a consortium could structure the data stored on or referenced by a distributed ledger network so that they could share information securely and track individual parts or items throughout a supply chain.

According to Robert Beideman, vice president of retail at GS1, "What attracts many organizations to blockchain technology is the possibility of sharing data across corporate boundaries while maintaining a high degree of rigor and accuracy."[437] The BRBC is in a position to refer, create, and use standards for blockchain applications. All the transactional data are secured and encrypted, and no one can use the information for other purposes.

As a new revenue strategy, members can hash their intellectual property (such as a design, patentable, or copyrightable material) onto the blockchain and then monetize it immediately or at a later date by licensing it. They need not build supply-chain capabilities or logistics to leverage their IP. With this strategy, they can focus on leveraging existing capabilities.

Supply chains are opaque. Even in the current system, participants encrypt data unless they have the authority to make them transparent. The decision comes down to what information is on the blockchain. Public blockchains may not be viable. To succeed, many parties need to come together to set the protocols. On the e-commerce side, users will be able to order customized items. E-commerce with customization is picking up. To ensure instant gratification, producers need it to keep the consumer posted at every step of the way.

Cyberport: Engaging players with the platform

Hong Kong Cyberport Management Company (Cyberport) harbors around 1,000 digital tech companies within the innovative digital community. The clusters of digital technology that it focuses on range from fintech, e-commerce, AI, and IoT; and it predicts that blockchain as an underpinning technology will hold them all together. After the initial tech workshops, Cyberport's leaders are trying to help its teams with scaling operations. Cyberport has an incubation program with start-ups to provide the infrastructure to build the

blockchain platform and its components. Of the future of blockchain and trade, Herman Lam, former CEO of Cyberport, said, "Trade can be complex, but some functions of blockchain can be decompressed. The challenge lies in engaging the industry players, not in code."[438]

KPMG: Preparing for the future of audits and consulting

KPMG and other audit firms are investing in blockchain capabilities. From an audit perspective, they foresee value arising from visibility of earlier transactions and digital audit trails to provide assurance. With the onset of smart contracts, they also envision new auditor teams who can read and write legal code. These capabilities could also move the needle for routine business streams. Tax services audits could move toward real-time revenue recognition.

KEY TAKEAWAYS IN LARGE-SCALE PROJECT MANAGEMENT

- **Identify the most compelling common interests and shared goal.** Diversity of interests can be challenging for a consortium. However, a healthy representation of public and private participants is also key to developing a strong proof of concept, especially as we think about global supply chains. While individual incentives can differ, members must have a common mandate and agree on the consortium's primary objective.

- **Cultivate government representation.** Government representation can help drive policy change and create an environment for economic cooperation. For Belt and Road consortia to succeed, government representation is almost of necessity, as much of technology infrastructure will require government approval and governance. We cannot undermine the importance of cybersecurity implications for an open trade system.

- **Create a structure for stewardship.** The governance structure continues to remain the most essential aspect of the consortium. The BRBC depends on the progress made by the Belt and Road Initiative. However, globally, governments and businesses can learn from the BRBC to develop their digital trade platforms.

- **Develop training programs for monitoring and evaluation.** The Belt and Road Initiative is both the most expensive global infrastructure project and China's most ambitious global policy initiative.[439] China may not be the only player seeking to create global connectivity. Real-time monitoring and evaluation of projects at scale can be complex. We need to develop a new stream of education for a variety of roles (e.g., audit, project management).

- **Be mindful of geopolitical ties.** Geopolitical affiliations often drive global trade. Breakdown of international trust and cybersecurity threats may have implications for trust among participants from the 130-plus nation states. The current US president has a different perspective on the trade deals that his predecessors were pursuing, and the Brexit vote has challenged Great Britain to evolve its trade agreements with the European Union and the rest of the world.

- **Factor in political risk and impact over time.**
Belt and Road will have implications for industries
and public policy for years to come. Regime
change and political stability within the 130 or so
countries add another layer of risk and complexity
for implementation. While political risk is inherent
for Belt and Road and hard to predict, the economic
incentives will likely trump political challenges in
the long term. China's ambitious economic vision
is gaining momentum and will likely top the trade
agenda for most countries over the next 10 years.

ACRONYMS AND ABBREVIATIONS

3D printer, general-purpose additive manufacturing device

ACE, Automated Commercial Environment

ADM, aircraft demolition management

AI, artificial intelligence

AIS, automatic information service

AM, additive manufacturing

AML, anti-money laundering

AMS, aircraft maintenance systems

AOC, airline operations center

API, application programming interface

API/PNR, advance passenger information/passenger name records

APIS, Advance Passenger Information System

B2B, business-to-business

B2C, business-to-consumer

BRBC, Belt and Road Blockchain Consortium

BRI, Blockchain Research Institute

CA, certification authority

CAD, computer-aided design

CBP, US Customs and Border Protection

CBV, Core Business Vocabulary

CDC, Centers for Disease Control and Prevention

CDD, customer due diligence

CEPA, Mainland and Hong Kong Closer Economic Partnership Agreement

CPS, cyber-physical systems

C-TPAT, Customs-Trade Partnership Against Terrorism

DAG, directed acyclic graph

Dapp, decentralized application

DARPA, US Defense Advanced Research Projects Agency

DAVN, decentralized autonomous value network

DHS, US Department of Homeland Security

DLT, distributed ledger technology

DOD, US Department of Defense

DPD, digital product definition

EHR, electronic historical record (aviation)

E-ID, electronic identity

EPCIS, Electronic Product Code Information Services

ERP, enterprise resource planning

ESB, enterprise service bus

ETO, Hong Kong Electronic Transactions Ordinance

FAST, Free and Secure Trade for Commercial Vehicles

FDI, foreign direct investment

GAO, US Government Accountability Office

GDPR, general data privacy regulation (Europe)

GS1, Global Specifications 1 (standards)

GTIN, Global Trade Identification Number (standards)

GUID, Globally Unique Identification Number

HKMA, Hong Kong Monetary Authority

IaaS, infrastructure-as-a-service

ICO, initial coin offering aka token offering

IDSA, Industrial Data Space Association

IIoT, industrial Internet of Things

IoT, Internet of Things

IP, intellectual property

ISCRM, International Supply Chain Reference Model

IT, information technology

JIT, just-in-time

KP, Kimberley Process (diamonds)

KPI, key performance indicator

KYB, know your business

KYC, know your customer

KYIP, know your intellectual property

KYM, know your machine

M2M, machine-to-machine

MES, manufacturing execution system

MOM, manufacturing operations management

MRO, maintenance, repair, and overhaul (aviation)

MSLA, master service level agreement

MVE, minimum viable ecosystem

MVP, minimum viable product

NAFTA, North American Free Trade Agreement

NFL, National Football League (American football)

NIST, National Institute of Standards and Technology

NOE, notice of escape

OEM, original equipment manufacturer

OTIF, on time in full

OUOD, one up, one down (food chain)

P&L, profit and loss statement

PCS, port community systems

PII, personally identifiable information

PLM, product life-cycle management

PO, purchase order

POC, proof of concept

QR code, quick response code

RFID, radio frequency identification

RFP, request for proposal

RFQ, request for quotation

ROA, return on asset

ROI, return on investment

SaaS, software-as-a-service

SAMPL, secure additive manufacturing platform

SAR, Hong Kong Special Administrative Region

SENTRI, Secure Electronic Network for Travelers Rapid Inspection

sGTIN, serialized Global Trade Identification Number (GTIN)

SME, small and medium-sized enterprise

SWIFT, Society for Worldwide Interbank Financial Telecommunication

TCP/IP, transmission control protocol/Internet protocol

TMS, transportation management system

TPP, Trans-Pacific Partnership

TQM, Total Quality Management

UCP, Uniform Customs and Practice for Documentary Credits

UHD, ultra-high-definition

UID, unique identification numbers (US Department of Defense)

UN/CEFACT, United Nations Centre for Trade Facilitation and Electronic Business

UPC, universal product code

VMI, vendor-managed inventory

WTO, World Trade Organization

XRF, X-ray fluorescence

zk-SNARK, zero knowledge Succinct Noninteractive ARgument of Knowledge

ACKNOWLEDGMENTS

We thank the Blockchain Research Institute's members for their ongoing participation: Accenture, Aon, Bank of Canada, Bell Canada, BioLife, BPC Banking Technologies, Brightline (a Project Management Institute initiative), Canada Health Infoway, Canadian Imperial Bank of Commerce, Capgemini, Centrica, Cimcorp, Cisco Systems Inc., City of Toronto, the Coca-Cola Company, Deloitte, Delta Air Lines Inc., Depository Trust & Clearing Corporation, ExxonMobil Global Service Company, FedEx Corporate Services, Fujitsu, Government of Ontario, Gowling WLG, Huobi, IBM, ICICI Bank, INSEAD, Institute on Governance, Interac, Intuit, ISED Canada, JumpStart, KPMG, Loblaw Companies, Manulife, Microsoft, MKS (Switzerland) SA, Moog, Nasdaq, Navigator, Ontario Ministry of Health and Long-Term Care, Orange, PepsiCo, Philip Morris International Management, PNC Bank, Procter & Gamble, Raymond Chabot Grant Thornton, Reliance Industries, Revenu Québec, Salesforce, SAP SE, Standard Bank, Sun Life Financial, Tata Consultancy Services, Teck Resources, TELUS, Tencent, Thomson Reuters, TMX Group, University of Arkansas, University Health Network, University of Texas-Dallas, and WISeKey.

We are grateful for our pioneer members: Access Copyright, Aion, Artlery, Attest, Blockchain Guru, Bloq, CarbonX, Cosmos, Decentral Inc., EVRYTHNG, Huobi, Jumpstart, Liechtenstein Cryptoassets Exchange, LongHash, Matic, Medicalchain, Navigator Ltd., NEM Foundation, Numeracle, Ownum, Paycase Financial, PermianChain Technologies Inc., Polymath, SGInnovate, Slant AG, SpaceChain, Stride Africa, Sweetbridge, Telos Foundation, Veriphi, and YouBase.

Thanks, too, to our affiliate organizations: Alastria, Blockchain in Transport Alliance, Blockchain Research Institute Nanjing,

Chamber of Digital Commerce, Coalition of Automated Legal Applications, Enterprise Ethereum Alliance, Healthcare Information and Management Systems Society, Hyperledger hosted by The Linux Foundation, and Illinois Chamber of Commerce.

Finally, we thank Hilary Carter for assembling such an expert group of blockchain researchers and overseeing the research pipeline in addition to her role as managing director. We also thank Kirsten D. Sandberg for creating a compelling manuscript out of this important set of research projects. She prepared and sequenced the chapters so that each built upon and reinforced the key ideas. It was a big project, one for which Kirsten has both the vision and the perseverance required.

ABOUT THE BLOCKCHAIN RESEARCH INSTITUTE

Co-founded in 2017 by Don and Alex Tapscott, the Blockchain Research Institute is an independent, global think tank established to help realize the new promise of the digital economy. For several years now, we have been investigating the transformative and disruptive potential of blockchain technology on business, government, and society.

Our syndicated research program, which is funded by major corporations and government agencies, aims to fill a large gap in the global understanding of blockchain protocols, applications, and ecosystems, and their strategic implications for enterprise leaders, supply chains, and industries. Deliverables include lighthouse cases, big idea white papers, research briefs, roundtable reports, infographics, videos, and webinars.

Our global team of blockchain experts is dedicated to exploring, understanding, documenting, and informing leaders about the market opportunities and implementation challenges of this nascent technology. Research areas include financial services, manufacturing, retail, energy and resources, technology, media, telecommunications, healthcare, and government as well as the management of organizations, the transformation of the corporation, and the regulation of innovation. We also explore blockchain's potential role in the Internet of Things, robotics and autonomous machines, artificial intelligence and machine learning, and other emerging technologies.

Our findings are initially proprietary to our members and are ultimately released under a Creative Commons license to help achieve our mission. To find out more, please visit **www.blockchainresearchinstitute.org**.

ABOUT THE CONTRIBUTORS

LOUISA BAI

Louisa Bai is a senior manager in Deloitte's Technology Consulting practice and is leading the firm's market development and partnerships in the blockchain ecosystem. She leads a group of strategy specialists engaged in assisting clients to understand and apply blockchain and DLT concepts to their business models, technology infrastructure, and operating processes.

KSHITISH BALHOTRA

Kshitish Balhotra is a manager in the Canadian consulting practice at Deloitte. He leads the Program Delivery for Blockchain for Deloitte Canada. Kshitish has over 11 years of experience in the financial services industry and has primarily been engaged on both functional and technical projects in capital markets space. In addition to blockchain, he also has expertise in SWIFT payments, regulatory frameworks and technology, front and middle office systems (trading and reconciliation), and mergers and acquisitions. He enjoys working in innovative, complex, and demanding environments.

NOLAN BAUERLE

Nolan Bauerle is the director of research at Manhattan-based *CoinDesk*. His work with bitcoin and blockchain technology began in 2013 with a long-term study of cryptocurrencies for the Canadian Senate Banking Committee where he dreamed up a fun publicity stunt: as the report was tabled in parliament, it was also simultaneously hashed into the Bitcoin blockchain. This was perhaps the first government usage of the blockchain for something other than buying or selling bitcoin. Over the last few years, Nolan's work has involved research and writing deep dives into tokens, supply chains, trade finance, insurance, Internet of Things, cryptography, privacy, and confidentiality.

SOUMAK CHATTERJEE

Soumak Chatterjee is a partner in Deloitte's Technology Consulting practice. He leads Deloitte's payments and blockchain team in Canada. Soumak is focused on assisting clients in driving business value through new disruptive products, services, and partnerships—leveraging his deep expertise at the intersection of innovation, business, and technology from strategy to execution.

ALAN COHN

Alan D. Cohn is an attorney and consultant in Washington, DC. He is co-chair of the Blockchain and Digital Currency practice at Steptoe & Johnson LLP, and the principal of ADC/Strategy.Works LLC, an independent consulting firm. Alan previously served as assistant secretary for strategy, planning, analysis, and risk at the Department of Homeland Security, and in similar policy and strategy roles at DHS for nine years. Alan is counsel to the Blockchain Alliance, a nonprofit organization that creates a forum for bitcoin and blockchain companies to engage with law enforcement and regulatory agencies. He is also an adviser to several blockchain technology companies. Alan is an adjunct professor at Georgetown University Law Center and the co-chair of the World Economic Forum's Global Future Council on Cybersecurity.

CARA ENGELBRECHT

Cara Englebrecht is an analyst in the Canadian Technology Consulting practice at Deloitte. She focuses on assisting clients with large-scale delivery and program management in the financial services space. Prior to joining Deloitte, Cara authored an undergraduate thesis paper,

"Empirical Prediction of Wind Farm Power Output Using Historical Data," which summarized and tested a method of estimating power output using Markov theory.

STEFAN HOPF

Dr. Stefan Hopf studied management at Ludwig-Maximilians-University in Munich (LMU), the University of Cape Town, and Columbia University of New York. In addition to various consulting and research activities in the public and private sector, he completed a postgraduate program in technology management at the Center for Digital Technology and Management. As research assistant at the LMU Research Center for Information, Organization, and Management, he spent a semester at the UC Berkeley School of Information and graduated with a Master of Business Research at LMU. After completing his doctorate in 2016, he started working as a senior consultant at The Nunatak Group—a Munich-based digital-strategy boutique. He has previously worked for Airbus on a blockchain market study. He currently works in strategy and corporate development, electronics, and automated driving at the BMW Group. Otherwise, he has no affiliation with or ownership stake in any other company discussed in his chapter.

RESHMA KAMATH

Reshma Kamath is a law graduate of Northwestern University Pritzker School of Law, Class of 2017, and the inaugural NextGen fellow at the American Bar Association. She pursued a graduate degree in international studies, specializing in international cooperation, under the guidance of world-class faculty and students at Seoul National University. She obtained a dual undergraduate degree in psychology and global studies at San Jose State University and spent her last undergraduate year at the University of KwaZulu-Natal's Howard Campus in South Africa. Reshma published "Blockchain for Women: Next Generation for Sustainable Development Goal 5" in

Asian Development Perspectives (formerly *Journal of Poverty Alleviation and International Development*). She has spoken at and moderated several events such as "Women on the Block" held in New York, the Emerging Technologies Symposium hosted by Freeborn and Peters LLP, and the Chicago Blockchain Project's "Blockchain for Social Good."

HENRY KIM

Dr. Henry Kim is associate professor at Schulich School of Business at York University and co-director of Blockchain Lab. As one of the leading blockchain scholars in Canada, he is engaged in blockchain research projects with the United Nations on cross-border activity, Toronto and Region Conservation Authority on electricity microgrids, the Canadian blockchain start-up Aion Network (formerly Nuco) on AI-based consensus mechanisms, Ontario Ministry of Agriculture on food traceability, and NIST on the manufacturing supply chain. He is co-organizer of University of Toronto's Fields Institute seminar series on blockchain and an adviser on the Government of Canada's white paper on blockchain and digital ledger technologies. He is a scientific adviser on several Canadian blockchain start-ups in the financial services and mining and natural resources industries.

MAREK LASKOWSKI

In 2011, Dr. Marek Laskowski completed his PhD in computer engineering at the University of Manitoba, where he developed a data-driven evidence-based decision support system for healthcare based on emergent AI. Since then, he has been studying the impact of public health intervention strategies within the Canadian population, with the sponsorship of the pharmaceutical industry. Marek teaches data science at the graduate level at the Schulich School of Business at York University where he co-founded the Blockchain Lab. He is a pioneer of on-chain analytics with high-fidelity virtual and augmented reality visualization and knowledge translation. He is a consultant for blockchain start-ups using Hyperledger and Ethereum and is working with NIST on a blockchain standard for digital assets and with UN/CEFACT on cross-border business process standards. His research involves blockchain, decision support systems for healthcare delivery, and population modeling of the effectiveness of such public health interventions as vaccine.

VINEET NARULA

Vineet Narula spent the better part of his 15-year corporate career focused on building operations and developing partnerships for diverse global businesses in retail and healthcare. He is passionate about understanding industry shifts enabled by technology and their impact on the global ecosystem—economic, social, and environmental. His interest in distributed ledger technology peaked while obtaining his MBA at MIT, where he advanced his research on digital transformation—blockchain—of supply chains and additive manufacturing. Vineet is currently a customer success leader responsible for helping to build expert (supply) platform to support Intuit's global ecosystem. He's developing exchange-to-exchange experience for experts with artificial intelligence and machine learning strategies.

PREMA SHRIKRISHNA

Prema Shrikrishna is a blockchain enthusiast. She spent over 13 years building sustainable business operations for Fortune 500 companies such as The Walt Disney Company, ABB, and Vodafone across Asia Pacific markets. She created strategies to address international environmental compliance requirements, built ethical supply chains, and used technology for last-mile innovation. Currently, she works at the World Bank Group's technology innovation lab, where she demonstrates the use of blockchain technology in projects on supply chain, health, agriculture, and trade finance.

VIKAS SINGLA

Vikas Singla is a senior manager in the Canadian consulting practice at Deloitte and leads the Canadian Blockchain team, a group of individuals dedicated to assisting clients in understanding and applying blockchain (or, broadly distributed ledger technology) concepts to their business models, technology infrastructure, and operating processes. He has over nine years of experience and has led multiple blockchain-based experimentation projects.

DON TAPSCOTT

Don Tapscott, CEO of the Tapscott Group and co-founder and executive chairman of the Blockchain Research Institute, is one of the world's leading authorities on the impact of technology on business and society. He has authored 16 books, including *Wikinomics: How Mass Collaboration Changes Everything* (with Anthony Williams), which has been translated into more than 25 languages. Don's most recent book was co-authored with his son, Alex Tapscott, a globally recognized investor, adviser, and speaker on blockchain technology and cryptocurrencies. The paperback edition of *Blockchain Revolution: How the Technology Behind Bitcoin and Other Cryptocurrencies Is Changing the World* was published in June 2018. According to Harvard Business School's Clay Christensen, it is "the book, literally, on how to survive and thrive in this next wave of technology-driven disruption." Don is a member of the Order of Canada and joined Professors Christensen and Michael Porter in the Thinkers50 Hall of Fame, which recognizes the world's most influential management thinkers. He is an adjunct professor at INSEAD and former two-term chancellor of Trent University in Ontario.

ANTHONY D. WILLIAMS

Anthony D. Williams is co-founder and president of the DEEP Centre and an internationally recognized authority on the digital revolution, innovation, and creativity in business and society. He is co-author (with Don Tapscott) of the groundbreaking bestseller, *Wikinomics: How Mass Collaboration Changes Everything*, and its follow-up, *Macrowikinomics: New Solutions for a Connected Planet*. Among other current appointments, Anthony is an expert adviser to the Markle Foundation's Initiative for America's Economic Future, a senior fellow with the Lisbon Council in Brussels and the Institute on Governance in Ottawa, and chief adviser to Brazil's Free Education Project, a national strategy to equip two million young Brazilians with the skills required for a twenty-first-century workforce. His work on technology and innovation has appeared in publications such as the *Huffington Post*, *Harvard Business Review*, and *The Globe and Mail*.

NOTES

1. Don Tapscott, "How the Blockchain Is Changing Money and Business," TED Summit, Banff, June 2016. www.ted.com/talks/don_tapscott_how_the_blockchain_is_changing_money_and_business/transcript. As of 13 Jan. 2020, there were 4.36 million views of this talk.

2. Please see Tom Serres and Bettina Warburg, "Introducing Asset Chains: The Cognitive, Friction-free, and Blockchain-enabled Future of Supply Chains," foreword by Don Tapscott, Blockchain Research Institute, 28 Nov. 2017. www.blockchainresearchinstitute.org/7914-2, accessed 20 Jan. 2020.

3. Bettina Warburg, "How the Blockchain Will Radically Transform the Economy," TED Summit, Banff, June 2016. www.ted.com/talks/bettina_warburg_how_the_blockchain_will_radically_transform_the_economy, as of 13 Jan. 2020.

4. "The Belt and Road Initiative: Country Profiles," HKTDC, Hong Kong Trade Development Council, as of 30 Oct. 2019. china-trade-research.hktdc.com/business-news/article/The-Belt-and-Road-Initiative/The-Belt-and-Road-Initiative-Country-Profiles/obor/en/1/1X000000/1X0A36I0.htm, accessed 30 Oct. 2019.

5. "Integral Study of the Silk Roads: Roads of Dialogue, 1988–1997," *UNESCO Digital Library* (2002): 1–22. United Nations Educational, Scientific, and Cultural Organization, unesdoc.unesco.org/images/0015/001591/159189E.pdf, accessed 24 March 2018.

6. "Trends in World Trade: Looking Back over the Past Ten Years," *World Trade Statistical Review 2017*, World Trade Organization (5 Oct. 2017): 11–12. www.wto.org/english/res_e/statis_e/wts2017_e/WTO_Chapter_02_e.pdf, accessed 24 March 2018.

7. "Trends in World Trade: Looking Back Over the Past Ten Years."

8. Kaustubh Das, "Hyperconvergence Should Bust IT Silos, Not Make New Ones," *Data Center Journal,* 11 Sept. 2017. www.datacenterjournal.com/hyperconvergence-bust-silos-not-make-new-ones, accessed 18 June 2018.

9. To learn more about the concept of the *symphonic enterprise,* see Ken Corless et al., "Tech Trends 2018: The Symphonic Enterprise," ed. Bill Briggs, Deloitte, Deloitte Touche Tohmatsu Ltd., 2018, pp. 12–13. www2.deloitte.com/tr/en/pages/technology-media-and-telecommunications/articles/tech-trends-2018.html, accessed 21 Feb. 2019.

10. Definitions of *smart contract* and *distributed application* are adapted from COALA Blockchain Workshops, "Blockchain Glossary," Version 1.0, Coalition of Automated Legal Applications, 7 Dec. 2015. coala.global/wp-content/uploads/2019/02/COALA-GLOSSARY-DEC-2015.pdf, accessed 23 Feb. 2019.

11. Krishna N. Das, Aditya Kalra, Devidutta Tripathy, and Tom Lasseter, "Eyes Wide Shut: The $1.8 Billion Indian Bank Fraud that Went Unnoticed," *Reuters*, Thomson Reuters, 19 Feb. 2018. www.reuters.com/article/us-punjab-natl-bank-fraud-insight/eyes-wide-shut-the-1-8-billion-indian-bank-fraud-that-went-unnoticed-idUSKCN1G20OZ, accessed 23 Feb. 2019.

12. Bloomberg, "Fraud in US$4 Trillion Trade Finance Turns Banks to Digital Ledger," *The Business Times*, Singapore Press Holdings Ltd., 23 May 2016. www.businesstimes.com.sg/banking-finance/fraud-in-us4t-trade-finance-turns-banks-to-digital-ledger, accessed 24 June 2018.

13. Simon Bowers, "Metals Trader Fraudster Given Extra Seven Years," *The Guardian*, Guardian News & Media Ltd., 24 Feb. 2012. www.theguardian.com/business/2012/feb/24/metals-trader-fraudster-extra-seven-years-prison, accessed 24 June 2018.

14. Marc Auboin and Isabella Blengini, "The Impact of Basel III on Trade Finance: The Potential Unintended Consequences of the Leverage Ratio," Staff Working Paper ERSD-2014-02, Economic Research and Statistics Division, World Trade Organization, 17 Jan. 2014. www.imf.org/external/np/seminars/eng/2014/trade/pdf/auboin.pdf, accessed 10 June 2018.

15. Stefan Dab et al., "Embracing Digital in Trade Finance," Working Paper, Boston Consulting Group, Oct. 2015. www.swift.com/sites/default/files/resources/swift_oursolutions_paper_embracingdigitalintradefinance.pdf, accessed 21 Feb. 2019.

16. David Bischof and Doina Buruiana, eds., "Rethinking Trade & Finance: An ICC Private Sector Development Perspective," International Chamber of Commerce, 2016. cdn.iccwbo.org/content/uploads/sites/3/2016/10/ICC-Global-Trade-and-Finance-Survey-2016.pdf, accessed 10 June 2018.

17. Leslie Wayne, "Boeing Is Delaying Delivery of Its 787," *New York Times*, New York Times Company, 11 Oct. 2007. www.nytimes.com/2007/10/11/business/11boeing.html, accessed 21 Feb. 2019.

18. "Trade Finance and SMEs: Bridging the Gaps in Provision," World Trade Organization, 2016. www.wto.org/english/res_e/booksp_e/tradefinsme_e.pdf, accessed 9 June 2018.

19. "Cash Cows—How Blockchain Is Transforming Trade Finance," Press Release, Barclays, 1 Nov. 2016. www.home.barclays/news/2016/11/how-blockchain-is-transforming-trade-finance.html, accessed 21 Feb. 2019.

20. Patrick Gillespie, "Chipotle Profits Tank after *E. coli* Scare," *CNN*, Turner Broadcasting System, 2 Feb. 2016. money.cnn.com/2016/02/02/investing/chipotle-earnings-e-coli/index.html, accessed 21 Feb. 2019.

21. Anthony Whiteing, "The Future of Sustainable Freight Transport and Logistics," European Parliament, 2010. www.europarl.europa.eu/RegData/etudes/note/join/2010/431578/IPOL-TRAN_NT(2010)431578_EN.pdf, accessed 9 June 2018.

22. Rolf Bax, "Maritime Transport Invoicing & Payment Processing Are Costing the Industry $34.4bn Annually," *ControlPay*, 4 May 2018. www.controlpay.com/blog/current-freight-invoicing-and-payment-processing-are-costing-the-industry-$34.4bn-annualy, accessed 21 Feb. 2019.

23. Natalie Southwick, "Counterfeit Drugs Kills 1 Mn People Annually: Interpol," *InSight Crime*, 24 Oct. 2013. www.insightcrime.org/news/brief/counterfeit-drugs-kill-1-million-annually-interpol, accessed 1 Nov. 2018.

24. Burney Simpson, "Cargo Theft Rising in Canada," *Transport Topics*, 11 July 2018. www.ttnews.com/articles/cargo-theft-rising-canada, accessed 1 Nov. 2018. The amount was reported as CAD 46.2 million; the average exchange rate from USD to CAD in 2017 was 1.297846.

25. "DHL and Accenture Unlock the Power of Blockchain in Logistics," News Release, Accenture, 12 March 2018. newsroom.accenture.com/news/dhl-and-accenture-unlock-the-power-of-blockchain-in-logistics.htm, accessed 1 Nov. 2018.

26. Michael del Castillo, "IBM's Biggest-Ever Blockchain Trade Finance Trial Could Go Global," *CoinDesk*, Digital Currency Group, 8 Feb. 2018. www.coindesk.com/ibms-biggest-ever-blockchain-trade-finance-trial-go-global, accessed 1 Nov. 2018; "IBM Launches Blockchain Initiative with Dubai Gov Agencies," Press Release, IBM Corporation, 7 Feb. 2017. www-03.ibm.com/press/us/en/pressrelease/51541.wss, accessed 26 Feb. 2019.

27. "The OLAF Report 2017," European Anti-Fraud Office, 2018. ec.europa.eu/anti-fraud/sites/antifraud/files/olaf_report_2017_en.pdf, accessed 21 Feb. 2019.

28. "Customs Fraud Results in SR437m Revenue Loss," *Saudi Gazette*, 3 July 2018. saudigazette.com.sa/article/538200/SAUDI-ARABIA/Customs-fraud-results-in-SR437m-revenue-loss, accessed 1 Nov. 2018.

29. "Port Community Systems," IPCSA, n.d. www.epcsa.eu/pcs, accessed 12 June 2018.

30. Olivier Moreau, "Port Community Systems: Achieving Interconnectivity between Public and Private Sectors," Bureau Veritas, June 2016. www.eiseverywhere.com/file_uploads/5cc93af549aedb3134cda63191eea530_Roundtable1Presentation3MrMoreau-pdfformat.pdf, accessed 13 June 2018.

31. Rena S. Miller, Liana W. Rosen, and James K. Jackson, "Trade-Based Money Laundering: Overview and Policy Issues," Congressional Research Service, 22 June 2016. fas.org/sgp/crs/misc/R44541.pdf, accessed 12 June 2018.

32. "Illicit Financial Flows to and from Developing Countries: 2005–2014," Global Financial Integrity, April 2017. www.gfintegrity.org/wp-content/uploads/2017/05/GFI-IFF-Report-2017_final.pdf, accessed 12 June 2018.

33. "Bank of Ireland and Deloitte Announce Blockchain Proof-of-Concept Focused on Trade Reporting," Bank of Ireland, Bank of Ireland Group PLC, n.d. www.bankofireland.com/about-bank-of-ireland/press-releases/2016/bank-of-ireland-and-deloitte-announce-blockchain-proof-of-concept-focused-on-trade-reporting, accessed 21 June 2018.

34. "Deloitte, HKMA and Leading Trade Finance Banks in Hong Kong Have Developed a Distributed Ledger Technology Proof of Concept for Trade Finance," News Release, Deloitte, Deloitte Touche Tohmatsu Ltd., 30 March 2017. www2.deloitte.com/cn/en/pages/about-deloitte/articles/pr-deloitte-hkma-dlt-proof-of-concept-for-trade-finance.html, accessed 24 June 2018.

35. "Import and Export Trade Industry in Hong Kong," *HKTDC Research*, Hong Kong Trade Development Council, 16 July 2018. hong-kong-economy-research.hktdc.com/business-news/article/Hong-Kong-Industry-Profiles/Import-and-Export-Trade-Industry-in-Hong-Kong/hkip/en/1/1X000000/1X006NJK.htm, accessed 24 June 2018.

36. "About the HKMA," Hong Kong Monetary Authority, last updated 11 July 2018. www.hkma.gov.hk/eng/about-the-hkma/hkma/about-hkma.shtml, accessed 24 June 2018.

37. "Distributed Ledger Technology," White Paper 2.0, Hong Kong Monetary Authority, 25 Oct. 2017. www.hkma.gov.hk/media/eng/doc/key-functions/finanical-infrastructure/infrastructure/20171024e1.pdf, accessed 18 June 2018.

38. "Distributed Ledger Technology—Annex," White Paper 2.0, Hong Kong Monetary Authority, 25 Oct. 2017. www.hkma.gov.hk/media/eng/doc/

key-functions/finanical-infrastructure/infrastructure/20171025e1a1.pdf, accessed 18 June 2018.

39. "Fintech Collaboration between the Hong Kong Monetary Authority and the Monetary Authority of Singapore," News Release, Hong Kong Monetary Authority, 25 Oct. 2017. www.hkma.gov.hk/eng/key-information/press-releases/2017/20171025-4.shtml; "Fintech Co-operation between the Hong Kong Monetary Authority and the Financial Services Regulatory Authority of Abu Dhabi Global Market," Press Release, Hong Kong Monetary Authority, 26 June 2018. www.hkma.gov.hk/eng/key-information/press-releases/2018/20180626-4.shtml, both accessed 30 June 2018.

40. Sanne Wass, "Trade Finance Blockchain Platform Soon Available to Clients of Nine European Banks," *Global Trade Review*, Exporta Publishing and Events, 13 April 2018. www.gtreview.com/news/fintech/trade-finance-blockchain-platform-soon-available-to-clients-of-nine-european-banks, accessed 18 July 2018.

41. Carlo R.W. De Meijer, "we.trade on Blockchain: Yes We Can!" *Finextra*, Finextra Research, 3 July 2018. www.finextra.com/blogposting/15519/wetrade-on-blockchain-yes-we-can, accessed 18 July 2018.

42. Shannon Manders, "Banks Unveil Roadmap for we.trade Blockchain Platform," *Global Trade Review*, Exporta Publishing and Events, 24 Oct. 2017. www.gtreview.com/news/fintech/banks-unveil-roadmap-for-we-trade-blockchain-platform, accessed 16 July 2018.

43. "we.trade Banking Partners," *we.trade*, we.trade Innovation DAC, as of 27 Feb. 2019. we-trade.com/banking-partners, accessed 27 Feb. 2019.

44. "we.trade Businesses," *we.trade*, we.trade Innovation DAC, as of 27 Feb. 2019. we-trade.com/businesses, accessed 27 Feb. 2019.

45. Shannon Manders, "Banks Unveil Roadmap for we.trade Blockchain Platform."

46. Shannon Manders, "Banks Unveil Roadmap for we.trade Blockchain Platform."

47. "we.trade—Nordea Co-Developed Blockchain Platform Has Performed Its First Trades," Press Release, Nordea, 3 July 2018. www.nordea.com/en/press-and-news/news-and-press-releases/news-group/2018/2018-07-03-we-trade-nordea-co-developed-blockchain-platform-has-performed-its-first-trades.html, accessed 16 July 2018.

48. Tom Allen, "Maersk Forced to Reinstall 45,000 PCs and 4,000 Servers Following NotPetya Attack," *The Inquirer*, Incisive Business Media (IP) Ltd., 26 Jan. 2018. www.theinquirer.net/inquirer/news/3025347/maersk-

forced-to-reinstall-45-000-pcs-and-4-000-servers-following-notpetya-attack, accessed 6 July 2018.

49. Tom Allen, "Maersk Forced to Reinstall 45,000 PCs and 4,000 Servers Following NotPetya Attack."

50. "Maersk and IBM to Form Joint Venture Applying Blockchain to Improve Global Trade and Digitize Supply Chains," Press Release, IBM Corporation, 16 Jan. 2018. www-03.ibm.com/press/us/en/pressrelease/53602.wss, accessed 20 June 2018.

51. "Maersk and IBM to Form Joint Venture."

52. Michael White, "Digitizing Global Trade with Maersk and IBM," *Blockchain Pulse: IBM Blockchain Blog*, IBM Corporation, 16 Jan. 2018. www.ibm.com/blogs/blockchain/2018/01/digitizing-global-trade-maersk-ibm, accessed 10 June 2018.

53. "Maersk and IBM to Form Joint Venture Applying Blockchain to Improve Global Trade and Digitize Supply Chains," News Release, IBM Corporation, 16 Jan. 2018. www-03.ibm.com/press/us/en/pressrelease/53602.wss, accessed 20 June 2018.

54. "Maersk and IBM to Form Joint Venture."

55. "Maersk and IBM to Form Joint Venture."

56. To learn more about the concept of the *minimum viable economy*, see Corless et al., "Tech Trends 2018: The Symphonic Enterprise." www2.deloitte.com/tr/en/pages/technology-media-and-telecommunications/articles/tech-trends-2018.html, accessed 21 Feb. 2019.

57. Lory Kehoe et al., "Six Control Principles for Financial Services Blockchains," Deloitte, Deloitte Touche Tohmatsu Ltd., Oct. 2017. www2.deloitte.com/content/dam/Deloitte/cn/Documents/financial-services/deloitte-cn-fs-six-principles-for-blockchains-report-en-171121.pdf, accessed 14 June 2018.

58. "ISO 20022-1:2013 Financial Services—Universal Financial Industry Message Scheme—Part 1: Metamodel," International Standards Organization, last reviewed 2017. www.iso.org/standard/55005.html; "Introducing UN/EDIFACT," United Nations Economic Commission for Europe, n.d. www.unece.org/cefact/edifact/welcome.html, both accessed 28 June 2018; and Lory Kehoe et al., "Six Control Principles for Financial Services Blockchains."

59. "ISO/ TC 307 Blockchain and Distributed Ledger Technologies," International Standards Organization, 2016. www.iso.org/committee/6266604.html, accessed 28 June 2018.

60. Blockchain in Transport Alliance, n.d. bita.studio; Sovrin, Sovrin Foundation, n.d. sovrin.org, both accessed 21 Feb. 2019.

61. "UCP 600 Part 1," Citigroup, Citigroup Inc., 2006. www.citigroup. com/transactionservices/home/trade_svcs/trade_u/docs/latem_32207. pdf?lid=UCPP1engpdf; "MT 798," SWIFT, n.d. www.swift.com/our-solutions/corporates/drive-trade-digitisation/mt-798, both accessed 21 Feb. 2019.

62. "ISO/IEC 27000 Family—Information Security Management Systems," International Standards Organization, n.d. www.iso.org/isoiec-27001-information-security.html, accessed 22 June 2018.

63. Bisade Asolo, "Breaking Down the Blockchain Scalability Trilemma," *Bitcoinist.com*, 10 June 2018. bitcoinist.com/breaking-down-the-scalability-trilemma, accessed 22 June 2018.

64. "Sharding FAQs," ed. James Ray, *Ethereum/Wiki*, GitHub Inc., last modified 28 Jan. 2018. github.com/ethereum/wiki/wiki/Sharding-FAQs; Raiden Network, n.d. raiden.network; Kyle Croman et al., "On Scaling Decentralized Blockchains," Position Paper, 26 Jan. 2016. fc16.ifca.ai/bitcoin/papers/CDE+16.pdf; "Basic Primer: Blockchain Consensus Protocol," *Blockgeeks,* n.d. blockgeeks.com/guides/blockchain-consensus; and Adam Back et al., "Enabling Blockchain Innovations with Pegged Sidechain," 22 Oct. 2014. kevinriggen.com/files/sidechains. pdf, all accessed 21 Feb. 2019.

65. David D. Clark, "The Design Philosophy of the DARPA Internet Protocols," *Proc. SIGCOMM* 18, no. 4 (Aug. 1988): 106–114. *Computer Communication Review,* ccr.sigcomm.org/archive/1995/jan95/ccr-9501-clark.pdf, accessed 16 July 2018.

66. David D. Clark, "The Design Philosophy of the DARPA Internet Protocols," p. 2. ccr.sigcomm.org/archive/1995/jan95/ccr-9501-clark.pdf, accessed 27 Feb. 2019.

67. Thomas Hardjono, Alexander Lipton, and Alex Pentland, "Towards a Design Philosophy for Interoperable Blockchain Systems," MIT Connection Science, Massachusetts Institute of Technology, 16 May 2018. arxiv.org/pdf/1805.05934.pdf, accessed 16 July 2018.

68. "The Birth of the Web," French Conseil Européen pour la Recherche Nucléaire (CERN), n.d. home.cern/topics/birth-web, accessed 16 July 2018.

69. Jacob Eberhardt and Stefan Tai, "On or Off the Blockchain? Insights on Off-Chaining Computation and Data," Information Systems Engineering, TU Berlin, 2017. www.ise.tu-berlin.de/fileadmin/fg308/

publications/2017/2017-eberhardt-tai-offchaining-patterns.pdf, accessed 1 July 2018.

70. IPFS, Protocol Labs, n.d. ipfs.io/#why, accessed 21 Feb. 2019.

71. "Blockchain: Legal Implications, Questions, Opportunities and Risks," *Deloitte Legal*, Deloitte Touche Tohmatsu Ltd., March 2018. www2.deloitte.com/content/dam/Deloitte/be/Documents/legal/ Blockchain%20Booklet%20March2018.pdf, accessed 1 July 2018.

72. Lory Kehoe et al., "Six Control Principles for Financial Services Blockchains."

73. John MacKenna, "Hyperledger's Brian Behlendorf and How Blockchains Will Change the Enterprise World," *Nasdaq*, Nasdaq.com, 10 Jan. 2018. www.nasdaq.com/article/hyperledgers-brian-behlendorf-and-how-blockchains-will-change-the-enterprise-world-cm903367, accessed 21 Feb. 2019.

74. Walter Isaacson, *Steve Jobs* (New York City, NY: Simon & Schuster, 2011): 189.

75. Charles Duhigg and Keith Bradsher, "How the US Lost Out on iPhone Work," *New York Times*, New York Times Company, 22 Jan. 2012. www. nytimes.com/2012/01/22/business/apple-america-and-a-squeezed-middle-class.html, accessed 22 Sept. 2017.

76. The first three industrial revolutions were steam power and mechanization, electricity, and computing and telecommunications.

77. "Financials Information for Hon Hai Precision Industry Co. Ltd.," *D&B Hoovers*, n.d. www.hoovers.com/company-information/cs/ revenue-financial.HON_HAI_PRECISION_INDUSTRY_CO_LTD. d987375fdd77c3f8.html, accessed 22 Sept. 2017.

78. Jack Lee, interviewed by Nolan Bauerle, 23 May 2017.

79. Jack Lee, interviewed by Nolan Bauerle, 23 May 2017.

80. Michael del Castillo, "Foxconn Reveals Plan for Blockchain Supply Chain Domination," *CoinDesk*, Digital Currency Group, 13 March 2017. www.coindesk.com/foxconn-wants-take-global-supply-chain-blockchain, accessed 22 Sept. 2017.

81. Jack Lee, interviewed by Nolan Bauerle, 23 May 2017.

82. Jack Lee, interviewed by Nolan Bauerle, 23 May 2017.

83. John Schmid, "Foxconn Founder Gou Maintains Low Profile even as He Transforms the Tech World," *Milwaukee Journal Sentinel*, 26 July 2017. www.jsonline.com/story/money/2017/07/27/foxconn-founder-

gou-maintains-low-profile-even-he-transforms-tech-world/514646001, accessed 26 Sept. 2017.

84. Jack Lee, interviewed by Nolan Bauerle, 23 May 2017.

85. Jack Lee, interviewed by Nolan Bauerle, 23 May 2017.

86. James Manyika et al., "Unlocking the Potential of the Internet of Things," McKinsey & Company, June 2015. www.mckinsey.com/ business-functions/digital-mckinsey/our-insights/the-internet-of-things-the-value-of-digitizing-the-physical-world, accessed 22 Sept. 2017.

87. Liam Tung, "Raspberry Pi Compute Module 3 Launches at $30, Ready to Power Up in Other Products," *ZDnet.com*, CBS Interactive, 16 Jan. 2017. www.zdnet.com/article/raspberry-pi-compute-module-3-launches-at-30-ready-to-power-up-in-other-products, accessed 26 Sept. 2017.

88. Jonathan Luk, "GREATS Unveil Revamped BEASTMODE 2.0 Royale Chukka," *Highsnobiety*, 24 Nov. 2015. www.highsnobiety. com/2015/11/24/greats-beastmode-2-royale-chukka, accessed 22 Sept. 2017.

89. Takashi Mochizuki, "Taiwan's Foxconn Completes Acquisition of Sharp," *Wall Street Journal*, Dow Jones & Company, 13 Aug. 2016. www.wsj.com/ articles/taiwans-foxconn-completes-deal-to-acquire-sharp-1470994207, accessed 22 Sept. 2017.

90. Jack Lee, interviewed by Nolan Bauerle, 23 May 2017.

91. Nick Szabo, "Trusted Third Parties as Security Holes," Nakamoto Institute, 2001. nakamotoinstitute.org/trusted-third-parties, accessed 26 Sept. 2017.

92. Ann Cavoukian, "Privacy by Design: The Seven Foundational Principles," Information and Privacy Commissioner of Ontario, Aug. 2009, revised Jan. 2011. www.ipc.on.ca/wp-content/uploads/ resources/7foundationalprinciples.pdf, accessed 18 Sept. 2017.

93. "General Data Protection Regulation Key Changes," European Union, n.d. www.eugdpr.org/the-regulation.html, accessed 18 Sept. 2017.

94. Ann Cavoukian, "Privacy by Design: The Seven Foundational Principles."

95. "The Game of Stones," Global Witness, n.d. www.globalwitness.org/en/ campaigns/central-african-republic-car/game-of-stones, accessed 23 Nov. 2017.

96. UN General Assembly, "General Assembly Urges Finalization of International Certification Scheme for Rough Diamonds," Plenary, 96th Meeting (AM), Press Release GA/10011, United Nations, 13 March

2002. www.un.org/press/en/2002/GA10011.doc.htm, accessed 14 Dec. 2017.

97. Aryn Baker, "The Fight against Blood Diamonds Continues," *Time* 186, no. 9, 7 Sept. 2015. time.com/blood-diamonds, accessed 15 Nov. 2017.

98. The Central African Republic (CAR), for example, is among the poorest and most fragile states in the world. Yet its rivers and soil are rich in both gold and diamonds. Rather than fueling development, these riches have been plundered by those in power—and by violent rebel groups wishing to seize it. While the international community—including the Kimberley Process—is working with CAR's government and diamond companies to establish legitimate supply chains, a Global Witness investigation found that smugglers and traders operating in CAR are thriving in a parallel black market. Several traders spoke openly to undercover reporters of the ease with which diamonds could be smuggled, and some spoke openly of working with international dealers. Ironically, many smugglers market their illicit diamonds using Facebook Messenger and WhatsApp to connect directly with opportunistic buyers in a virtual global supply chain for conflict diamonds. "The Game of Stones," Global Witness, n.d. www.globalwitness.org/en/campaigns/central-african-republic-car/game-of-stones, accessed 23 Nov. 2017.

99. Greg Campbell, *Blood Diamonds: Tracing the Deadly Path of the World's Most Precious Stones* (New York, NY: Basic Books, 2012): 121.

100. Greg Campbell, *Blood Diamonds: Tracing the Deadly Path of the World's Most Precious Stones*: 121.

101. William Yu, *De Beers—Rulers of the Diamond Industry: The Rise and Fall of a Monopoly* (Berkeley, CA: Berkeley University, 2005). are.berkeley.edu/~sberto/DeBeersDiamondIndustry.pdf, accessed 29 Nov. 2017.

102. Ian Smillie, "Conflict Diamonds—Unfinished Business," International Development Research Centre, 22 July 2011. www.idrc.ca/en/article/conflict-diamonds-unfinished-business, accessed 15 Nov. 2017.

103. Letter sent 21 Jan. 2000, by Robert P. Kaplan (director in Rex Diamond Mining Corporation, Canada) to Hon. Lloyd Axworthy, P.C., M.P., Minster of Foreign Affairs of Canada.

104. About the Kimberley Process, n.d. www.kimberleyprocess.com/en/about, accessed 16 Nov. 2017.

105. The 28 member states of the European Union are represented collectively by the European Commission. For the full list of Kimberley Process participants, see "Participants," Kimberley Process, n.d. www.kimberleyprocess.com/en/participants, accessed 15 Jan. 2020.

106. "What Is the KP," Kimberley Process, n.d. www.kimberleyprocess.com/en/what-kp, accessed 16 Nov. 2017.

107. See, for example, Diamond Development Initiative, www.ddiglobal.org/artisanal-mining/issues; and Global Witness, www.globalwitness.org/en/campaigns/conflict-diamonds, both accessed 17 Nov. 2017.

108. "Why We Are Leaving the Kimberley Process," Global Witness, 3 Dec. 2011. www.globalwitness.org/en/archive/why-we-are-leaving-kimberley-process-message-global-witness-founding-director-charmian-gooch, accessed 16 Nov. 2017.

109. Jon Yoemans, "Blood Diamonds, Synthetics, and Ethical Supply: The Diamond Industry Fights Its Corner," *Daily Telegraph*, Telegraph Media Group, 18 Nov. 2016. www.telegraph.co.uk/business/2016/11/18/blood-diamonds-synthetics-and-ethical-supply-the-diamond-industr, accessed 16 Nov. 2017.

110. Leanne Kemp, "Blockchain Technology for the Diamond Industry," remarks at IBM InterConnect 2017, 21 March 2017. www.youtube.com/watch?v=-zYnYXpmtoc, accessed 22 Nov. 2017.

111. "Enforcement," Kimberley Process, n.d. www.kimberleyprocess.com/en/enforcement, accessed 16 Nov. 2017.

112. Arvind Krishna, "Keynote Address," remarks at Consensus 2017: Making Blockchain Real, New York City, 22 May 2017.

113. Arvind Krishna, "Power of Blockchain + Watson," *IBM Research Blog*, IBM Corporation, 22 May 2017. www.ibm.com/blogs/research/2017/05/power-blockchain-watson, accessed 22 Nov. 2017.

114. Arvind Krishna, "Keynote Address," 22 May 2017.

115. Dimitris Karapiperis, "Fraud Insurance," *CIPR Newsletter* 13, The Center for Insurance Policy and Research, Oct. 2014. www.naic.org/cipr_newsletter_archive/vol13_insurance_fraud.pdf, accessed 23 Nov. 2017.

116. Dimitris Karapiperis, "Fraud Insurance," *CIPR Newsletter* 13, The Center for Insurance Policy and Research, Oct. 2014.

117. Survey conducted by the Fair Isaac Corporation (FICO) and the Property Casualty Insurers Association of America (PCI), 2013. www.fico.com/en/node/8140?file=5858, accessed 23 Nov. 2017.

118. Survey conducted by the Fair Isaac Corporation (FICO), 2013.

119. Leanne Kemp, "Blockchain Technology for the Diamond Industry," remarks at IBM InterConnect 2017, 21 March 2017. www.youtube.com/watch?v=-zYnYXpmtoc, accessed 22 Nov. 2017.

120. "Maureen Downey and Everledger Join Forces to Combat Counterfeit Wine with the Introduction of the Chai Wine Vault," *Winefraud.com*, 18 Nov. 2016. www.winefraud.com/wp-content/uploads/Chai-Wine-Vault-Press-Release.pdf, accessed 29 Nov. 2017.

121. See the Chai Wine Vault, www.winefraud.com/chai-wine-vault, accessed 29 Nov. 2017.

122. "Maureen Downey and Everledger Join Forces to Combat Counterfeit Wine with the Introduction of the Chai Wine Vault," *Winefraud.com*, 18 Nov. 2016.

123. Bernadine Brocker, "The Fine Line between Transparency and Confidentiality in the Art World," *Vastari Blog*, 3 May 2016. blog.vastari.com/post/144351319189/the-fine-line-between-transparency-and, accessed 29 Nov. 2017.

124. Leanne Kemp, interviewed by Anthony Williams, 30 Nov. 2017.

125. Leanne Kemp, interviewed by Anthony Williams, 30 Nov. 2017.

126. Leanne Kemp, interviewed by Anthony Williams, 30 Nov. 2017.

127. Leanne Kemp, interviewed by Anthony Williams, 30 Nov. 2017.

128. Leanne Kemp, interviewed by Anthony Williams, 30 Nov. 2017.

129. Leanne Kemp, interviewed by Anthony Williams, 30 Nov. 2017.

130. Leanne Kemp, interviewed by Anthony Williams, 30 Nov. 2017.

131. UN FAO, "FAO Statistical Yearbook 2012: World Food and Agriculture," foreword by Pietro Gennari, *www.fao.org*, Food and Agricultural Organization of the United Nations, 17 April 2012, p. 11. issuu.com/faosyb/docs/fao_statistical_yearbook_2012_issuu; Carl Haub et al., "World Population Data Sheet 2011: The World at Seven Billion," Population Reference Bureau, July 2011. assets.prb.org/pdf11/2011population-data-sheet_eng.pdf, both accessed 5 Dec. 2017.

132. "Kenya's Farmers Demand Coffee Break," *Gro Intelligence Insights*, Gro Intelligence, 26 Feb. 2016. gro-intelligence.com/insights/kenyas-farmers-demand-coffee-break, accessed 29 Nov. 2017.

133. "WHO Estimates of the Global Burden of Foodborne Diseases," World Health Organization, 12 March 2015. www.who.int/foodsafety/publications/foodborne_disease/fergreport/en, accessed 29 Nov. 2017.

134. Michael del Castillo, "Walmart, Kroger & Nestle Team with IBM Blockchain to Fight Food Poisoning," *CoinDesk*, Digital Currency Group, 22 Aug. 2017. www.coindesk.com/walmart-kroger-nestle-team-with-ibm-blockchain-to-fight-food-poisoning, accessed 29 Nov. 2017.

135. National Geographic, "Sustainable Agriculture," *National Geographic Reference*, n.d. www.nationalgeographic.com/environment/habitats/sustainable-agriculture, accessed 29 Nov. 2017.

136. Nathaniel Popper and Steve Lohr, "Blockchain: A Better Way to Track Pork Chops, Bonds, Bad Peanut Butter?" *New York Times*, New York Times Company, 4 March 2017. www.nytimes.com/2017/03/04/business/dealbook/blockchain-ibm-bitcoin.html, accessed 29 Nov. 2017.

137. Alicia Noel, "Blockchain Is Now Being Used on the Food Supply Chain," *LinkedIn Pulse*, LinkedIn Corp., 27 June 2017. www.linkedin.com/pulse/blockchain-now-being-used-food-supply-chain-alicia-noel-凤兰-, accessed 29 Nov. 2017.

138. Provenance, "Provenance: Every Product Has a Story," *Provenance.org*, n.d. www.provenance.org, accessed 29 Nov. 2017.

139. Alicia Noel, "Blockchain Is Now Being Used on the Food Supply Chain."

140. Marek Laskowski, "A Blockchain-Enabled Participatory Decision Support Framework," *Social, Cultural, and Behavioral Modeling*, Proceedings of the International Conference on Social Computing, Behavioral-Cultural Modeling and Prediction and Behavior Representation in Modeling and Simulation, Washington, DC, 5–8 July 2017, pp. 329–334. www.springer.com/us/book/9783319602394, accessed 29 Nov. 2017.

141. Alicia Noel, "Blockchain Is Now Being Used on the Food Supply Chain."

142. Martin Gooch and Brian Sterling, "Traceability Is Free: Competitive Advantage of Food Traceability to Value Chain Management," VCM International, 12 Aug. 2013. vcm-international.com/wp-content/uploads/2013/08/Traceability-Is-Free.pdf, accessed 29 Nov. 2017.

143. Brian Sterling, interviewed by the Henry Kim and Marek Laskowski, 11 July 2017.

144. Don Tapscott and Alex Tapscott, "Realizing the Potential of Blockchain: A Multistakeholder Approach to the Stewardship of Blockchain and Cryptocurrencies," World Economic Forum, June 2017. www3.weforum.org/docs/WEF_Realizing_Potential_Blockchain.pdf, accessed 29 Nov. 2017.

145. Stan Higgins, "Nuco Builds Tokenized Blockchain 'Bridge' for Enterprise Applications," *CoinDesk*, Digital Currency Group, 17 July 2017. www.coindesk.com/nuco-builds-tokenized-blockchain-bridge-enterprise-applications, accessed 29 Nov. 2017.

146. Henry M. Kim and Marek Laskowski, "Towards an Ontology-Driven Blockchain Design for Supply Chain Provenance," Workshop on

Information Systems and Technology (WITS), Dublin, Ireland, 2016. yoda.lab.yorku.ca/files/2016/08/wits-2016-hk-ver2.1.pdf; and Kim and Laskowski, "A Perspective on Blockchain Smart Contracts: Reducing Uncertainty and Complexity in Value Exchange," The Third IEEE Workshop on Workshop on Privacy, Security, Trust and Blockchain Technologies, Vancouver, BC, 31 July–3 Aug. 2017. doi:10.1109/ICCCN.2017.8038512, both accessed 29 Nov. 2017.

147. Tim Lea, "b3 Blockchain Interview with the Founders of AgriLedger. com: The International Philanthropic Blockchain Application to Protect Third World Farmers," *LinkedIn*, LinkedIn Corp., 10 Aug. 2016. www. linkedin.com/pulse/b3-blockchain-interview-founders-agriledgercom-application-lea, accessed 29 Nov. 2017.

148. Joshua Althauser, "Arkansas Livestock Cooperative Planning Use Blockchain Technology in Meat Products Monitoring," *Cointelegraph.com*, 7 Aug. 2017. cointelegraph.com/news/arkansas-livestock-cooperative-planning-use-blockchain-technology-in-meat-products-monitoring, accessed 29 Nov. 2017.

149. Paul Stothard, Xiaoping Liao, Adriano S. Arantes, et al., "A Large and Diverse Collection of Bovine Genome Sequences from the Canadian Cattle Genome Project," *Gigascience* 4, 1 (2015): 49. doi:10.1186/s13742-015-0090-5, accessed 29 Nov. 2017.

150. Ellen Goddard, interviewed by Henry Kim, 17 Aug. 2017.

151. Marieke de Ruyter de Wildt, interviewed by Henry Kim and Marek Laskowski, 17 Oct. 2017.

152. William E. Bodell III, "FarmShare: Blockchain Community-Supported Agriculture," White Paper, modified 1 Nov. 2017. docs.google.com/document/d/1jntZtiw0VQQ6ZctVyWsCcg-ZGvv6MCSvlFIIPG5GDSg/edit, accessed 5 Dec. 2017.

153. Ether, CoinMarketCap.com. coinmarketcap.com/currencies/ethereum/historical-data/?start=20130428&end=20181026, accessed 26 Oct. 2018.

154. See matthew-lohry-kded.squarespace.com. As of 5 Dec. 2017, this page indicated that FarmShare is "currently on hold."

155. Julien Hall, "AgriDigital Pioneers Blockchain Use with First Farmer-Buyer Agriculture Settlement," *The Barrel Blog*, 2 Feb. 2017. blogs.platts. com/2017/02/02/agridigital-pioneers-blockchain-agriculture, accessed 29 Nov. 2017.

156. Gro Intelligence, "Blockchain: Beyond Bitcoin to Agriculture," *Gro Intelligence Insights*, 2 Aug. 2017. gro-intelligence.com/insights/blockchain-in-agriculture, accessed 29 Nov. 2017.

157. Daily Fintech, "IOT Meets DLT and Blockchain Meets M-Pesa in Africa," *Daily Fintech*, 24 March 2017. dailyfintech.com/2017/03/24/iot-meets-dlt-and-blockchain-meets-m-pesa-in-africa, accessed 29 Nov. 2017.

158. Everex, "Problems with Microlending and How Blockchain Solves Them," *Everex Blog*, 22 Aug. 2017. blog.everex.io/problems-with-microlending-and-how-blockchain-solves-them-1582f98e2a7c, accessed 29 Nov. 2017.

159. Anne Connelly, interviewed by Henry Kim, 22 Oct. 2017.

160. Michael del Castillo, "No Token Response: UNICEF Is Open to Doing Its Own ICO," *CoinDesk*, Digital Currency Group, 13 Oct. 2017. www.coindesk.com/no-token-response-unicef-is-open-to-doing-its-own-ico, accessed 29 Nov. 2017.

161. Frank Yiannas and Rebecca Liu, e-mail to Reshma Kamath, 6 Sept. 2017.

162. IBM, "Hyperledger—Open Source Blockchain for Business—IBM Blockchain," *IBM Cognitive Advantage Reports*, IBM Corporation, 2017. www.ibm.com/blockchain/hyperledger.html, accessed 7 Aug. 2017. Frank Yiannas, interviewed by Reshma Kamath, 28 June 2017.

163. Frank Yiannas, interviewed by Reshma Kamath, 28 June 2017.

164. Frank Yiannas, interviewed by Reshma Kamath, 28 June 2017.

165. Brigid McDermott, interviewed by Reshma Kamath, 23 June 2017; edited by McDermott, 12 Sept. 2017.

166. "Foodborne Illnesses and Germs," Centers for Disease Control and Prevention, June 2011. www.cdc.gov/foodsafety/foodborne-germs.html, accessed 29 June 2017.

167. "Food Safety: Key Facts," World Health Organization, 31 Oct. 2017. www.who.int/mediacentre/factsheets/fs399/en, accessed 30 June 2017.

168. Stephen Castle, "Europe Says Tests Show Horse Meat Scandal Is 'Food Fraud,'" *New York Times*, New York Times Company, 16 April 2013. www.nytimes.com/2013/04/17/business/global/european-study-affirms-role-of-fraud-in-horsemeat-scandal.html, accessed 29 June 2017.

169. Rudy Ruitenberg, "Horse-Meat Suspect Spanghero Denies Beef Scam Responsibility," *Bloomberg News*, Bloomberg LP, 15 Feb. 2013. www.bloomberg.com/news/2013-02-15/horse-meat-suspect-spanghero-denies-scam-admits-some-negligence.html, accessed 9 July 2017.

170. Search for "horsemeat scandal," *Financial Times*. www.ft.com/topics/themes/Horsemeat_scandal?mhq5j=e1, accessed 30 June 2017.

171. "Fighting $40bn Food Fraud to Protect Food Supply,"
PricewaterhouseCoopers and Safe and Secure Approaches in Field
Environments, 14 Jan. 2016. press.pwc.com/News-releases/fighting–
40bn-food-fraud-to-protect-food-supply/s/44fd6210-10f7-46c7-8431-
e55983286e22, accessed 30 June 2017.

172. Keith Bradsher, "Chinese City Shuts Down 13 Walmarts," *New
York Times*, New York Times Company, 11 Oct. 2011. www.nytimes.
com/2011/10/11/business/global/wal-marts-in-china-city-closed-for-
pork-mislabeling.html, accessed 8 Sept. 2017. Steve Clemons, "China's
Latest Food Scandal: Fox-Tainted Donkey Meat," *The Atlantic,* Atlantic
Monthly Group LLC, 2 Jan. 2014. www.theatlantic.com/international/
archive/2014/01/chinas-latest-food-scandal-fox-tainted-donkey-
meat/282776, accessed 30 June 2017.

173. Celia Hatton, "Will China's New Food Safety Rules Work?" *BBC News,*
Beijing, 30 Sept. 2015. www.bbc.com/news/blogs-china-blog-34398412;
Keith Bradsher, "Chinese City Shuts Down 13 Walmarts," *New
York Times*, New York Times Company, 10 Oct. 2011. www.nytimes.
com/2011/10/11/business/global/wal-marts-in-china-city-closed-for-
pork-mislabeling.html, accessed 7 Aug. 2017. "Reuse of rancid cooking
oil by restaurants has become a national scandal, and where the deliberate
mixing of powdered infant formula with industrial waste from plastics
manufacturing to meet minimum protein standards has sickened an
estimated 50,000 babies."

174. Gang Liu, "Food Losses and Food Waste in China: A First Estimate,"
Office of Economic Cooperation and Development, 15 June 2013. www.
oecd.org/site/agrfcn/Food%20losses%20and%20waste%20in%20China_
Gang%20Liu.pdf, accessed 30 June 2017.

175. Gang Liu, "Food Losses and Food Waste in China: A First Estimate,"
Office of Economic Cooperation and Development, 15 June 2013.

176. "FDA Statement on Foodborne E. coli O157:H7 Outbreak in Spinach,"
Press Release, US Food and Drug Administration, 6 Oct. 2006. wayback.
archive-it.org/7993/20170113132906/www.fda.gov/NewsEvents/
Newsroom/PressAnnouncements/2006/ucm108761.htm, accessed
17 July 2018.

177. Frank Yiannas, e-mail to Reshma Kamath, 6 Sept. 2017.

178. Frank Yiannas, e-mail to Reshma Kamath, 6 Sept. 2017.

179. Center for Food Safety and Applied Nutrition, "FDA Investigates
Multiple Salmonella Outbreak Strain Linked to Papayas," US Food
and Drug Administration, 18 Aug. 2017. www.fda.gov/food/
RecallsOutbreaksEmergencies/Outbreaks/ucm568097.htm, accessed
24 Aug. 2017.

180. Frank Yiannas, e-mail to Reshma Kamath, 6 Sept. 2017.

181. Steve Culp, "Supply Chain Disruption a Major Threat to Business," *Forbes*, Forbes Media LLC, 15 Feb. 2013. www.forbes.com/sites/steveculp/2013/02/15/supply-chain-disruption-a-major-threat-to-business/#2ed93c7673b6, accessed 7 Aug. 2017. Frank Yiannas, e-mail to Reshma Kamath, 6 Sept. 2017.

182. J. Ralph Blanchfield and Bruce Welt, "Food Traceability," *The International Union of Food Science and Technology*, March 2012. www.iufost.org/iufostftp/IUF.SIB.Food%20Traceability.pdf, accessed 8 Aug. 2017.

183. J. Ralph Blanchfield and Bruce Welt, "Food Traceability," *The International Union of Food Science and Technology*, March 2012.

184. Stuart Hodge, "Can Blockchain Technology Transform Safety Standards in the Global Food Supply Chain?" *Supply Chain Digital*, 25 Aug. 2017. www.supplychaindigital.com/technology/can-blockchain-technology-transform-safety-standards-global-food-supply-chain, accessed 25 Aug. 2017.

185. Frank Yiannas, interviewed by Reshma Kamath, 28 June 2017. J. Ralph Blanchfield and Bruce Welt, "Food Traceability," *Scientific Information Bulletin*, The International Union of Food Science and Technology, March 2012. www.iufost.org/iufostftp/IUF.SIB.Food%20Traceability.pdf, accessed 8 Aug. 2017.

186. Teeka Tiwari, "Profit Alert: Walmart Is Adopting the Blockchain Right Now," Palm Beach Research Group, 6 Dec. 2016. palmbeachgroup.com/content/palm-beach-daily/profit-alert-walmart-is-adopting-the-blockchain-right-now/32499, accessed 7 Aug. 2017; "Walmart, IBM Developing a Food Safety Solution," The Association for Convenience and Fuel Retailing, 28 Feb. 2017. www.nacsonline.com/Media/Daily/Pages/ND0228171.aspx#.WZNwQlGGPIV, accessed 7 Aug. 2017.

187. Brigid McDermott, interviewed by Reshma Kamath, 23 June 2017.

188. Brigid McDermott, interviewed by Reshma Kamath, 23 June 2017.

189. The Global Traceability Standard (GTS) is promulgated by GS1, an international not-for-profit association with member organizations in over 100 countries. GTS enables traceability systems of global supply chains, regardless of the number of companies involved, borders crossed, or technologies used. See J. Ralph Blanchfield and Bruce Welt, "Food Traceability," *Scientific Information Bulletin*, The International Union of Food Science and Technology, March 2012. www.iufost.org/iufostftp/IUF.SIB.Food%20Traceability.pdf, accessed 8 Aug. 2017.

190. GS1 AISB, "GS1 Recommends Use of Existing Data Standards in Enterprise Blockchain Implementations," *The Global Language of Business,* 2017. www.gs1.org/sites/default/files/docs/internet-of-things/gs1-blockchain-pov-paper-a4.pdf, accessed 30 June 2017.

191. GS1 AISB, "GS1 Recommends Use of Existing Data Standards in Enterprise Blockchain Implementations," *The Global Language of Business,* 2017.

192. IBM, "Hyperledger–Open Source Blockchain for Business–IBM Blockchain," *IBM Cognitive Advantage Reports*, IBM Corporation, 2017. www.ibm.com/blockchain/hyperledger.html, accessed 7 Aug. 2017.

193. Brigid McDermott, interviewed by Reshma Kamath, 23 June 2017.

194. Brigid McDermott, interviewed by Reshma Kamath, 23 June 2017.

195. Brigid McDermott, interviewed by Reshma Kamath, 23 June 2017.

196. Fred Gale, "China's Pork Imports Rise Along with Production Costs," *Economic Research Services,* US Department of Agriculture, Jan. 2017. www.ers.usda.gov/webdocs/publications/81948/ldpm-271-01.pdf?v=42745, accessed 30 June 2017.

197. Fred Gale, "China's Pork Imports Rise along with Production Costs," *Economic Research Services,* US Department of Agriculture, Jan. 2017. www.ers.usda.gov/webdocs/publications/81948/ldpm-271-01.pdf?v=42745, accessed 30 June 2017. See section on "Food Distribution and Aggregation" to see effect on small-scale producers and farmers.

198. Jacob Bunge, "How to Satisfy the World's Surging Appetite for Meat," *Wall Street Journal,* Dow Jones & Company, 4 Dec. 2015. www.wsj.com/articles/how-to-satisfy-the-worlds-surging-appetite-for-meat-1449238059, accessed 30 June 2017.

199. Laurie Burkitt, "Walmart to Triple Spending on Food Safety in China," *Wall Street Journal,* Dow Jones & Company, 17 June 2014. www.wsj.com/articles/Walmart-to-triple-spending-on-food-safety-in-china-1402991720, accessed 29 June 2017; Brigid McDermott, interviewed by Reshma Kamath, 23 June 2017; "Walmart to Invest 25 Million in China Food Safety Research," *Bloomberg News,* Bloomberg LP, 19 Oct. 2016. www.bloomberg.com/news/articles/2016-10-19/Walmart-to-invest-25-million-in-china-food-safety-research, accessed 30 June 2017.

200. Walmart, "Walmart Invites Global Collaboration on Food Safety in China," Press Release, 19 Oct. 2016. www.wal-martchina.com/english/news/2016/20161130-4.htm, accessed 12 Sept. 2017.

201. "Walmart to Invest 25 Million in China Food Safety Research," *Bloomberg News*, Bloomberg LP, 19 Oct. 2016. www.bloomberg.com/news/articles/2016-10-19/Walmart-to-invest-25-million-in-china-food-safety-research, accessed 30 June 2017.

202. Kim S. Nash, "Walmart Readies Blockchain Pilot for Tracking US Produce China Pork," *Wall Street Journal CIO Journal*, Dow Jones & Company, 16 Dec. 2016. blogs.wsj.com/cio/2016/12/16/wal-mart-readies-blockchain-pilot-for-tracking-u-s-produce-china-pork, accessed 15 Aug. 2017.

203. Brigid McDermott, interviewed by Reshma Kamath, 23 June 2017.

204. Brigid McDermott, interviewed by Reshma Kamath, 23 June 2017.

205. Ian Allison, "IBM Enlists Walmart, Nestlé, Unilever, Dole for Food Safety Blockchain," *International Business Times*, 24 Aug. 2017. www.ibtimes.com/ibm-enlists-walmart-nestle-unilever-dole-food-safety-blockchain-2582490, accessed 28 Aug. 2017.

206. Rachel Ralte, "IFA Accuses Pig Processors of Undermining Pigmeat Market," *ThePigSite News Desk*, 5m Enterprises Inc., 7 Aug. 2017 www.thepigsite.com/swinenews/43938/ifa-accuses-pig-processors-of-undermining-pigmeat-market; Rachel Ralte, "Pig Premise ID Registrations Top 13 Thousand & Growing," *ThePigSite News Desk*, 5m Enterprises Inc., 2 Aug. 2017. www.thepigsite.com/swinenews/43919/pig-premise-id-registrations-top-13-thousand-growing, accessed 7 Aug. 2017.

207. Fred Gale, "China's Pork Imports Rise along with Production Costs," *Economic Research Services*, US Department of Agriculture, Jan. 2017. www.ers.usda.gov/webdocs/publications/81948/ldpm-271-01.pdf?v=42745, accessed 30 June 2017.

208. Leon Kaye, "Responding to Food Safety Concerns, Walmart Invests $25 Million in China," *Triple Pundit*, 25 Oct. 2016. www.triplepundit.com/story/2016/responding-food-safety-concerns-walmart-invests-25-million-china/21896, accessed 30 June 2017.

209. Dan Murphy, "Meat of the Matter: When Solutions Are Seen as Problems," *Farm Journal's Pork*, 29 Nov. 2016. www.porknetwork.co/community/contributors/meat-matter-when-solutions-are-seen-problems, accessed 29 June 2017.

210. J. Ralph Blanchfield and Bruce Welt, "Food Traceability," *The International Union of Food Science and Technology*, March 2012. www.iufost.org/iufostftp/IUF.SIB.Food%20Traceability.pdf, accessed 8 Aug. 2017.

211. "Production and Post-Harvest Best Practices," *Mango.org*, National Mango Board, 2017. www.mango.org/postharvest-practices-research, accessed 8 Aug. 2017.

212. Helena Bottemelier, "IBM and China Team Up to Build Pork Traceability System," *Food Safety News*, 19 Dec. 2011. www.foodsafetynews.com/2011/12/ibm-and-china-team-up-to-build-pork-traceability-system/#.WZjWBCiGPIU, accessed 15 Aug. 2017.

213. Tom Doyle, "Enabling Trusted Trade through Secure Track and Trace Technology," *World Customs Journal* 8, 1 (2), Practitioner's Perspective, International Network of Customs Universities, March 2014. worldcustomsjournal.org/Archives/Volume%208%2C%20Number%201%20(Mar%202014)/14%20Doyle.pdf, accessed 3 July 2017.

214. Michael del Castillo, "Walmart Blockchain Pilot China Pork Market" *CoinDesk*, Digital Currency Group, 19 Oct. 2016. www.coindesk.com/walmart-blockchain-pilot-china-pork-market, accessed 7 Aug. 2017.

215. Frank Yiannas, e-mail to Reshma Kamath, 6 Sept. 2017.

216. Brigid McDermott, interviewed by Reshma Kamath, 23 June 2017. Frank Yiannas, e-mail to Reshma Kamath, 6 Sept. 2017.

217. James Andrews, "Mango Outbreaks Connected through Interviews," *Food Safety News*, 26 Oct. 2012. www.foodsafetynews.com/2012/10/mango-outbreaks-connected-through-interviews/#.WYtxMneGPBI, accessed 15 Aug. 2017; "Organic Mangoes Recalled for Possible Listeria Contamination," 26 May 2014. www.foodsafetynews.com/2014/05/organic-mangos-recalled-for-possible-listeria-contamination/#.WYtxqneGPBI, both accessed 15 Aug. 2017.

218. Laurie Burkitt, "Walmart to Triple Spending on Food Safety in China," *Wall Street Journal*, Dow Jones & Company, 17 June 2014. www.wsj.com/articles/Walmart-to-triple-spending-on-food-safety-in-china-1402991720, accessed 29 June 2017.

219. "Production and Post-Harvest Best Practices," *Mango.org*, National Mango Board, 2017. www.mango.org/about-the-nmb/what-is-the-nmb-doing/research-program/postharvest-practices-research, accessed 8 Aug. 2017.

220. Sanne van der Wal, "Peruvian Mango Production: Not Enough Improvements," *Centre for Research on Multinational Corporations (SOMO)*, 30 July 2013. www.somo.nl/peruvian-mango-production-not-enough-improvements, accessed 8 Aug. 2017

221. Franziska Humbert, "Mangoes with Blemishes: The Market Power of German Supermarket Chains and Unfair Working Conditions in Peru,"

Oxfam.de, Oxfam Deutschland eV, June 2013. www.oxfam.de/system/files/130705_oxfam_mangostudie_englisch_web.pdf, accessed 8 Sept. 2017.

222. Sanne van der Wal, "Peruvian Mango Production: Not Enough Improvements," *Centre for Research on Multinational Corporations (SOMO)*, 30 July 2013. www.somo.nl/peruvian-mango-production-not-enough-improvements, accessed 8 Aug. 2017

223. Rachel Ralte, "IFA Accuses Pig Processors of Undermining Pigmeat Market," *ThePigSite News Desk*, 5m Enterprises Inc., 7 Aug. 2017 www.thepigsite.com/swinenews/43938/ifa-accuses-pig-processors-of-undermining-pigmeat-market; John Brittell, Shashwat Gautam, Stephen Keefe, et al., "Mango Supply Chain: Who Is More Sustainable—MNC or Co-operative Society?" The George Washington University—School of Business, 7 March 2013. talkaboutfoodjb.files.wordpress.com/2013/08/f_brittell_gautam_keefe_mata_shah_wang.pdf, accessed 8 Aug. 2017.

224. Rachel Ralte, "IFA Accuses Pig Processors of Undermining Pigmeat Market," *ThePigSite News Desk*, 5m Enterprises Inc., 7 Aug. 2017. www.thepigsite.com/swinenews/43938/ifa-accuses-pig-processors-of-undermining-pigmeat-market, accessed 15 Jan. 2020.

225. "Precision Agri-Food Scoping Study," Precision Strategic Solutions, 1 Sept. 2016. static1.squarespace.com/static/583f561af7e0ab824c0b77c8/t/586ad4a23e00bec12e6c1ff7/1483396389489/User+Needs+Assessment.pdf, accessed 9 July 2017.

226. M.S. Mazhar et al., "Managing Mango Fruit Quality through the Supply Chain: A Pakistan Case Study," Institute of Horticultural Sciences, University of Agriculture, Nov. 2010. www.researchgate.net/publication/235258157_Managing_Mango_Fruit_Quality_through_the_Supply_Chain_A_Pakistan_Case_study, accessed 7 Aug 2017.

227. John Brittell, Shashwat Gautam, Stephen Keefe, et al., "Mango Supply Chain: Who Is More Sustainable—MNC or Co-operative Society?" The George Washington University—School of Business, 7 March 2013. talkaboutfoodjb.files.wordpress.com/2013/08/f_brittell_gautam_keefe_mata_shah_wang.pdf; M.S. Mazhar et al., "Managing Mango Fruit Quality through the Supply Chain: A Pakistan Case Study," Institute of Horticultural Sciences, University of Agriculture, Nov. 2010. www.researchgate.net/publication/235258157_Managing_Mango_Fruit_Quality_through_the_Supply_Chain_A_Pakistan_Case_study, both accessed 7 Aug. 2017.

228. "Mango Production and Post-Harvest Practices," *Mango.org*, National Mango Board, May 2017. www.mango.org/professionals/industry/

improving-mango-quality/production-postharvest-best-practices; *Mango Postharvest Best Management Practices Manual*, edited by Dr. Jeffrey K. Brecht, National Mango Board, University of Florida, revised May 2017. www.mango.org/wp-content/uploads/2019/09/Mango_Postharvest_ Best_Management_Practices_Manual_English.pdf, accessed 15 Jan. 2020.

229. Amitranjan Gantait, Joy Patra, and Ayan Mukherjee, "Integrate Device Data with Smart Contracts in IBM Blockchain," IBM Corporation, 9 Jan. 2017, updated 1 June 2017. developer.ibm.com/articles/cl-blockchain-for-cognitive-iot-apps-trs, accessed 15 Jan. 2020.

230. essDOCS, "2017 Blockchain for Freight Panel," 3 March 2017. www.essdocs.com/blog/essdocs-tpm-2017-blockchain-for-freight-panel, accessed 7 Aug. 2017.

231. Robert Hackett, "Walmart Blockchain Drones Patent," *Fortune*, Fortune Media Group, 30 May 2017. fortune.com/2017/05/30/walmart-blockchain-drones-patent, accessed 7 Aug. 2017.

232. "Maersk and IBM Unveil First Industry-Wide Cross-Border Supply Chain Solution on Blockchain," Press Release, IBM Corporation, 5 March 2017. www-03.ibm.com/press/us/en/pressrelease/51712.wss, accessed 16 Aug. 2017.

233. John Webb, "Tracking Pork from Pen to Plate," *Advances in Pork Production*, 2004. www.prairieswine.com/pdf/2426.pdf, accessed 7 Aug. 2017.

234. Olga Kharif, "Walmart Tackles Food Safety with Trial of Blockchain," *Bloomberg News*, Bloomberg LP, 18 Nov. 2016. www.bloomberg.com/news/articles/2016-11-18/wal-mart-tackles-food-safety-with-test-of-blockchain-technology, accessed 30 June 2017.

235. Greg Simon, "Supply Chain Loyalty—The Evolution of Coupons," *Loyyal*, 15 Feb. 2016. medium.com/@Loyyal/supply-chain-loyalty-the-evolution-of-coupons-766192d3c6a7, accessed 30 June 2017.

236. Olga Kharif, "Walmart Tackles Food Safety with Trial of Blockchain," *Bloomberg News*, Bloomberg LP, 18 Nov. 2016. www.bloomberg.com/news/articles/2016-11-18/wal-mart-tackles-food-safety-with-test-of-blockchain-technology, accessed 30 June 2017.

237. Frank Yiannas, e-mail to Reshma Kamath, 6 Sept. 2017.

238. Bridget van Kralingen, "Blockchain's Role in Improving Global Food Safety," *IBM THINK Blog*, IBM Corporation, 19 Oct. 2016. www.ibm.com/blogs/think/2016/10/blockchain-food-safety, accessed 30 June 2017.

239. Amitranjan Gantait, Joy Patra, and Ayan Mukherjee, "Integrate Device Data with Smart Contracts in IBM Blockchain," IBM Corporation, 9 Jan. 2017, updated 1 June 2017. developer.ibm.com/articles/cl-blockchain-for-cognitive-iot-apps-trs, accessed 15 Jan. 2020.

240. Robert Hackett, "Walmart and Nine Food Giants Team Up on IBM Blockchain Plans," *Fortune*, Fortune Media Group, 22 Aug. 2017. Fortune.com/2017/08/22/walmart-blockchain-ibm-food-nestle-unilver-tyson-dole, accessed 24 Aug. 2017.

241. "IBM Announces Major Blockchain Collaboration with Dole, Driscoll's, Golden State Foods, Kroger, McCormick and Company, McLane Company, Nestlé, Tyson Foods, and Unilever, and Walmart to Address Food Safety Worldwide," Press Release, IBM Corporation, 22 Aug. 2017. www-03.ibm.com/press/us/en/pressrelease/53013.wss, accessed 24 Aug. 2017.

242. Brigid McDermott, interviewed by Reshma Kamath, 23 June 2017.

243. IAEA Technical Food Programme, Agriculture and Food Security, *International Atomic Energy*. www.iaea.org/technicalcooperation/documents/Factsheets/Agri_Eng.pdf, accessed 19 Aug. 2017.

244. Laurie Burkitt, "Walmart to Triple Spending on Food Safety in China," *Wall Street Journal*, Dow Jones & Company, 17 June 2014. www.wsj.com/articles/Walmart-to-triple-spending-on-food-safety-in-china-1402991720, accessed 29 June 2017.

245. Frank Yiannas, interviewed by Reshma Kamath, 28 June 2017.

246. Tom Doyle, "Enabling Trusted Trade through Secure Track and Trace Technology," *World Customs Journal* 8, 1 (2), Practitioner's Perspective, International Network of Customs Universities, March 2014. worldcustomsjournal.org/Archives/Volume%208%2C%20Number%201%20(Mar%202014)/14%20Doyle.pdf, accessed 3 July 2017.

247. John Brittell, Shashwat Gautam, Stephen Keefe, et al., "Mango Supply Chain: Who Is More Sustainable—MNC or Co-operative Society?" The George Washington University—School of Business, 7 March 2013. talkaboutfoodjb.files.wordpress.com/2013/08/f_brittell_gautam_keefe_mata_shah_wang.pdf, accessed 8 Aug. 2017.

248. Thorsten Wuest, "Identifying Product and Process State Drivers in Manufacturing Systems Using Supervised Machine Learning," WTI-Frankfurt-digital GmbH, 2015. www.wti-frankfurt.de/images/top-themen/Identifying-Product-and-Process-State-Drivers-in-Manufacturing-Systems-Using-Supervised-Machine-Learning.pdf, accessed 30 June 2017.

249. Can-Trace Secretariat, "Can-Trace Pork Pilot Project Report," Can-Trace, Electronic Commission of Canada, Agriculture and Agri-Foods Canada, 2004. www.can-trace.org/portals/0/docs/Can-TracePorkPilotProjectReport.pdf, accessed 8 Aug. 2017.

250. Laurie Burkitt, "Walmart to Triple Spending on Food Safety in China," *Wall Street Journal,* Dow Jones & Company, 17 June 2014. www.wsj.com/articles/Walmart-to-triple-spending-on-food-safety-in-china-1402991720, accessed 29 June 2017.

251. Can-Trace Secretariat, "Can-Trace Pork Pilot Project Report," Can-Trace, Electronic Commission of Canada, Agriculture and Agri-Foods Canada, 2004. www.can-trace.org/portals/0/docs/Can-TracePorkPilotProjectReport.pdf, accessed 8 Aug. 2017.

252. Amitranjan Gantait, Joy Patra, and Ayan Mukherjee, "Integrate Device Data with Smart Contracts in IBM Blockchain," IBM Corporation, 9 Jan. 2017, updated 1 June 2017. developer.ibm.com/articles/cl-blockchain-for-cognitive-iot-apps-trs, accessed 15 Jan. 2020.

253. Don Tapscott, "The Dynamics of Development," *Innovations: Technology, Governance, Globalization* (Cambridge: MIT Press, 2014). dontapscott.com/wp-content/uploads/Innovations.pdf, accessed 15 Jan. 2020.

254. Crystall Lindell, "Walmart to Invest in $25M in Food Safety in China," *Food Engineering,* BNP Media, 20 Oct. 2016. www.foodengineeringmag.com/articles/96277-walmart-to-invest-25m-in-food-safety-in-china, accessed 25 Aug. 2017.

255. Laurie Burkitt, "Walmart to Triple Spending on Food Safety in China," *Wall Street Journal,* Dow Jones & Company, 17 June 2014. www.wsj.com/articles/Walmart-to-triple-spending-on-food-safety-in-china-1402991720, accessed 29 June 2017.

256. US Customs and Border Protection, "Snapshot: A Summary of CBP Facts and Figures," 1 June 2017. www.cbp.gov/document/fact-sheets/cbp-snapshot-fy2016#, accessed 19 Nov. 2017; "Weight of Shipments by Transportation Mode: 2007, 2013, and 2040" (table) in "Freight Facts and Figures, 2015," p. 3. www.rita.dot.gov/bts/sites/rita.dot.gov.bts/files/FFF_complete.pdf, accessed 17 Oct. 2017.

257. This 23,000 figure does not include the approximately 20,000-strong border patrol.

258. US Department of Justice, "Justice Department Recovers over $4.7 Billion from False Claims Act Cases in Fiscal Year 2016," 14 Dec. 2016. www.justice.gov/opa/pr/justice-department-recovers-over-47-billion-false-claims-act-cases-fiscal-year-2016, accessed 17 Oct. 2017.

259. "CBP Facilitates Record Level of Travelers and Modernizes Trade Systems in FY2016," US Customs and Border Protection, 12 Jan. 2017. www.cbp.gov/newsroom/national-media-release/cbp-facilitates-record-level-travelers-and-modernizes-trade-systems, accessed 19 Nov. 2017.

260. These people and corporations did so by claiming that the merchandise was "in-bond" cargo to be trans-shipped to other countries, and instead importing the cargo into the United States; US Department of Justice, "$100 Million Customs Fraud Uncovered; President of the San Diego Customs Brokers Association and Ten Others Charged in Scheme," 25 July 2012. www.fda.gov/ForConsumers/ConsumerUpdates/ucm313527.htm, accessed 19 Nov. 2017.

261. The United States began production of the passports in 2005, offered them in 2006, and has issued only so-called "e-passports" since 2007.

262. Billy Mitchell, "US Will Use Facial Recognition at Airports," *fedscoop*, Scoop News Group, 19 Jan. 2016. www.fedscoop.com/customs-pushing-facial-recognition-tech-nationwide, accessed 19 Nov. 2017.

263. "Fact Sheet: APIS," US Customs and Border Protection, 12 Nov. 2013. www.cbp.gov/sites/default/files/documents/apis_factsheet_3.pdf, accessed 19 Nov. 2017.

264. "Secure Freight Initiative," US Customs and Border Protection, 23 Sept. 2015. www.dhs.gov/secure-freight-initiative, accessed 19 Nov. 2017.

265. "Container Security Initiative," US Customs and Border Protection, 26 June 2014. www.cbp.gov/border-security/ports-entry/cargo-security/csi/csi-brief, accessed 19 Nov. 2017.

266. "Secure Freight Initiative," US Customs and Border Protection, 23 Sept. 2015. www.dhs.gov/secure-freight-initiative, accessed 19 Nov. 2017.

267. The final rule for 10+2 went into effect in 2010. See "Importer Security Filing and Additional Carrier Requirements," 19 CFR 4, 12, 18, 101, 103, 113, 122, 123, 141, 143, 149, 178, and 192. www.cbp.gov/sites/default/files/documents/import_sf_carry_3.pdf, accessed 15 Jan. 2020.

268. "CBP Aims to Prevent High-Risk Travelers from Boarding US-Bound Flights, but Needs to Evaluate Program Performance," US Government Accountability Office, Jan. 2017, pp. 31–32. www.gao.gov/assets/690/682255.pdf, accessed 19 Nov. 2017.

269. "CBP: Improved Planning Needed to Strengthen Trade Enforcement," US Government Accountability Office, June 2017, pp. 39–40. www.gao.gov/assets/690/685215.pdf, accessed 19 Nov. 2017.

270. William Mougayar, *The Business Blockchain* (Hoboken, NJ: John Wiley & Sons, Inc. 2016): 4.

271. Blockchains that use an open-consensus model (where no single party controls the administration of the blockchain) result in a transaction ledger that is very difficult to corrupt. Business logic protocols can be layered on an open-consensus blockchain, such as the Bitcoin blockchain or Ethereum, to establish permissions to participate in a particular set of processes, and add functions such as identity validation and reputation scoring. Blockchains can also be established in permissioned environments, where a single entity hosts the platform and sets permissions. In these environments, the administrator and participants set participation permissions and transaction rules more directly, but transactions and validations occur in a similar manner, and a similar record of transactions is generated that is maintained across the participants within the permissioned environment.

272. Kevin K. McAleenan, interviewed by Alan Cohn, 21 Aug. 2017. McAleenan was nominated by President Trump to serve as the permanent commissioner of CBP on 22 May 2017; he served as acting secretary for the Department of Homeland Security until his resignation in October 2019.

273. Anil John, interviewed by Alan Cohn, 21 Aug. 2017.

274. Kevin K. McAleenan, interviewed by Alan Cohn, 21 Aug. 2017.

275. Jim Manning, "Factom Receives Second DHS Grant for Blockchain IoT Project," *ETHNews*, 30 Jan. 2017. www.ethnews.com/factom-receives-second-dhs-grant-for-blockchain-iot-project, accessed 19 Nov. 2017. Department of Homeland Security, "DHS S&T Awards $199K to Austin Based Factom Inc. for Internet of Things Systems Security," 17 June 2016. www.dhs.gov/science-and-technology/news/2016/06/17/st-awards-199k-austin-based-factom-inc-iot-systems-security, accessed 19 Nov. 2017.

276. Kevin K. McAleenan, interviewed by Alan Cohn, 21 Aug. 2017.

277. Anil John, interviewed by Alan Cohn, 21 Aug. 2017.

278. Stan Higgins, "US Government Awards $2.25 Million to Blockchain Research Projects," *CoinDesk*, Digital Currency Group, 12 May 2017. www.coindesk.com/us-government-awards-2-25-million-blockchain-research-projects; Department of Homeland Security, "DHS S&T awards $9.7M for 13 Phase II Small Business Innovation Research Projects," 2 May 2017. www.dhs.gov/science-and-technology/news/2017/05/02/press-release-dhs-st-awards-97m-13-phase-ii-sbir-projects#, both accessed 19 Nov. 2017.

279. Kevin K. McAleenan, interviewed by Alan Cohn, 21 Aug. 2017.

280. Identity2020 Systems, "ID2020: Concept for Public/Private Partnership," Concept Note, Identity2020 Systems, Inc., Jan. 2017.

281. CBP is already working with blockchain start-up Factom Inc. on Internet of Things-related applications. See US Customs and Border Protection, "CBP Announces Initial Awards under Silicon Valley Innovation Program," 20 Dec. 2016. www.factom.com/news/cbp-announces-initial-awards-under-silicon-valley-innovation-program, accessed 19 Nov. 2017.

282. Michael del Castillo, "Inside Bank of America's New Microsoft-Powered Blockchain Project," *CoinDesk*, Digital Currency Group, 29 Sept. 2016. www.coindesk.com/bank-of-america-blockchain-microsoft-trade-finance, accessed 19 Nov. 2017.

283. Stan Higgins, "R3 Completes Blockchain Test with 11 Banks," *CoinDesk*, Digital Currency Group, 20 Jan. 2016. www.coindesk.com/r3cev-blockchain-test-11-banks; Stan Higgins, "8 R3 Banks Test Intel Blockchain Platform," *CoinDesk*, Digital Currency Group, 26 Sept. 2016. www.coindesk.com/8-r3-banks-test-intel-blockchain-platform; "Calypso and R3 Successfully Test FX Trade Matching on Corda DLT Platform," *CryptoNinjas*, 25 April 2017. www.cryptoninjas.net/2017/04/25/calypso-r3-successfully-test-fx-trade-matching-corda-dlt-platform, all accessed 19 Nov. 2017.

284. See, e.g., Carlo R.W. De Meijer, "Blockchain: Accelerated Activity in Trade Finance," *Finextra*, Finextra Research, 26 Jan. 2017. www.finextra.com/blogposting/13593/blockchain-accelerated-activity-in-trade-finance, accessed 19 Nov. 2017.

285. Brenda B. Smith, interview responses provided to Alan Cohn, 21 Aug. 2017.

286. Brenda B. Smith, interview responses provided to Alan Cohn, 21 Aug. 2017.

287. Kevin K. McAleenan, interviewed by Alan Cohn, 21 Aug. 2017.

288. Kevin K. McAleenan, interviewed by Alan Cohn, 21 Aug. 2017.

289. Marley Gray, "Ethereum Blockchain as a Service now on Azure," Microsoft, 9 Nov. 2015. azure.microsoft.com/en-us/blog/ethereum-blockchain-as-a-service-now-on-azure, accessed 19 Nov. 2017; "Calypso and R3 Successfully Test FX Trade Matching on Corda DLT Platform," *CryptoNinjas*, 25 April 2017. www.cryptoninjas.net/2017/04/25/calypso-r3-successfully-test-fx-trade-matching-corda-dlt-platform; Robert Hackett, "Walmart and IBM and Partnering to Put Chinese Pork on a Blockchain," *Fortune*, Fortune Media Group, 19 Oct. 2016. fortune.com/2016/10/19/walmart-ibm-blockchain-china-pork, both accessed 19 Nov. 2017.

290. Anil John, interviewed by Alan Cohn, 21 Aug. 2017.

291. Brenda B. Smith, interview responses provided to Alan Cohn, 21 Aug. 2017.

292. General Notice, "Air Cargo Advance Screening (ACAS) Pilot Program," *Federal Register* 77, 206 (Government Publishing Office, 24 Oct. 2012): 65006. www.gpo.gov/fdsys/pkg/FR-2012-10-24/pdf/2012-26031.pdf, accessed 19 Nov. 2017.

293. General Notice, "Air Cargo Advance Screening (ACAS) Pilot Program."

294. General Notice, "Air Cargo Advance Screening (ACAS) Pilot Program."

295. General Notice, "Air Cargo Advance Screening (ACAS) Pilot Program."

296. Leanne Kemp, "Everledger Pitch," YouTube.com, 22 April 2016. www.youtube.com/watch?v=aow2hxPI5DI; US CBP, "Fact Sheet: APIS," 12 Nov. 2013. www.cbp.gov/sites/default/files/documents/apis_factsheet_3.pdf, both accessed 19 Nov. 2017.

297. Carlo R.W. De Meijer, "Blockchain: Can It Be of Help for the Agricultural Industry?" *Finextra*, Finextra Research, 23 Oct. 2016. www.finextra.com/blogposting/13286/blockchain-can-it-be-of-help-for-the-agricultural-industry, accessed 19 Nov. 2017.

298. Brenda B. Smith, interview responses provided to Alan Cohn, 21 Aug. 2017.

299. Anil John, interviewed by Alan Cohn, 21 Aug. 2017.

300. Brenda B. Smith, interview responses provided to Alan Cohn, 21 Aug. 2017.

301. The World Bank, "Industry, Value Added (% of GDP)," *The World Bank Group*, n.d. data.worldbank.org/indicator/NV.IND.TOTL.ZS, accessed 13 Sept. 2017. Stefan Hopf would like to thank Prof. Dr. Dres. h.c. Arnold Picot (Ludwig-Maximilians-University Munich), Güngör Kara (EOS–Electro Optical Systems), Dr. Alexander Duisberg (Bird & Bird), Dr. Reinhold Achatz (Industrial Data Space/Thyssenkrupp), Ronny Fehling (Airbus), and Dr. Leon Zucchini (Airbus) for their valuable input and feedback. Moreover, he is grateful to everyone at The Nunatak Group who assisted in research and preparation of the white paper from which this chapter was adapted.

302. Henning Kagermann, Wolfgang Wahlster, and Johannes Helbig, "Securing the Future of German Manufacturing Industry: Recommendations for Implementing the Strategic Initiative Industrie 4.0," *Forschungsunion and Acatech*, April 2013. www.acatech.de/fileadmin/user_upload/Baumstruktur_nach_Website/Acatech/root/de/Material_ fuer_Sonderseiten/Industrie_4.0/Final_report__Industrie_4.0_ accessible.pdf, accessed 13 Sept. 2017.

303. In this chapter, *blockchain technology* is used as a term to capture various underlying elements (e.g., blockchain, smart contracts, tokens).

304. Figure 1 is based on the work of Henning Kagermann, Wolfgang Wahlster, Johannes Helbig, and Johannes Helbig, "Im Fokus: Das Zukunftsprojekt Industrie 4.0 – Handlungsempfehlungen zur Umsetzung," *Forschungsunion*, 1 March 2012. www.bmbf.de/pub_hts/ kommunikation_bericht_2012-1.pdf, accessed 13 Sept. 2017.

305. Henning Kagermann, Wolfgang Wahlster, and Johannes Helbig, "Securing the Future of German Manufacturing Industry: Recommendations for Implementing the Strategic Initiative Industrie 4.0," *Forschungsunion and Acatech*, April 2013. www.acatech.de/fileadmin/ user_upload/Baumstruktur_nach_Website/Acatech/root/de/Material_ fuer_Sonderseiten/Industrie_4.0/Final_report__Industrie_4.0_ accessible.pdf, accessed 13 Sept. 2017.

306. Jürgen Gausemeier and Fritz Klocke, "Industrie 4.0: Internationaler Benchmark, Zukunftsoptionen und Handlungsempfehlungen für die Produktionsforschung," *Acatech*, Heinz Nixdorf Institut, RWTH Aachen University, June 2016. www.acatech.de/fileadmin/user_upload/ Baumstruktur_nach_Website/Acatech/root/de/Publikationen/ Sonderpublikationen/INBENZHAP_dt_web_verlinkt.pdf, accessed 13 Sept. 2017. Figure 2 is based on the work of Harald Foidl and Michael Felderer, "Research Challenges of Industry 4.0 for Quality Management," University of Innsbruck, April 2016. www.researchgate. net/publication/300319076_Research_Challenges_of_Industry_40_for_ Quality_Management, accessed 13 Sept. 2017.

307. Henning Kagermann, Wolfgang Wahlster, and Johannes Helbig, "Securing the Future of German Manufacturing Industry: Recommendations for Implementing the Strategic Initiative Industrie 4.0," *Forschungsunion and Acatech*, April 2013. www.acatech.de/fileadmin/ user_upload/Baumstruktur_nach_Website/Acatech/root/de/Material_ fuer_Sonderseiten/Industrie_4.0/Final_report__Industrie_4.0_ accessible.pdf, accessed 13 Sept. 2017.

308. Venkat N. Venkatraman, "IT-Enabled Business Transformation: From Automation to Business Scope Redefinition," *Sloan Management Review* 35, 2 (1994): 73–87. Massachusetts Institute of Technology, sloanreview. mit.edu/article/itenabled-business-transformation-from-automation-to- business-scope-redefinition, accessed 13 Sept. 2017.

309. Joseph Lubin, "The Basics of Blockchain and Ethereum," *Lift Conference*, 11 Feb. 2016. liftconference.com/lift16/speakers/4623, accessed 13 Sept. 2017.

310. Monax, "Explainer: Ecosystem Applications," *Monax Explainer*, n.d. monax.io/explainers/ecosystem_applications, accessed 13 Sept. 2017.

311. Thomas Fedkenhauer, Dr. Yvonne FritzscheSterr, Lars Nagel, et al., "Datenaustausch als wesentlicher Bestandteil der Digitalisierung," *PwC*, PricewaterhouseCoopers, 25 April 2017. www.pwc.de/de/digitale-transformation/studie-datenaustausch-digitalisierung.pdf, accessed 13 Sept. 2017.

312. IDSA, "Innovative Ways for Adding Value," Industrial Data Space Association, as of 8 Oct. 2016. web.archive.org/web/20161008001338/http://www.industrialdataspace.org:80/en/industrial-data-space, accessed 15 Jan. 2020. Please see IDSA's current site here: www.internationaldataspaces.org.

313. Strictly speaking and similar to previous general-purpose technologies (e.g., electricity), blockchain technology will enable the development of over-the-top applications and standards that will become the actual platforms—similar to the Internet and e-mails.

314. Table 7-1 is based on Monax, "Explainer: Ecosystem Applications," *Monax Explainer*, n.d. monax.io/explainers/ecosystem_applications, accessed 23 Aug. 2017.

315. Sachin Karadgi, "Warm-up to the Idea of Blockchain in Manufacturing," *LinkedIn*, LinkedIn Corp., 12 June 2016. www.linkedin.com/pulse/warm-up-idea-blockchain-manufacturing-sachin-karadgi, accessed 13 Sept. 2017.

316. Nick Szabo, "Formalizing and Securing Relationships on Public Networks," *First Monday*, 1 Sept. 1997. firstmonday.org/ojs/index.php/fm/article/view/548/469, accessed 23 Aug. 2017.

317. Antony Lewis, "A Gentle Introduction to Digital Tokens," *Bits on blocks*, 28 Sept. 2015. bitsonblocks.net/2015/09/28/a-gentle-introduction-to-digital-tokens, accessed 23 Aug. 2017.

318. Burkhard Blechschmidt and Carsten Stöcker, "How Blockchain Can Slash the Manufacturing 'Trust Tax,'" Genesis of Things, 2016. www.genesisofthings.com/pdf/whitepaper.pdf, accessed 23 Aug. 2017.

319. Burkhard Blechschmidt and Carsten Stöcker, "How Blockchain Can Slash the Manufacturing 'Trust Tax.'"

320. SyncFab, "Decentralized Manufacturing," Version 15, 3 Aug. 2018. blockchain.syncfab.com/SyncFab_MFG_WP.pdf, accessed 15 Jan. 2020. Hermann Simon, *Hidden Champions: Lessons from 500 of the World's Best Unknown Companies* (Boston, MA: Harvard Business School Press, 1996).

321. Hillary Ohlmann, "Top 10 Biggest Procurement Challenges," *Deltabid Blog*, 19 April 2016. blog.deltabid.com/top-10-biggest-procurement-challenges, accessed 23 Aug. 2017.

322. Tai Ming Cheung, Thomas Mahnken, Deborah Seligsohn, et al., "Planning for Innovation: Understanding China's Plans for Technological, Energy, Industrial, and Defense Development," *Institute on Global Conflict and Cooperation*, 18 Sept. 2015. www.uscc.gov/sites/default/files/Research/Planning%20for%20Innovation-Understanding%20China%27s%20Plans%20for%20Tech%20Energy%20Industrial%20and%20Defense%20Development072816.pdf, accessed 23 Aug. 2017.

323. "A Brief History of SyncFab," SyncFab, 10 Nov. 2017. medium.com/syncfabmfg/a-brief-history-of-syncfab-9c9a8cf64402, accessed 13 Dec. 2017.

324. "Decentralized Hardware Manufacturing," SyncFab, 2017. blockchain.syncfab.com/SyncFab_MFG_One_Pager.pdf, accessed 13 Dec. 2017.

325. "Decentralized Manufacturing," Version 15, SyncFab, 3 Aug. 2018. blockchain.syncfab.com/SyncFab_MFG_WP.pdf, accessed 15 Jan. 2020.

326. For an image of how SyncFab works, see syncfab.com/assets/img/press/high-res/how-it-works.png, accessed 22 Feb. 2020.

327. "Decentralized Manufacturing," Version 15, SyncFab, 3 Aug. 2018. blockchain.syncfab.com/SyncFab_MFG_WP.pdf, accessed 15 Jan. 2020.

328. "Decentralized Manufacturing," Version 15, SyncFab, 3 Aug. 2018.

329. Stefan Hopf and Arnold Picot, "Crypto-Property and Trustless P2P Transactions: Blockchain as a Disruption of Property Rights and Transaction Cost Regimes?" *1. interdisziplinäre Konferenz zur Zukunft der Wertschöpfung*, Jens Wulfsberg, Tobias Redlich, and Manuel Moritz (2016): 159–172, Helmut-Schmidt-Universität. Hamburg.

330. "Decentralized Manufacturing," Version 15, SyncFab, 3 Aug. 2018. blockchain.syncfab.com/SyncFab_MFG_WP.pdf, accessed 15 Jan. 2020.

331. Duck Bong Kim, Paul Witherell, Yan Lu, and Shaw Feng, "Toward a Digital Thread and Data Package for Metals-Additive Manufacturing," ResearchGate, March 2017. www.researchgate.net/publication/314246208_Toward_a_Digital_Thread_and_Data_Package_for_Metals-Additive_Manufacturing#pf17, accessed 23 Aug. 2017.

332. Mark Cotteleer, Stuart Trouton, and Ed Dobner, "3D Opportunity for Blockchain," Deloitte University Press, 17 Nov. 2016. dupress.deloitte.com/dup-us-en/focus/3d-opportunity/3d-printing-blockchain-in-manufacturing.html, accessed 23 Aug. 2017.

333. Mark Cotteleer, Stuart Trouton, and Ed Dobner, "3D Opportunity for Blockchain," Deloitte University Press, 17 Nov. 2016.

334. Cubichain is a partnership of 3D Systems, Boeing, CalRAM, and Northrop Grumman; and Genesis of Things is a partnership of EOS, Innogy, Cognizant, BigchainDB, Riddle&Code, 3yourmind, 3D makers zone, Commerzbank, and Intel.

335. Mark Cotteleer, Stuart Trouton, and Ed Dobner, "3D Opportunity for Blockchain," Deloitte University Press, 17 Nov. 2016. dupress.deloitte. com/dup-us-en/focus/3d-opportunity/3d-printing-blockchain-in-manufacturing.html, accessed 23 Aug. 2017. Cubichain Technologies, cubichain.com, accessed 23 Aug. 2017.

336. Burkhard Blechschmidt and Carsten Stöcker, "How Blockchain Can Slash the Manufacturing 'Trust Tax,'" White Paper, Genesis of Things, 2016. www.genesisofthings.com/pdf/whitepaper.pdf, accessed 23 Aug. 2017.

337. Jess Holl, "Blockchain: The Trust Protocol," News Release, Airbus SAS, 27 March 2017. www.airbus.com/newsroom/news/en/2017/03/Blockchain.html, accessed 23 Aug. 2017.

338. Mark Cotteleer, Stuart Trouton, and Ed Dobner, "3D Opportunity and the Digital Thread," Deloitte University Press, 3 March 2016. dupress. deloitte.com/dup-us-en/focus/3d-opportunity/3d-printing-digital-thread-in-manufacturing.html, accessed 23 Aug. 2017.

339. AEROTEC, EOS, and Daimler, "Industrial 3D Printing: The New Era Has Begun," Press Release, EOS, 19 April 2017. www.eos.info/eos_binaries0/eos/442ea5fb8cf30609/184aa887b21d/EOS_Press_Release_2017_04_19_NextGenAM.pdf, accessed 23 Aug. 2017.

340. Karen Lewis, "Blockchain: Four Use Cases Transforming Business," *IBM Internet of Things Blog*, IBM Corporation, 25 May 2017. www.ibm. com/blogs/internet-of-things/iot-blockchain-use-cases, accessed 23 Aug. 2017.

341. Stefanie Kowallick, "How Blockchain Can Help to Prevent Odometer Fraud," *Bosch ConnectedWorld Blog*, Bosch.IO GmbH, 5 Dec. 2017. blog.bosch-si.com/blockchain/how-blockchain-can-help-to-prevent-odometer-fraud, accessed 13 Dec. 2017.

342. Stan Higgins, "GE Patent Filings Hint at Blockchain Role in Aircraft Management," *CoinDesk*, Digital Currency Group, 9 Nov. 2017. www. coindesk.com/ge-patent-filings-hint-at-blockchain-role-in-aircraft-management, accessed 13 Dec. 2017.

343. Carly Sheridan, "Digitizing Vehicles: The First Blockchain-Backed Car Passport," *BigchainDB Blog*, 24 March 2017. blog.bigchaindb.

com/digitizing-vehicles-the-first-blockchain-backed-car-passport-
b55ead6dbc71; Woodrow Bellamy III, "Air France KLM Is Evaluating
MRO Potential for Blockchain," *Aviation Today*, 3 Oct. 2017. www.
aviationtoday.com/2017/10/03/air-france-klm-evaluating-mro-potential-
blockchain; and Patrick Götze, "Generating More Transparency in
Aviation with Blockchain Technology," Lufthansa Industry Solutions,
n.d. www.lufthansa-industry-solutions.com/de-en/solutions-products/
aviation/generating-more-transparency-in-aviation-with-blockchain-
technology, all accessed 13 Dec. 2017.

344. David Noller and Robert Rencher, "IoT for Blockchain and the Life
of an Asset," *IBM and Boeing at Interconnect 2017*, IBM Corporation,
13 March 2017. www-304.ibm.com/events/tools/ic/2017ems/REST/
presentations/PDF/IC2017_2227.pdf, accessed 13 Dec. 2017.

345. David Noller and Robert Rencher, "IoT for Blockchain and the Life of
an Asset."

346. David Noller and Robert Rencher, "IoT for Blockchain and the Life of
an Asset."

347. Jeremy Coward, "Planes Are Getting Smarter as Aviation IoT Takes Off,
Says Boeing," Internet of Things Institute, 27 Feb. 2017. www.ioti.com/
industrial-iot/planes-are-getting-smarter-aviation-iot-takes-says-boeing,
accessed 13 Dec. 2017.

348. George A. Akerlof, "The Market for 'Lemons': Quality Uncertainty and
the Market Mechanism, " *Quarterly Journal of Economics* 84, 3 (1970):
488–500.

349. Bitkom, "Industrie 4.0 als unternehmerische Gestaltungsaufgabe,"
Bitkom, 2017. www.bitkom.org/noindex/Publikationen/2017/
Positionspapiere/Geschaeftsmodelle-Industrie-40/FirstSpirit-
1496912702488170608-Faktenpapier-Geschaeftsmodelle-Industrie-40-
Online.pdf, accessed 13 Dec. 2017; Peter Weill, Tom Malone, Victoria
D'Urso, George Herman, and Stephanie Woerner, "Do Some Business
Models Perform Better than Others? A Study of the 1000 Largest
US Firms," Working Paper, MIT Center for Coordination Science, 2005.
ccs.mit.edu/papers/pdf/wp226.pdf, accessed 30 Oct. 2019.

350. Rolls-Royce, "Rolls-Royce Celebrates 50th Anniversary of Power-by-
the-Hour," Press Release, Rolls-Royce PLC, 30 Oct. 2012. www.rolls-
royce.com/media/press-releases/yr-2012/121030-the-hour.aspx, accessed
13 Dec. 2017.

351. Council of Supply Chain Management Professionals, "Definitions
of Supply Chain Management," *CSCMP Supply Chain Management
Definitions and Glossary*, n.d. cscmp.org/CSCMP/Educate/SCM_
Definitions_and_Glossary_of_Terms/CSCMP/Educate/SCM_

Definitions_and_Glossary_of_Terms.aspx?hkey=60879588-f65f-4ab5-8c4b-6878815ef921, accessed 13 Dec. 2017.

352. Ben Dickson, "Blockchain Has the Potential to Revolutionize the Supply Chain," *TechCrunch*, Verizon Media, 24 Nov. 2016. techcrunch.com/2016/11/24/blockchain-has-the-potential-to-revolutionize-the-supply-chain, accessed 13 Dec. 2017.

353. Doug Gates, Tom Mayor, and Erich L. Gampenrieder, "Global Manufacturing Outlook," KPMG, May 2016. home.kpmg.com/content/dam/kpmg/pdf/2016/05/global-manufacturing-outlook-competing-for-growth.pdf, accessed 13 Dec. 2017.

354. Pete Rizzo, "World's Largest Mining Company to Use Blockchain for Supply Chain," *CoinDesk*, Digital Currency Group, 23 Sept. 2016. www.coindesk.com/bhp-billiton-blockchain-mining-company-supply-chain, accessed 13 Dec. 2017.

355. Robert Hackett, "Walmart and IBM Are Partnering to Put Chinese Pork on a Blockchain," *Fortune*, Fortune Media Group, 19 Oct. 2016. fortune.com/2016/10/19/walmart-ibm-blockchain-china-pork, accessed 13 Dec. 2017.

356. Michael del Castillo, "Foxconn Reveals Plan for Blockchain Supply Chain Domination" *CoinDesk*, Digital Currency Group, 13 March 2017. www.coindesk.com/foxconn-wants-take-global-supply-chain-blockchain; Mahindra, "Mahindra and IBM to Develop Blockchain Solution for Supply Chain Finance," Press Release, Mahindra & Mahindra Ltd., 30 Nov. 2016. www.mahindra.com/news-room/press-release/Mahindra-and-IBM-to-Develop-Blockchain-Solution-for-Supply-Chain-Finance; and Tatsiana Yablonskaya, "IBM and Sichuan Hejia Launched a Blockchain Platform for Pharmaceutical Procurement," *Coinspeaker*, 11 April 2017. www.coinspeaker.com/2017/04/11/ibm-sichuan-hejia-launched-blockchain-platform-pharmaceutical-procurement, all accessed 13 Dec. 2017.

357. Michael del Castillo, "Foxconn Reveals Plan for Blockchain Supply Chain Domination," *CoinDesk*, Digital Currency Group, 13 March 2017. www.coindesk.com/foxconn-wants-take-global-supply-chain-blockchain, accessed 13 Dec. 2017.

358. Angel Versetti, "Blockchain for Pharma—Ambrosus," *Ambrosus Blog*, 2 Sept. 2017. blog.ambrosus.com/blockchain-for-pharma-ambrosus-ec732e61f732, accessed 13 Dec. 2017.

359. Ian Allison, "Blockchain IoT Firm Chronicled Creates MediLedger Project to Safeguard Pharmaceuticals," *International Business Times*, 20 Sept. 2017. www.ibtimes.co.uk/blockchain-iot-firm-chronicled-creates-mediledger-project-safeguard-pharmaceuticals-1640054, accessed 13 Dec. 2017.

360. Josef Maichle, "Teileverfolgung in der Supply Chain," blockLAB Stuttgart, 28 Aug. 2017. www.youtube.com/watch?v=u_Z2yI6CHDQ, accessed 13 Dec. 2017.

361. Table 7-3 is based on Chris Skinner, "What Does the Blockchain Mean for Our Payment Systems?" *Chris Skinner's Blog*, The Finanser, 3 Nov. 2017. thefinanser.com/2015/11/what-does-the-blockchain-mean-for-our-ccps-and-achs.html, accessed 13 Dec. 2017.

362. Tom Fuerstner, "Resilient Identity Services" *9984 Summit*, 10 Nov. 2017. www.youtube.com/watch?v=06VJPTf7DSo; and Chronicled, "How and Why We Invented the CryptoSeal," *Chronicled Blog*, 17 Nov. 2017. blog. chronicled.com/how-and-why-we-invented-the-cryptoseal-6577d8633a2, both accessed 13 Dec. 2017.

363. Christoph Malmo, "Bitcoin's Surge in Price Has Sent Its Electricity Consumption Soaring," *Motherboard*, Vice Media LLC, 1 Nov. 2017. motherboard.vice.com/en_us/article/ywbbpm/bitcoin-mining-electricity-consumption-ethereum-energy-climate-change, accessed 13 Dec. 2017.

364. Store of Value, "List of High Profile Cryptocurrency Hacks So Far," *Store of Value Blog*, Github Inc., 24 Aug. 2017. storeofvalue.github.io/posts/cryptocurrency-hacks-so-far-august-24th, accessed 13 Dec. 2017.

365. Pete Rizzo, "In Formal Verification Push, Ethereum Seeks Smart Contract Certainty," *CoinDesk*, Digital Currency Group, 28 Sept. 2016. www.coindesk.com/ethereum-formal-verification-smart-contracts, accessed 13 Dec. 2017.

366. Ian Roderick Macneil, "The Many Futures of Contracts," *Southern California Law Review* 47 (1974): 691–816.

367. Stefan Hopf and Arnold Picot, "Crypto-Property and Trustless P2P Transactions: Blockchain as a Disruption of Property Rights and Transaction Cost Regimes?" in Jens Wulfsberg, Tobias Redlich, and Manuel Moritz, *Interdisziplinäre Konferenz zur Zukunft der Wertschöpfung* (Hamburg: Helmut-Schmidt-Universität, 2016): 159–172.

368. Trusted IoT Alliance, www.trusted-iot.org, accessed 13 Dec. 2017.

369. Sebastien Meunier, "When Do You Need Blockchain? Decision Models," *Sebastien Meunier Blog*, Medium, 4 Aug. 2016. medium. com/@sbmeunier/when-do-you-need-blockchain-decision-models-a5c40e7c9ba1, accessed 13 Dec. 2017.

370. Vincent Dietrich, Marko Ivanovic, Thomas Meier, et al., "Application of Blockchain Technology in the Manufacturing Industry," Frankfurt School Blockchain Center Working Paper, Nov. 2017. explore-ip. com/2017_Blockchain-Technology-in-Manufacturing.pdf. Table 7-4 is based on information in Gunther Dütsch and Neon Steinecke, "Use Cases for Blockchain Technology in Energy and Commodity Trading," *PwC*, PricewaterhouseCoopers, July 2017. www.pwc-energiewirtschaft. de/de/wp-content/uploads/2017/07/PwC_Broschuere_Blockchain_ Commodity_Mgmt_EN_Juli-2017_FINAL.pdf, both accessed 13 Dec. 2017.

371. Abby Mayer, "Supply Chain Metrics that Matter: A Focus on Aerospace and Defense Industry," Supply Chain Insights LLC, 18 March 2014. Supplychaininsights.com/supply-chain-metrics-that-matter-a-focus-on-aerospace-defense, accessed 24 Aug. 2017.

372. 44 U.S.C. Chapter 33, Sec. 3301. National Archives, www.archives.gov/ about/laws/disposal-of-records.html, accessed 15 Jan. 2020.

373. "2016 Index of US Military Strength," The Heritage Foundation, n.d. index.heritage.org/military/2015/chapter/us-power/us-air-force, accessed 24 Aug. 2017.

374. Patrick Boyd, "These Industries Are the Future of Additive Manufacturing," *IndustryWeek*, Endeavor Business Media, 17 Nov. 2016. www.industryweek.com/future-additive-manufacturing, accessed 24 Aug. 2017; "Enabling the Next Production Revolution: The Future of Manufacturing and Services: Interim Report," *Meeting of the OECD Council at Ministerial Level*, Paris, 1–2 June 2016. www.oecd.org/mcm/ documents/Enabling-the-next-production-revolution-the-future-of-manufacturing-and-services-interim-report.pdf, accessed 3 July 2018.

375. Moog, "About Us," n.d. www.moog.com/about-us.html, accessed 24 Aug. 2017.

376. Martina F. Ferracane, "Shaking and Reshaping: Industry 4.0 and Industry 4.1," *Paris Innovation Review*, 30 Nov. 2015. parisinnovationreview.com/2015/11/30/industry-4-0-and-industry-4-1, accessed 24 Aug. 2017.

377. Stuart Trouton, Mark Vitale, and Jason Killmeyer, "3D Opportunity for Blockchain," Deloitte University Press, 17 Nov. 2016. dupress.deloitte. com/dup-us-en/focus/3d-opportunity/3d-printing-blockchain-in-manufacturing.html; Enrico Camerinelli, "Blockchain in the Supply Chain," *Finextra*, Finextra Research, 13 May 2016. www.finextra.com/ blogposting/12597/blockchain-in-the-supply-chain, both accessed 24 Aug. 2017.

378. George Small, e-mail message to Vineet Narula and Prema Shrikrishna, 10 May 2017.

379. Vineet Narula and Prema Shrikrishna extend their appreciation to Moog Inc., especially James Allen Regenor (business unit director,

transformative technologies) and George Small (chief technology officer), for collaborating with them throughout the research process.

380. James Allen Regenor, interviewed by Vineet Narula and Prema Shrikrishna, 18 April 2017.

381. James Allen Regenor, interviewed by Vineet Narula and Prema Shrikrishna, 18 April 2017.

382. James Allen Regenor, interviewed by Vineet Narula and Prema Shrikrishna, 18 April 2017.

383. Ronan Mahoney, "Blockchain Technology Brings Watertight Security to Additive Manufacturing," *3DPrinting.com*, 18 Nov. 2016. 3dprinting. com/news/blockchain-technology-brings-watertight-security-additive-manufacturing, accessed 24 Aug. 2017.

384. Atos SE, " Securing 3D-Printing: Could Blockchain Be the Answer?" 8 Feb. 2017. ascent.atos.net/securing-3d-printing-could-blockchain-be-the-answer, accessed 24 Aug. 2017.

385. A shipset is a quantity of parts greater than the quantity needed to ensure safety.

386. "DHL White Paper Makes the Case for 'Plug and Play' Supply Chains," *Post & Parcel*, 23 Nov. 2016. postandparcel.info/76704/news/dhl-white-paper-makes-the-case-for-plug-and-play-supply-chains, accessed 24 Aug. 2017.

387. Jeffrey Frankel, "The Brexiting British, Donald Trump and Globalisation's Have-Nots," *The Guardian*, Guardian News & Media Ltd., 17 July 2016. www.theguardian.com/business/2016/jul/17/donald-trump-eu-referendum-brexit-globalisation, accessed 24 Aug. 2017.

388. "Will 3-D Printing Reshape the Dynamics of Global Trade?" *The Economist*, The Economist Newspaper Ltd., 13 April 2017. destinationinnovation.economist.com/2017/04/13/will-3-d-printing-reshape-the-dynamics-of-global-trade, accessed 24 Aug. 2017.

389. Richard McCormick, "Amazon Wants to Fit Trucks with 3D Printers to Speed Up Deliveries," *The Verge*, 27 Feb. 2015 www.theverge. com/2015/2/27/8119443/amazon-3d-printing-trucks-patent, accessed 24 Aug. 2017.

390. Bret Boyd, "3D Printing and the Regionalization of Economic Activity," Grayline Group, 22 Jan. 2017. graylinegroup.com/manufacturing-catalyst-overview, accessed 24 Aug. 2017.

391. Mritiunjoy Mohanty, "The Growth Model Has Come Undone," *The Hindu*, 19 July 2016. www.thehindu.com/opinion/lead/the-growth-model-has-come-undone/article3621241.ece, accessed 24 Aug. 2017.

392. Richard D'Aveni, "The 3-D Printing Revolution," *Harvard Business Review*, May 2015. hbr.org/2015/05/the-3-d-printing-revolution, accessed 24 Aug. 2017.

393. Management Study Guide, "Supply Chains as Sources of Competitive Advantage," n.d. www.managementstudyguide.com/supply-chains-as-sources-of-competitive-advantage.htm, accessed 24 Aug. 2017.

394. An Baijie, "Xi Jinping Thought Approved for Party Constitution," *ChinaDaily.com.cn*, China Daily Information Co, 24 Oct. 2017. www.chinadaily.com.cn/china/19thcpcnationalcongress/2017-10/24/content_33644524.htm, accessed 1 May 2018.

395. "Belt and Road Portal," *eng.yidaiyilu.gov.cn*, n.d. eng.yidaiyilu.gov.cn/info/iList.jsp?cat_id=10076, accessed 1 May 2018.

396. Kevin Sneader and Joe Ngai, "China's One Belt, One Road: Will It Reshape Global Trade?" hosted by Cecilia Ma Zecha, *McKinsey Podcast*, McKinsey & Company, July 2016. www.mckinsey.com/featured-insights/china/chinas-one-belt-one-road-will-it-reshape-global-trade, accessed 11 May 2018.

397. Kane Wu and Sumeet Chatterjee, "China's Belt and Road Acquisitions Surge Despite Outbound Capital Crackdown," *Reuters*, Thomson Reuters, 15 Aug. 2017. www.reuters.com/article/china-ma/chinas-belt-and-road-acquisitions-surge-despite-outbound-capital-crackdown-idUSL4N1L03XF, accessed 1 May 2018.

398. Forrester, "Cross-Border Ecommerce Will Reach $627 Billion by 2022," Forrester Research Inc., 28 June 2017. www.forrester.com/CrossBorder+eCommerce+Will+Reach+627+Billion+By+2022/-/E-PRE10033, accessed 1 May 2018.

399. "Cap. 553 Electronic Transactions Ordinance," Hong Kong e-Legislation, Hong Kong Department of Justice, last modified 7 July 2017. www.elegislation.gov.hk/hk/cap553, accessed 29 April 2018.

400. Pindar Wong, interviewed by Vineet Narula and Prema Shrikrishna, 22 April 2018. See also Aaron Pittman, "Push vs. Pull in Your Supply Chain … What's The Difference?" *The Network Effect: Beyond Supply Chains*, 5 Dec. 2014. supplychainbeyond.com/push-vs-pull-supply-chain-whats-difference, accessed 1 May 2018.

401. Nick Robins, "2017: What Next for Green Finance?" *The Huffington Post*, Oath Inc., 16 Jan. 2017, updated 17 Jan. 2018. www.huffingtonpost.com/nick-robins/2017-what-next-for-green_b_14203706.html, accessed 3 May 2018. Robins is the co-director of the UN Environment Inquiry into a Sustainable Financial System.

402. "WRAP and the Circular Economy," *WRAP UK*, Waste and Resources Action Programme, 24 Jan. 2013. www.wrap.org.uk/about-us/about/wrap-and-circular-economy, accessed 3 May 2018.

403. Peter Gratzke, David Schatsky, and Eric Piscini, "Banding Together for Blockchain: Does It Make Sense for Your Company to Join a Consortium?" *Deloitte Insights*, Deloitte LLP, 16 Aug. 2017. www2. deloitte.com/insights/us/en/focus/signals-for-strategists/emergence-of-blockchain-consortia.html, accessed 1 May 2018.

404. VeChain, "VeChain Is Co-Founder of the Belt and Road Initiative Blockchain Alliance," *Cision PRNewswire*, PR Newswire Association LLC, 30 Dec. 2019. www.prnewswire.com/news-releases/vechain-is-co-founder-of-the-belt-and-road-initiative-blockchain-alliance-briba-300979679.html; for a running total and updates, see "The Belt and Road Initiative: Country Profiles," *HKTDC*, Hong Kong Trade Development Council, china-trade-research.hktdc.com/business-news/article/The-Belt-and-Road-Initiative/The-Belt-and-Road-Initiative-Country-Profiles/obor/en/1/1X000000/1X0A36I0.htm, and the data tab of the official One Belt One Road Portal, eng.yidaiyilu.gov.cn/dsjym.htm.

405. "Pricing Guide," "Join Hyperledger," Hyperledger, The Linux Foundation, 2018. www.hyperledger.org/members/join, accessed 11 May 2018.

406. Anna Irrera, "JPMorgan Chase & Co Leaves Blockchain Consortium R3," *Reuters*, Thomson Reuters, 27 April 2017. www.reuters.com/article/us-jpmorgan-r3/jpmorgan-chase-co-leaves-blockchain-consortium-r3-idUSKBN17T2T4, accessed 1 May 2018.

407. Alex Batlin, "Crypto 2.0 Musings: Decentralised Business Models," *LinkedIn Pulse*, LinkedIn Corp., 23 Oct. 2016. www.linkedin.com/pulse/crypto-20-musings-digital-business-models-alex-batlin?articleId=6195870281790218240, accessed 1 May 2018.

408. Fred Ehrsam, "Blockchain Tokens and the Dawn of the Decentralized Business Model," *The Coinbase Blog*, Medium, 1 Aug. 2016. blog.coinbase.com/app-coins-and-the-dawn-of-the-decentralized-business-model-8b8c951e734f#.z0k2pec4u, accessed 1 May 2018.

409. For more information about alternative dispute resolution—essentially any process such as arbitration or mediation that resolves disputes without litigation—see "Alternative Dispute Resolution," Legal Information Institute, Cornell Law School, 6 Aug. 2007. www.law.cornell.edu/wex/alternative_dispute_resolution. For examples of patent nonaggression pacts, see the Open Innovation Network, launched in 2005 by IBM, NEC, Novell, Philips, Red Hat, and Sony. "OIN License

Agreement," Open Invention Network LLC, 6 March 2017, www.
openinventionnetwork.com/joining-oin/oin-license-agreement; and
"Open Patent Non-Assertion Pledge," Google Search, Google LLC, n.d.,
www.google.com/patents/opnpledge/pledge, all accessed 11 May 2018.

410. "Economy Rankings," *Doing Business*, World Bank, June 2017. www.
doingbusiness.org/rankings, accessed 1 May 2018.

411. United Nations Conference on Trade and Development, "World
Investment Report 2017," United Nations, 2017. unctad.org/en/
PublicationsLibrary/wir2017_en.pdf, accessed 1 May 2018.

412. "Why Hong Kong Remains Vital to China's Economy," *The Economist*,
The Economist Newspaper Ltd., 1 Oct. 2014. www.economist.com/
blogs/economist-explains/2014/09/economist-explains-22, accessed
1 May 2018.

413. "Hong Kong Retains Second Place in Global FDI Inflows," InvestHK,
2016. www1.investhk.gov.hk/news-item/hong-kong-retains-second-
place-in-global-fdi-inflows, accessed 1 May 2018.

414. PricewaterhouseCoopers, "Paying Taxes 2016," 10th ed., World
Bank Group, 2016. www.pwc.com/gx/en/paying-taxes-2016/paying-
taxes-2016.pdf, accessed 1 May 2018.

415. Cap. 553 Electronic Transactions Ordinance, Hong Kong e-Legislation,
7 Jan. 2000. www.elegislation.gov.hk/hk/cap553, accessed 15 Jan. 2020.

416. "Certificate Authorities and Trust Hierarchies," *GlobalSign SSL
Information Center*, GMO Internet Group. www.globalsign.com/en/ssl-
information-center/what-are-certification-authorities-trust-hierarchies,
accessed 3 May 2018.

417. "Certificate Authorities and Trust Hierarchies," *GlobalSign SSL
Information Center*, GMO Internet Group.

418. Eva Chan, interviewed in person by Vineet Narula and Prema
Shrikrishna, 11 Sept. 2017.

419. Pindar Wong, interviewed by Vineet Narula and Prema Shrikrishna,
22 April 2018.

420. Christiana Imafidon, "The Spiraling Costs of KYC for Banks and
How FinTech Can Help," *ITProPortal*, Future plc, 6 June 2016. www.
itproportal.com/2016/06/06/the-spiralling-costs-of-kyc-for-banks-and-
how-fintech-can-help, accessed 1 May 2018.

421. "Hong Kong Fact Sheet," The Postmaster General's Statement,
Hongkong Post, Government of Hong Kong, Dec. 2016. www.
hongkongpost.hk/about_us/corp_info/publications/fact_sheet/index.
html, accessed 11 May 2018.

422. Infoteam SA, "UPU Member Countries," Universal Postal Union, United Nations Specialized Agency, n.d. www.upu.int/en/the-upu/member-countries.html; "History," Asia Pacific Post Cooperative, Asia Pacific Postal Union, n.d. www.app.coop/about-us/history; and "Express Delivery Management Programme for China Express Association," *APPU Newsletter*, Asian-Pacific Postal Union, June 2016. appu-bureau.org/wp-content/uploads/2016/07/June-20163.pdf, all accessed 11 May 2018. In the region, the Asian-Pacific Postal Union has 32 member countries and the Asia Pacific Post Cooperative has 27 member countries. The Universal Postal Union is the United Nations specialized agency for the postal sector with 192 member countries.

423. "Hong Kong Fact Sheet," The Postmaster General's Statement, Hongkong Post, Government of Hong Kong, Dec. 2016. www.hongkongpost.hk/en/about_us/corp_info/publications/fact_sheet/index.html, accessed 11 May 2018.

424. "Frequently Asked Questions on e-Cert," *Hongkong Post e-Cert*, Government of Hong Kong, n.d. www.hongkongpost.gov.hk/support/faq/index.html#J, accessed 11 May 2018.

425. Charles D'Haussy, interviewed in person by Vineet Narula and Prema Shrikrishna, 5 Sept. 2017.

426. Finbarr Bermingham, "Hong Kong-Singapore Blockchain Trade Platform to Go Live in 2019," *Global Trade Review*, 16 Nov. 2017. www.gtreview.com/news/asia/hong-kong-singapore-blockchain-project-to-go-live-in-2019, accessed 11 May 2018. Banks involved in Singapore include the Development Bank of Singapore (DBS), Overseas Chinese Banking Corporation (OCBC), Bank United Overseas Bank (UOB), Japan's Mitsubishi UFJ Financial Group MUFG, and Standard Chartered. On the Hong Kong side are Bank of East Asia, Hang Seng, as well as Standard Chartered.

427. The Belt and Blockchain Consortium, n.d. www.beltandroadblockchain.org, accessed 1 May 2018.

428. Vinay Gupta, "The Internet of Agreements," *Building the Hyperconnected Future on Blockchains*, Hexyurt Capital, 12 Feb. 2017. internetofagreements.com/files/WorldGovernmentSummit-Dubai2017.pdf, accessed 27 April 2018.

429. "Cyberport Hosts 'Blockchain Strategies for Business' Conference to Spearhead FinTech Development in Hong Kong and Beyond," Press Release, Hong Kong Cyberport Management Company Ltd., 28 July 2016. tinyurl.com/y8xuu4qy, accessed 29 April 2018.

430. R.J. Whitehead, "One Belt One Road a Boon for Global Halal Supply," *Food Navigator-Asia.com*, William Reed Business Media Ltd.,

10 Sept. 2017, updated 11 Sept. 2017. www.foodnavigator-asia.com/ Article/2017/09/11/One-Belt-One-Road-a-boon-for-global-halal-supply, accessed 1 May 2018.

431. Marco Tieman, "Leveraging Blockchain Technology for Halal Supply Chains," *Building Logistics Blocks*, LBB International, 27 March 2018. lbbinternational.com/2018/03/27/leveraging-blockchain-technology-for-halal-supply-chains, accessed 1 May 2018.

432. According to the *Financial Times, mudaraba* is a trust financing contract between the provider of capital and the party that needs it. *Musharaka* is an instrument of participation, where two or more parties (for example, an Islamic bank and its clients) agree to contribute capital to a venture and share in its profits and losses. *Murabaha* is a type of sales contract where a bank buys an asset—often a costly asset—on behalf of a client and transfers it to the client at a markup, paid in installments. *Ijara* is a type of rental contract between a lessor and a lessee for the use of an asset over a specific period. For greater explanation, see the *Financial Times* lexicon, lexicon.ft.com. According to the Islamic Development Bank, *Istisna'a* is an instrument of pre-shipment financing, often to support manufacturing. For more information, see "Istisna'a Mode of Financing," Islamic Development Bank, 23 Jan. 2002. Duke University, faculty.fuqua.duke.edu/~charvey/Teaching/BA456_2002/isdb_intisna. pdf, accessed 27 April 2018. *Salam* is an upfront-payment forward sale for a commodity to be delivered later on a specified date. For more information, see the *Financial Encyclopedia*, ed. Majd Bakir, Investment and Finance, 28 Feb. 2013. www.financialencyclopedia.net/islamic-finance/s/salam.html, accessed 27 April 2018.

433. Liu Qin, "China Needs to Pave 'One Belt One Road' with Green Finance, Say Experts," *ChinaDialogue.net*, 7 Jan. 2016. www. chinadialogue.net/article/show/single/en/8532-China-needs-to-pave-One-Belt-One-Road-with-green-finance-say-experts-, accessed 3 May 2018.

434. "Blockchain in Logistics," Supply Chain Management Outsource, n.d. www.scmo.net/blockchain/?rq=IoT, accessed 28 April 2018.

435. Nicolas De Loisy, interviewed in person by Vineet Narula and Prema Shrikrishna, 6 Sept. 2017.

436. "SCMO Attends HKMW Blockchain in Shipping and Logistics Event," *SCMO Newsletter*, Supply Chain Management Outsource, 21 Nov. 2017. www.scmo.net/scmo-newsletter/2017/12/12/scmo-attends-hkmw-blockchain-in-shipping-and-logistics-event?rq=IoT, accessed 29 April 2018.

437. "Chain of Shipping," Case Study 3, Chain of Things Ltd., n.d. www. chainofthings.com/cs3chainofshipping, accessed 29 April 2018.

438. "About GS1," GS1 AISBL, n.d. www.gs1.org/about, accessed 27 April 2018.

439. "How Does GS1 Cloud Work?" GS1 AISBL, last modified 12 Sept. 2017. www.gs1.org/services/gs1-cloud/how-gs1-cloud-works, accessed 28 April 2018.

440. Dr. Stephen Lam, interviewed in person by Vineet Narula and Prema Shrikrishna, 7 Sept. 2017.

441. "GS1, IBM, and Microsoft Announce Collaboration to Leverage GS1 Standards in Enterprise Blockchain Applications," Press Release, GSI, 13 Sept. 2017. www.gs1.org/docs/news/GS1-Open-Standards-Promote-Interoperability-Blockchain-Applications.pdf, accessed 28 April 2018.

442. Herman Lam, former CEO, Cyberport, interviewed in person by Vineet Narula and Prema Shrikrishna, 6 Sept. 2017.

443. Sara Hsu, "How China's Asian Infrastructure Investment Bank Fared Its First Year," *Forbes*, Forbes Media LLC, 14 Jan. 2017. www.forbes. com/sites/sarahsu/2017/01/14/how-chinas-asian-infrastructure-investment-bank-fared-its-first-year/#778eb6b35a7f; Nikki Sun, "China Development Bank Commits $250bn to Belt and Road," *Nikkei Asian Review*, Nikkei Inc., 15 Jan. 2018. asia.nikkei.com/Politics-Economy/Policy-Politics/China-Development-Bank-commits-250bn-to-Belt-and-Road, both accessed 1 May 2018.

444. Here is a link to the report hash on Coin Sciences Ltd.'s website, coinsecrets.org/?to=361625.000003, block 361625, 19 Jun 2015, 12:20 GMT.

INDEX